# The Soul of Ireland

# The Soul of Ireland

## Issues of Society, Culture and Identity

*Edited by*
Joe Mulholland

The Liffey Press

Published by
The Liffey Press
Ashbrook House
10 Main Street
Raheny, Dublin 5, Ireland
www.theliffeypress.com

A catalogue record of this book is
available from the British Library.

ISBN 1-905785-12-7

Printed in Ireland by Futureprint Ltd.

# Contents

Contents

# 5. The Relevance of 1916

# 6. The Soul of Ireland in Traditional Music

# 7. The Death Throes of the Irish Language?

# 8. Secularisation and the Loss of Religious Identity

# Contents

# Acknowledgements

It is not an exaggeration to say that this book would not have seen the light of day without the kind and generous assistance of Mr. Paddy Kelly of Redquartz Developments, Mr. Maurice Regan, Mr. Tony Sheridan of CampusIT and Mr. Michael Norris, all of whom passionately believe in what we do in Glenties, and I am extremely grateful to them for their support.

Neither would we be in a position to organise the MacGill School year after year without the help of the Donegal County Council and, in particular, its Manager, Mr. Michael McLoone. We are also indebted to Dr. Martin Naughton, Executive Chairman of Glen Dimplex and to the Director-General and management of Radio Telefís Éireann. I am very grateful to Mr Martin Territt and his colleagues in the Office of the European Commission in Dublin for their help in the organisation of the Annual John Hume Lecture.

This is our first year to work with The Liffey Press in the production of this book and it was a very enjoyable and satisfying experience. I thank, in particular, their Managing Director, Mr. David Givens, for his unfailing professionalism and courtesy.

My gratitude also goes to Mr. Charles Byrne who, for many years, has provided excellent sound at our symposium and who is a continuous source of technical and, indeed, moral support and to Ms. Nuala Naughton whose transcribing skill was invaluable this year. I would also like to acknowledge the help and support of another former colleague, Mr. Tommie Gorman of RTE, who has always given assistance to the MacGill School and whose encouragement is always generous and unstinting.

As always, we are particularly indebted to our excellent contributors whose papers, slightly edited, are reproduced in this book. They are all very busy people and it is to their credit that they took time out of their schedules to write papers and to travel to Donegal to deliver them.

I would also like to thank our Committee in Glenties, who have always offered me their loyalty and support and, in particular, the Chairman, Michael Gallagher and Secretary, Mary Claire O'Donnell. St. Columba's School has been associated with MacGill since the beginning and I lament the passing, a few weeks ago, of its former Principal, Mr. Jim Gallagher, who was always helpful, as well as thank his successor, Mr. Michael Naughton and his staff who have continued in that tradition. A special word of thanks to the Boyle family of the Highlands Hotel and their wonderful staff who make all our speakers, guests and audiences so welcome.

Finally, my thanks to my family – my wife, Annie and children Fiona, Sylvain and Julien – for their loyalty, patience and support.

Joe Mulholland
November 2006

Rt. Hon. Peter Hain MP and Joe Mulholland

# Joe Mulholland

## Director of the MacGill Summer School & Arts Week

*Born in Donegal and educated at Stranorlar Boys' NS, the Finn College, Ballybofey, De La Salle Teachers' Training College, Manchester, University of Nancy (L.es L., Dr. es L.) and University of London (BA Hons). Held several executive positions in RTÉ and is an award winning documentary producer. With a local committee in Glenties, he founded the Patrick MacGill Summer School in 1981 and, with the exception of a few years, has been Director since then. Has been a contributor to French media including the newspaper,* Le Monde. *He is currently Chairman of the board of the National College of Art and Design (NCAD). Received a Donegal Person of the Year award in 2002.*

## Foreword

Minister Brian Cowen, in his incisive and wide-ranging paper which he delivered when he officially opened this year's MacGill Summer School, states his view that the soul of Ireland is in good shape and lists a number of key areas of life in this country which have changed beyond recognition – and for the better. The Minister is perfectly right to remind us that the Ireland of today is a much better place than the Ireland of 20 years ago with its mass unemployment and emigration. The MacGill School, in the 26 years of its existence, has reflected this phenomenal evolution. The Minister is also right to point to achievements other than the transformation of our economy, such as the stability of our democratic institutions, which sometimes we take for granted, the bringing about of peace on this island, the vitality of our cultural identity and its resilience in the face of globalisation and the regeneration of disadvantaged and decaying urban communities.

Another minister of Government, Michael McDowell, also points to the way in which the Irish people have accepted and welcomed waves of immigrants to our shores and to the fact that in such a short space of time we have become a multi-ethnic and multi-cultural society without the accompanying race-based or immigration-based politics that have surfaced in other European democracies. And, with some reservations perhaps about our use of the term "the Soul of Ireland", he unequivocally rejects any notion of a society which would have a simplistic and unreal view of itself as being a homogenous community with one set of values and beliefs, or of Irishness as being only Celtic or Gaelic or of any other single origin when the reality is that the blood in our veins is of many sources.

This year's MacGill School, then, was very much in the tradition of the previous 25 years – an attempt to analyse where this small island of ours now finds itself and, more importantly, an attempt to assess where it will find itself in another quarter of a century. To judge by the speed and the enormity of change which we have lived through in the past decade, there are few of us who, in spite of our concerns, and indeed fears, about the future would go back to what we had in the 40s, 50s and 60s – social deprivation, a declining population, disillusionment and despair. The independent Dáil deputy and MEP, Marian Harkin, dealing with the subject of loss of community spirit in Ireland, does not even accept the notion that communities in the Ireland of earlier decades were all that healthy. Yes, we do remember a time when people visited one another's homes constantly, when as children we could roam the countryside, safe and carefree, when the elderly could sleep without fear in their beds at night and when neighbours helped each other out at times of sickness or need. However, Deputy Harkin points to the other side of the coin, to how closed and hierarchical these communities were with nobody daring to step out of line, to those locked and hidden away in mental institutions, to the physical abuse of children in schools and the sexual abuse in homes and in sacristies, to the discrimination against women and so on. Recognising, of course, that we have lost much of what was good in our communities and that "the pendulum has swung too far", the task for Ms. Harkin is to try and get it on the way back and to get a balance.

Some of the other speakers, in fact, said that this will not be easy. It is easy to be nostalgic about the past but there are in our society quite widespread concerns that, to use the frequently used and abused cliché, "we have lost the run of ourselves". There are real fears for the way our society is evolving and fears, in particular, for the young who are the next generations of Irish men and women. With the Celtic Tiger has come affluence, and very quickly, and with affluence has come selfishness, self-gratification, the flaunting of huge personal wealth as well as greed and avarice. Recently, following the tragic deaths of five young men in a road accident in Monaghan, the parish priest, Fr. O'Reilly, who is also youth director in the diocese of Clogher, courageously made the point that material goods rather than emotional love are being plied on children by parents who are too busy benefiting from the Celtic Tiger. Prosperity has increased our choices but, as Brian Cowen states in his paper, with that prosperity must come personal responsibility and self-discipline. These two qualities, it has to be said, are not always in evidence in the Irish society of 2006 and their absence is partly due to the breakdown of relations between people, between families and within communities. As Father Harry Bohan, who has tried for many a year to build genuine communities, says in his paper, "Capitalism attacks the very roots of community by making the individual the centre of everything and suggesting that once individual wants and needs are met there is no need for other people".

There are, then, issues of society, culture and identity as Ireland embarks on a new millennium as one of the wealthiest countries in the world: an increasing population, a considerable part of which has not been born here; its official language on which much money and effort has been spent in real danger of disappearing forever; and religious practice falling away, particularly amongst the young with few priests being ordained thus changing radically the structure of society as a whole. There are issues when some urban housing estates are being destroyed by drugs, vandalism and crime. There are issues when we now have a multi-cultural, multi-ethnic society with all that this implies, not necessarily for the present but for the future, and David Begg, Lucy Gaffney and Michael McDowell deal with some of them. There are issues when youngsters are sexually active at a younger and younger age and sexually transmitted diseases are spiralling upwards, and there are issues when we have the problem of the largest consumption of alcohol in Europe, especially amongst the young. It is timely, therefore, to debate these issues when we still have choices, when, for example, we can put our wealth to good use by providing good public services, especially for those most in need of them and dealing with the painful issue of child poverty which continues to persist as described in this volume by John Monaghan, Helen Johnston and John Lonergan. We can still build on the goodwill and sense of duty and decency to be found in this country as well as on the kind of voluntary effort to be found in the GAA and described movingly by Sean Kelly.

We can use our affluence in so many ways to improve the society on this relatively small island so that we become a model for other states struggling to come to terms with globalisation and forces and events outside their control. One of the most obvious ways, as Mary Finan points out, is in support of the arts which have never had so much vitality and which, in the words of Mary Cloake, have a hugely important role to play in the forging of our national cultural identity but are in need of succour and constant attention. Our Gaelic games and our traditional music are a vital component of life in our communities throughout the island – North and South. Sean Kelly, Micheál Ó Muircheartaigh and Mike Cronin depict the GAA as an organisation which, in spite of the commercial and competitive pressures on it, retains its historic and crucially important role in the cultural and sporting life of the nation and of its communities.

As I said in the foreword to this year's MacGill programme, in the year when we celebrate the ninetieth anniversary of the Rising and remember the bravery and idealism of its leaders, it is fitting that we should stop and deliberate on the kind of society we have created, either by accident or design, look at the features it has which distinguish us as a nation with its own culture and identity and ask what are the steps we need to take to avail of our new-found prosperity in a responsible manner so as to build the society of which we can all be proud and with which we can be comfortable.

We still have much to cherish in Ireland but these things cannot be taken for granted. Without decrying the magnificent achievements of those men and women who have contributed to the transformation of Ireland in our lifetimes, it is time for stocktaking and reflection.

I hope that this tome, consisting of the excellent contributions made by our qualified and distinguished speakers in Glenties in July of this year, will assist in that process.

Michael Daly, Editor, *Donegal Democrat*

Nuala O'Loan
Police Ombudsman for NI

Part of the audience for *Secularisation and Loss of Religious Identity*

Brian Cowen TD, Minister for Finance

*Introduction*

# The Soul of Ireland is in Good Shape

Brian Cowen TD
**Minister for Finance**

# Brian Cowen TD

## Minister for Finance

*Born in Offaly in 1960, was educated at Clara National School, Cistercian College, Roscrea, UCD and Incorporated Law Society. First elected to Dáil Éireann in a by-election in 1984 caused by the death of his father, Bernard. He was Minister for Labour 1992-3, Minister for Transport, Energy and Communications 1993-4 and Minister for Health and Children 1997-2000. He served as Minister for Foreign Affairs from 2000 to 2004 when he was appointed to the Finance portfolio. He is also Deputy Leader of Fianna Fáil . He was a member of the Fianna Fáil Party Commission to review the aims and structures of the organisation.*

## The Soul of Ireland is in Good Shape

This year's overall theme, "The Soul of Ireland – Issues of Society, Culture and Identity", is a challenging and broad one. The question being posed by the Director this year seems to be: recognising that our economic fortunes have been transformed, do we need to take stock and reflect on what impact all of this change is having on our culture and sense of identity, and on the kind of society we would like and deserve to have?

**Recognising that our economic fortunes have been transformed, do we need to take stock and reflect on what impact all of this change is having on our culture and sense of identity, and on the kind of society we would like and deserve to have?**

My first reaction is to say that I am an optimist about the direction of this country. I am reminded of something the late Liam de Paor said in 1985, a period widely perceived as being one of national malaise and of identity crisis. He said then:

> "The country is young ... and the young country takes its identity and nationality for granted.... It is ... just possible to see that under the rapid and bewildering changes now occurring in Ireland, a completely new sense of national identity is taking shape.... We are living now in a period of extraordinary energy and productivity. The arts, particularly the literary arts, flourish. People are going back to first principles in politics. Unionists talk to nationalists, nationalists to unionists as never before ... the shape of an independent Ireland emerges."

I think that prescient observation resonates with the same impact now as it did with me then. Our people have responded every time the lead is given. There is no doubt that we have many serious problems to overcome and also that various trends, including globalisation, pose direct challenges to the ability of this island to be distinct. However,

I believe that a fair balancing of progress and opportunities on one side, with loss and threats on the other, suggests many reasons to be positive about the soul of Ireland. In fact, we have the potential to strengthen further our social fabric and to do this on the basis of an ever evolving culture and identity which is at its very core positive and outward looking.

A period of tremendous change brings with it many uncertainties – and a tendency to both fear change and see it as a destroyer of tradition. I do not subscribe to the idea that we have left behind us a pure and betrayed past. In fact, I believe that Ireland today is a significantly better place than it was 20, 40 or 80 years ago. Our economic transformation through the work of social partnership, the peace process in Ireland, and our membership of the EU are important contexts in which to see how our view of ourselves and how others see us has changed.

I completely disagree with those who say that progress has been all about an economy and nothing to do with a society. That assertion does a grave disservice to successive governments and the social partners who have worked at agreeing both economic and social priorities on the basis of a shared commitment.

I look at the situation today compared to the one faced by our economy and society 20 years ago when I entered politics. The most dramatic change is that we have overcome mass unemployment and emigration. There is no doubt in my mind that increasing the number of jobs in Ireland has provided a sense of contribution and participation for citizens that gives purpose and greater meaning to their lives than any other comparable economic factor could do. Young people expect to have four or five different jobs before they are 30, unlike their parents whose sense of security would be shattered by such a prospect! This genuinely historical progress means that this is the first generation of Irish people in over 200 years which has the opportunity to build a prosperous future in the land of their birth.

Prosperity has increased our choices and possibilities. Does it guarantee a better life? With that prosperity must come a sense of personal responsibility and self-discipline. We need to put value on developing a civic culture that insists on civility in our dealings, courtesy and consideration for others, especially our elderly and vulnerable, and respect to be shown for our laws and to those charged to uphold them. Such a communal attitude and approach is a necessary prerequisite to good social order and harmony. Our own individual sense of being a citizen with obligations to others who live in our communities, and indeed the wider society, will in large measure determine how positive a factor being better off will be in our lives. A community of engaged citizens, with the common sense

**I do not subscribe to the idea that we have left behind us a pure and betrayed past. In fact, I believe that Ireland today is a significantly better place than it was 20, 40 or 80 years ago.**

to contribute positively and give something back, will always enjoy better prospects of a fulfilled and better life than one characterised by viewing themselves as consumers of services with rights and entitlements regardless of how they behave themselves or towards others. The values of our civic culture must affirm the former and insist that the latter has no acceptable place in our society.

I think good government, both central and local, works best when it facilitates the participation of local communities in finding solutions to problems that affect them. A sense of citizenship is imparted when people work with, not against, authorities. There has to be a responsive approach where people get a sense of ownership of the problem and where the interaction with those in authority is results-driven.

## Community Life Remains Strong

High levels of employment, a rising population all over the country and the achievement of an unprecedented scale and pace of growth brings with it inevitable and serious pressures. There is no doubt that families and communities face challenges today which make it hard for them to maintain much of what was valuable in the past. But equally, there is no doubt that there are significant signs that, to use a term which is gaining wider acceptance all the time, the social capital of this country remains strong.

The scale of activism within communities and levels of involvement in joint activities like sports clubs are two important examples of this. In many areas you can actually point to a significant strengthening of the bonds within and between communities – the exact opposite of the alleged trends.

Look, for example, at many disadvantaged communities in Dublin. Areas once taken as bywords for decay are being regenerated through a combination of Europe's largest programme of state-funded renewal and a sustained partnership with the communities themselves. Places like Ballymun and Fatima Mansions are being physically transformed, but more importantly the community infrastructure, both formal and informal, is also being transformed by and with the people.

My basic point is that the agenda of Ireland is no longer about the inevitability of decline, but how to secure and make the most of historic opportunities. In this context, one of the great challenges for us is to develop a public discourse which is capable of playing a constructive role in shaping our future.

*Places like Ballymun and Fatima Mansions are being physically transformed, but more importantly the community infrastructure, both formal and informal, is also being transformed by and with the people.*

## The Role of the Public Discourse

A core requirement for this shaping of our future is to have substantial public engagement with politics and political issues. Unfortunately, I believe that there is a risk that we could see a growing alienation from politics because of factors beyond those which are commonly discussed.

For example, there is the very fact that so much has been achieved on what were the defining issues of modern Ireland. This is something which has been identified in most modern developed countries and it would be foolish for us to believe that we should be different.

Equally, there is evidence that we have a public discourse which is alienating in spite of its public goal of being inclusive. While we live in a world of colour and shade, we tend to debate in black and white. There is often a sense that, until everything is achieved, no progress can be acknowledged – and that every advance can be challenged with a negative counter example. In the challenge faced by ordinary citizens of trying to understand the state of their society, they experience substantial advocacy but very little perspective to allow them make up their own minds.

As part of this we are seeing an undeniable trend towards a more populist agenda which we once prided ourselves in rejecting. This was held to be in stark contrast to our near neighbours. It can safely be said that in the search for a competitive advantage with the public, no tactic is now off-limits.

This is an important part of the fact that it is increasingly less likely that serious areas of public policy can be debated in a constructive manner. To give one basic example of this: everyone knows that much practical political policy comes down to what something will cost and how it will be paid for. It is not possible to have an honest political discourse without a specific response to these questions. It's the difference between lightly-given empathy and a real commitment to action. In order to help parties in this challenge, resources to support them have been dramatically increased in recent years – yet, for all this, the policy of the opposition producing an alternative budget was abandoned four years ago.

We now have an incredibly dysfunctional situation where it is the stated policy of a large part of the political system not to allow the public see any specifics on what they would do differently if in government. In effect, the public is being told not to bother its head with specifics. It is really something new when soundbites are no longer used to summarise policies, they actually are the policies.

*... there is evidence that we have a public discourse which is alienating in spite of its public goal of being inclusive. While we live in a world of colour and shade, we tend to debate in black and white.*

## Our Democratic Tradition

Ninety years after the Easter Rising we are one of the world's longest continuous democracies. We also have strong public legitimacy for our democratic institutions – with a very recent survey showing that we have one of the highest levels of public satisfaction with our national democracy of any of the member states of the European Union.

To protect this valuable part of our inheritance, we need to work harder to make sure that we have a public discourse which is serious enough so that the public is given a real opportunity to understand and influence policy on issues of concern to them.

## Culture and Identity

**Circumstances change, and in our case we should all be thankful for this. National identity and culture should evolve, not stay rooted in the past.**

Just as I believe that our country has seen significant and sustained progress in many areas, I do not believe that our culture and identity are under threat. It is possible to take a snapshot in time, idealise it and call it a national culture. I reject this approach because it misses the essentially dynamic nature of a strong culture. Circumstances change, and in our case we should all be thankful for this. National identity and culture should evolve, not stay rooted in the past.

## Globalisation

One of the most remarkable developments of the modern era has been globalisation in its many forms. Globalisation has been an inescapable element in helping an island on the Atlantic periphery to develop and provide a future for its people. Without trade we cannot prosper. Equally, without the many and growing external influences to which we are exposed, our culture would be a museum piece and not a part of what we are – and our identity would hold us back, not empower us.

Pointing to growing similarities with other cultures is not the same as showing that we are losing our distinctiveness. For example, many of our foremost music groups do not play traditional music, but it would be a foolish person who tried to deny them their essential Irishness. They are not overt representatives, but they have undoubtedly been influenced by their country and, more importantly, they speak to the experience of Irish people.

In music, just like in sport and so many other areas, we are showing our ecumenical side and it is a very positive thing. The passion with which we now support our soccer and rugby teams has grown along with increased passion for the GAA. The sales of replica shirts for English clubs has not undermined or devalued our own distinctive sporting identity. Where once membership meant an occasional commitment, GAA clubs are now growing in their importance as centres of community life. Dublin, which is becoming more diverse and international by the day, and was once seen as fallow territory for Gaelic games, is witnessing a remarkable growth in club numbers and membership.

Tradition is important – and it is always worth protecting its history so that people can gain a perspective on why we are who we are. Equally, each generation receives its tradition in different ways and adds to it in ways which are incomprehensible to previous generations. This is normal, healthy and exactly what we are experiencing in Ireland today.

## Irish Language

The Irish language is a very good example of this. Many people fall into the trap of believing that the situation and promotion of the language is as it was when they were in school. In fact, there is a new engagement with the language which goes well beyond people who are part of a formal language movement. Those who laugh at the foisting of *Peig* on teenagers, or rail against the systematic imposition of inflexible rules which cause arbitrary harm to non-speakers, are missing the fact that times have changed.

The incredible growth of Gaelscoileanna is a development of recent years, as have been a range of curriculum reforms and a combination of the removal of many strict requirements and the introduction of flexible supports. Taken together, these factors mean that the Irish language is at an exciting time.

I believe the protection and promotion of the native language of this island is a fair and reasonable objective of public policy. We may well now be finally experiencing serious progress. We should acknowledge this and give it a fair opportunity to go further before taking any reactionary steps which might set this trend into reverse.

> I believe the protection and promotion of the native language of this island is a fair and reasonable objective of public policy. We may well now be finally experiencing serious progress.

## Immigration, Integration and Identity

Of course it is not possible to talk about Irish identity without mentioning the fact that we have, for the first time in our recent history, been experiencing significant immigration. Many are people who come from different cultures and who speak languages we have no comprehension of. For an island which was so relatively homogenous until recently, this poses a major challenge.

The only way in which this could be seen as a threat to our national identity would be if we were to accept the idea that national identity is something which only finds substance in opposition to an "other". This may indeed be true in the context of the original formation of national identity, and I believe this is a significant area for academic study at the moment, but beyond this initial formative phase, it is an approach which is neither inevitable nor desirable to the maintenance of national identity.

## The Influence of Europe

You can see this very clearly if you look at the experience of our participation in the great project of European integration. We comment a lot on the importance of what is now known as the European Union in our economic development, but its role in helping shape our modern identity is equally important. It taught us how to mediate interests both at home and abroad. Its institutions imposed disciplines on us that have helped modernise our economy in ways we would have found more difficult on our own, particularly in the context of the single market and our entry to the euro. It is our EU experience which has directly led us to be a self-confident, outward-looking and questioning country.

In the regular surveys which the European Commission carries out which touch on identity, Ireland is consistently one of the countries with the highest levels of pride in national identity – and also consistently one of the countries with the highest levels of pride in a shared European identity. The Irish people have rejected the false opposites of nation state versus Europe and embraced a more positive outlook. The essentially defensive and inward-looking nature of identity in many countries has found little resonance here.

We must obviously work hard to deal with pressures which arise inevitably from the scale and pace of immigration which we have seen in recent years – and also not casually dismiss as backward anyone who raises concerns – but equally we should see the growing diversity of the population of this island as something which will further enrich our resilient and evolving national identity.

## Peace

We should also make sure that we do not miss the opportunity presented to this generation to build a lasting peace and reconciliation between traditions on this island. The progress in conflict resolution over the last ten years has been drawn-out at times, but historic nonetheless. One of the greatest achievements has been that the crises and impasses which we must overcome involve politics not violence and death.

> **We must obviously work hard to deal with pressures which arise inevitably from the scale and pace of immigration which we have seen in recent years – and also not casually dismiss as backward anyone who raises concerns – but equally we should see the growing diversity of the population of this island as something which will further enrich our resilient and evolving national identity.**

The people of this island have, for the first time in our history, expressed a fixed will about how we will manage our shared future. In focusing on the next hurdle, we can often lose sight of how far we have come and how much the communities involved have directly benefited.

The prospect of conflict has been removed from the national identity espoused by all but a few fundamentalists. We have all agreed to a common journey consistent with democratic principles, in partnership with equality of esteem being accorded to both traditions. Both governments wish to see full institutional expression being given to the Good Friday Agreement by November 24th. Thereafter, if agreement is not reached, both governments have their duties to discharge in the interests of everyone. The logic of the situation is clear.

## The Soul of Ireland

For these and the other reasons which I have mentioned, I believe that the soul of Ireland is in good shape. Yes, we have lost many things and in this we are no different from any other society. With progress comes new challenges.

The challenge for us all is to understand the great lesson of our recent past: that we must continue to embrace change if we want to shape rather than be the victim of the future.

> The prospect of conflict has been removed from the national identity espoused by all but a few fundamentalists. We have all agreed to a common journey consistent with democratic principles ...

The Rt. Hon. Peter Hain MP, Secretary of State for Northern Ireland and Wales

*The Sixth Annual
John Hume Lecture*

# Facing Up
# to the Future

**THE RT. HON. PETER HAIN MP**
**Secretary of State for Northern Ireland and Wales**

# The Rt. Hon. Peter Hain MP

## Secretary of State for Northern Ireland and Wales

*He was born in 1950 in Nairobi of South African parents. In 1966 the family fled South Africa where they were involved in the anti-Apartheid movement and settled in London where, still in his teens, he became involved in the anti-Apartheid campaign. A case brought against him as a result of these activities led to a controversial ten-day trial at the Old Bailey in 1972. He joined the Liberal Party but in 1977 left to join the Labour Party. He studied at St. Mary's College, the University of London and the University of Sussex before taking up a post with the Union of Communication Workers. He was elected at a by-election in 1991 to Westminster as MP for Neath in Wales. Following the Labour Party's victory in the 1997 General Election, he was appointed to the Welsh Office, then to the Foreign and Commonwealth Office as Minister for Africa. In October 2002 he was made Secretary of State for Wales and in June 2003, Leader of the House of Commons and Lord Privy Seal. In 2005 he was appointed Secretary of State for Northern Ireland whilst continuing to hold the Welsh portfolio. He is the author of several books including,* Don't Play With Apartheid *(1971),* Reviving the Labour Party *(1980),* Political Trials in Britain *(1985) and* The End of Foreign Policy? *(with Robin Cook, 2001).*

## Facing Up to the Future

The contribution of men from the whole island of Ireland in the First World War is now widely recognised. Historians have begun to explore the social and economic impact of the loss of life across this island. The numbers are staggering: over 200,000 men – perhaps 20 per cent of the adult male population – fought on the Western Front, Gallipoli and elsewhere. The 16th Irish Division alone lost well over 4,000 men at the Somme.

There can hardly have been a family, North or South, which was not affected; we have contemporary accounts of the trauma within communities as thousands of telegrams were delivered in the days following the battle, announcing the deaths of loved ones.

The motivation of these men was diverse. Some fought for the promise of Home Rule, others from loyalty to the Crown. Others – perhaps even the majority – joined up out of economic necessity. But what united them was ultimately far, far greater than what divided them. That is a lesson which we are still helping each other to learn on this island of Ireland.

**... what united them was ultimately far, far greater than what divided them. That is a lesson which we are still helping each other to learn on this island of Ireland.**

Nor is it unique to the Irish experience. A few miles from the battlefields where the Ulster and Irish Divisions fought is Delville Wood, where there is a memorial to the South African brigade, and where my great uncle was badly wounded. As you can imagine, the role of South Africans fighting for the British Empire is overlaid by the legacy of apartheid and the separate roles of black and white soldiers – blacks being denied the right to carry guns, for example, even on the front line. It took a leader of Nelson Mandela's vision and moral courage to acknowledge the shared suffering and sacrifice of South African soldiers – black and white – on the Western Front.

The commemoration this year at Islandbridge attended by President McAleese, and the presence of the Irish Government through Education Minister, Mary Hanafin, at the Somme are very welcome developments in the same vein. The Taoiseach's personal interest in this has also been very significant. Some years ago he recognised the bravery of Irish soldiers in the British army as "part of the shared experience and history of the Irish and British peoples" – a point at which we should come together rather than being forced apart.

I mention the Somme, and the understanding of what unites rather than divides, because a shared future has been a central theme of my first year as Secretary of State. As you know, it is a job for which there is no shortage of history lessons. Everyone has a view of the past – at least one view of the past as I have only too often discovered – and nearly everyone wishes it had been different. Far too many people and politicians are so rooted in the past that they are unable or unwilling to look to the future.

I have tried to focus minds on what should unite politicians across Northern Ireland in facing up to the future. In pointing to the fierce forces of globalisation – for example low cost economic competition from India and China – and why Northern Ireland needs radical economic, educational and social reform to meet these challenges, some think I have been deliberately using shock tactics. I've even been accused by some Unionists of acting "like a Viceroy" – an odd comparison for someone reared on anti-colonialism and the struggle against apartheid.

But I make no apology for telling it straight. The time has long gone when Northern Ireland politicians could act as if the world could be stopped whilst they sorted out their differences. It most emphatically cannot. Western economies need to have highly skilled and flexible workforces if they are to compete with increasingly highly educated but very significantly lower paid workforces in Asia. The challenge from these rapidly emerging economic powers will not be met if politicians and community leaders in Northern Ireland are mired in ancient differences.

**But I make no apology for telling it straight. The time has long gone when Northern Ireland politicians could act as if the world could be stopped whilst they sorted out their differences. It most emphatically cannot.**

Nor will an economy which has to fund those differences be sustainable in the long term. The costs of division in Northern Ireland are staggering in almost every sector. In education, for example, there are now 50,000 empty school places in Northern Ireland (rising to 80,000 by 2015) – out of a school population of 333,000. This means a monumental waste of resources: teachers in the wrong places, empty class rooms and scores of small schools which are not viable; two segregated primary schools in a village doomed to closure where a merger might be viable and produce higher standards where separately they cannot; secondary schools with inadequate facilities where a rational school estate with integrated or shared facilities could produce high quality. No society can support this situation, least of all Northern Ireland, with its high skill standards at the top, dismal ones lower down and appalling ones at the bottom. The educational future of Northern Ireland must be shared and focused on what unites. Divided it will be bleak.

The same applies to the economy. Quite simply – and as Northern Ireland business readily agrees – the economy as it is currently structured is not sustainable. A weak private sector and a huge, heavily subsidised – and until now unreformed – public sector, means two things: radical reform within Northern Ireland and much more extensive North-South cooperation. Radical reform to cut stifling bureaucracy: seven councils with real powers devolved, each with a strong revenue base, boundaries co-terminus with policing and health, and a swingeing cull of the quangos. Radical reform to raise more local finance: through water charges and higher rates, all to bring Northern Ireland more into line with charges across the rest of the UK which have until now been more than double. Radical reforms also to promote competitiveness, encourage entrepreneurship and strengthen the private sector.

And deeper North-South co-operation which is practical rather than constitutional. The island of Ireland is a small place. As it looks out west across the Atlantic and east towards the mighty, galloping economies of Asia, it should increasingly operate in unison rather than in division: a shared economic strategy for investment and for clusters of excellence in new sectors; a common approach to the North West, for the regeneration of Derry and Donegal; a single energy market and a united policy to boost renewable energy; patients crossing the border to get treatment where it makes medical sense to do so; free cross border public transport for pensioners right across the island. These and many more – the triumph of commonsense over history, of cooperation over division. A shared future for the whole of Ireland and not just for north of the border.

**The island of Ireland is a small place. As it looks out west across the Atlantic and east towards the mighty, galloping economies of Asia, it should increasingly operate in unison rather than in division ...**

And, yes, a shared future for policing too – a subject of immediate importance to political progress in Northern Ireland.

Policing should unite us. I understand, of course, why it has been a source of division in Northern Ireland in the past. But looking to the future, a society which cannot agree on its policing and criminal justice arrangements cannot meet the challenges of social cohesion, still less tackle serious and organised crime. If we are to succeed in putting the last pieces of the Good Friday Agreement jigsaw in place then we need to extend support for policing right across the community, including in Republican areas.

**I want to take seriously the republican movement's reservations about policing and to deal with them directly. It is in everyone's interests that we work together to overcome them.**

I want to take seriously the Republican movement's reservations about policing and to deal with them directly. It is in everyone's interests that we work together to overcome them.

They seem to me to fall into two categories. First, Republicans continue to question the practical details of the reform of policing and its completion. When Chris Patten published his report in 1999, Irish historians could perhaps understand why Sinn Féin reserved judgement while the recommendations were translated into legislation. That process was tortuous but once the legislation was complete, and the process of implementation was underway, the Irish Government, the SDLP, the Catholic Church and broad nationalist opinion shifted towards supporting the change process. They knew that it was indeed a process rather than a state of perfection, but realised that their support was essential to achieving the very improvements that Nationalists wanted to see.

They opted to be part of the change and part of the future of policing. In the case of John Hume's SDLP, they led from the front and took the political risk of supporting the Patten governance arrangements for policing by joining the Policing Board.

Since that time, the PSNI has gone through one of the greatest change programmes of any public organisation in Europe. It is the most highly-regulated, inspected and independently monitored police service anywhere. The Police Ombudsman, Nuala O'Loan, has independent powers of investigation which are unparalleled and certainly greater than anything in Britain or here in Ireland. The commitment and personal integrity of Hugh Orde and of Nuala have been very significant factors in building public confidence across the community.

Of course, there will always be a need for further reassurance, particularly where the legacy of the Troubles is concerned, and steps are being taken to address the past. But I think Republicans recognise that people in both communities have seen the huge scale of change for themselves and welcome the arrival of a new style of community policing across Northern Ireland. Any outstanding issues of real concern should be discussed. The PSNI and the Government are ready to take part in a mature and sustained dialogue with the Sinn Féin leadership this autumn on any outstanding concerns about the change programme. There is no reason to delay this engagement on practical issues.

But I recognise that Republican reservations about policing go deeper than practicalities. The experience of Republican communities, the history of physical force Republicanism, and the basic constitutional aspirations of the Republican movement, make support for the policing institutions of Northern Ireland genuinely problematic. I do not underestimate those difficulties with the burden of history behind them. Nor do I underestimate the centrality for Republicans of the transfer of powers on policing and criminal justice to the Assembly.

Equally, Government recognises, and I think Republicans too should appreciate, the sheer depth of hurt amongst the Unionist community and the police themselves about the past, and the suspicions about Republican involvement in policing that arise from that hurt. Given the violence and pain of the last 30 years, that should not come as a surprise, nor should it be lightly dismissed. A visit to the RUC GC memorial garden, which I made not long before I visited the Somme, is a graphic reminder of the scale of sacrifice and suffering which took place. That is why Republicans need to help allay those concerns and dispel suspicions that they are somehow ambivalent about the rule of law itself, as opposed to the political prism through which they have traditionally viewed rule of law "by the Brits".

The only way to address the experience of policing in Republican areas is to begin a process of building trust between the police and Republican communities on the ground. The PSNI want to engage in this dialogue – indeed, increasingly are doing so, not least in County Derry and in South Armagh – and I hope that increasingly Sinn Féin will promote that. The approach of senior Sinn Féin figures in dealing with the PSNI over recent parades and their very significant efforts to bring about a peaceful summer on the streets has been encouraging.

No one expects the wounds of the past to be healed instantly. But it takes two sides to build trust. What everyone agrees is that these communities desperately need a police service to engage with – they need to be able to deal with serious crime, with rape, assault and burglary. Only the PSNI can deliver this service, and they can only deliver it in partnership with the community.

The world has changed. The commitments made by the IRA in July 2005 and delivered over the past year mean that a vacuum has opened up in communities which can only be filled by a policing

... these communities desperately need a police service to engage with – they need to be able to deal with serious crime, with rape, assault and burglary. Only the PSNI can deliver this service, and they can only deliver it in partnership with the community

service. Normalisation has brought with it the contemporary problems of normal societies: drunken yobbery on a Saturday night, anti-social behaviour, "joy riding", car crime and so on. And local residents are demanding action which can only come from the police.

There is simply no viable alternative. Community Based Restorative Justice has generated a lot of heat. It has a place, and has potential for the future, as the experience of other countries has shown. But it can never be a substitute for the criminal justice system. And everyone must agree that, where it operates, it must be within the rule of law and with full police cooperation.

But the heart of the problem is, of course, constitutional. Given the history of the Republican movement and its legitimate political aspirations, recognised in the Good Friday Agreement, it is not unreasonable that Sinn Féin should see a link between its official support for the institution of the Policing Board and devolution of policing and criminal justice. Both stem from the Agreement to which Republicans and Nationalists committed themselves. It is not entirely surprising that Republicans hesitate to officially endorse the tripartite governance arrangements for policing while I, as a British Secretary of State, occupy one part of that structure in place of a Northern Ireland Executive Minister. They argue strongly that the transfer of policing and criminal justice is central to them and that Patten and the Agreement envisaged this. That I understand. But equally, if the devolution point can be satisfied, Republican support for the PSNI becomes as constitutionally logical as support for the Garda.

While we work to resolve the issue of devolution, I would strongly urge the Republican leadership to draw a distinction between "constitutional" endorsement of the structures of policing, and support for the practical service of policing in the community. There should be no part of Northern Ireland where people are not actively encouraged to report crimes to the police so that they can take action. There should be no community where elected representatives do not routinely talk to PSNI officers. Sinn Féin Councillors refusing to talk to PSNI officers makes as much sense as DUP MLAs refusing to talk to Sinn Féin representatives. That is to say, it makes no sense. We need to move beyond this kind of politics–of–the–past if Northern Ireland is to move forward.

The reluctance of Sinn Féin to support the work of the PSNI is damaging both to the wider political process and to the interests of Republicans themselves and their voters. Once the legislation providing for the devolution of policing and justice receives Royal Assent (as we hope) in the next two weeks, we need to see a step-

**The reluctance of Sinn Féin to support the work of the PSNI is damaging both to the wider political process and to the interests of Republicans themselves and their voters.**

change in efforts by all parties to resolve the issue of policing. Everyone – including Unionists – has a responsibility to engage in the dialogue necessary to bring this about.

Reluctance in this area allows that minority of Unionists who will always look for reasons not to enter a power-sharing Executive to portray Sinn Féin as hostile to law and order itself. It allows them to argue that this reluctance stems from IRA involvement in criminality, even though the International Monitoring Commission (IMC) has made it clear that "the IRA continues to seek to stop criminal activity by its members and to prevent them from engaging in it".

Much more importantly, the vast majority of fair-minded Unionists, who would like to see devolution returned, cannot understand this reluctance to be associated with the institutions of law and order. Whatever allowances they may make for the painful history of Northern Ireland, Unionists – and many Nationalists – are simply puzzled at the prospect of Sinn Féin Ministers in an Executive being unable to endorse the practical activities of the PSNI in fighting crime and keeping the community safe. There are plenty of sophisticated political and historical answers – without doubt eminently suitable to a summer school debate – but none are as powerfully troubling as that question in the minds of people across Northern Ireland.

In short, holding back from being part of policing now, and in shaping its future, has meant that the historic IRA statement of a year ago, and the equally historic subsequent act of decommissioning, have not yet had the full impact they should in the wider community. The perception of Sinn Féin's position on policing acts as a brake on the massive political progress which Republicans have done so much to promote. Ironically, it also becomes an obstacle to the implementation of devolution of policing and justice which Republicans see as essential to their constitutional position on policing and which is a key part of the Good Friday Agreement.

I remain optimistic that we can set out a path for resolving the issue of policing in the timescale recently published by the Prime Minister and the Taoiseach. That optimism is based on the fact that the Good Friday Agreement holds the key. The genius of that Agreement was that it effectively removed the constitutional issue from policing. It allowed Nationalists and Unionists to pursue their constitutional aspirations through peaceful and democratic means but, in the meantime, constructed a new arrangement for policing which all could support, irrespective of their political goals.

Young Catholics have seen this and grasped the opportunity to be part of the new beginning: thousands have applied to join the PSNI in the past few years. Catholic membership of the police has jumped

**That optimism is based on the fact that the Good Friday Agreement holds the key. The genius of that Agreement was that it effectively removed the constitutional issue from policing.**

to over 20 per cent and is well on track to meet Patten's 30 per cent target by 2010. I hope that in time all young people from Republican areas will be actively encouraged to join them.

The gap between Republicans of goodwill who want to take positive steps on policing and Unionists of goodwill who want to acknowledge them is not wide.

As we approach the anniversary of the IRA statement and look back at the progress made, there is a responsibility on all of us involved in the political process not to lose momentum in the final and, I believe, inevitable path towards the restoration of power-sharing government.

This year has seen, for the first time since 1970, the 12th of July demonstrations take place – without the army on the streets of Belfast. Of course, strong feelings on all sides remain. And of course there still had to be a significant security presence, but what nobody can deny is that progress has been made in handling our differences in a peaceful way – and that is a credit to all involved: police, community leaders and politicians.

But as that new Northern Ireland emerges, politicians have to be careful that they do not get caught up in the old arguments when the reality and the grain of public opinion has moved on.

The balance we all have to achieve in the next few months is how, without denying people's genuine historical and current concerns, we acknowledge that reality has indeed moved on – whether in terms of policing or, indeed, the IRA – and that, therefore, politics has to move on too, and not be caught in what the public may see as dated and arcane arguments.

Everyone – Unionists and Republicans, Nationalists and Loyalists – will be faced with difficult moments of decision in the autumn. We will do all we can to encourage those who want to move forward and in this respect I want to welcome the efforts of those in the Loyalist community who are trying to lead their areas into a new future.

In approaching these decisions, I hope they will be guided by two thoughts. First, a clear focus on what unites rather than what divides. Second, a vision of the future, well represented by the young people from Ballymena schools who met with the Prime Minister and Taoiseach at Stormont recently. They are the generation who will need and want the benefits of devolution, of self-government and of social cohesion if they are to face the huge global challenges of the new century. They will not agree on everything, but they are already talking to each other and establishing common ground. They have a natural sense of the future and natural ability to leave the past behind. In that, as so often, young people may be ahead of their parents.

Let us hope that Northern Ireland's politicians catch up with

**The balance we all have to achieve in the next few months is how, without denying people's genuine historical and current concerns, we acknowledge that reality has indeed moved on – whether in terms of policing or, indeed, the IRA – and that, therefore, politics has to move on too, and not be caught in what the public may see as dated and arcane arguments.**

**Not much time for Northern Ireland's people to find out whether their politicians are trapped in old hatreds, or up to new challenges of making Northern Ireland world class.**

them. There is not much time left. Not just the four months to the November 24th deadline for restoration of devolved government. But not much time left for Northern Ireland's parties to decide, either to lead the way to a world class Northern Ireland or remain impotent and paralysed in the face of globalisation, with no answers and no policies. Not much time for Northern Ireland's people to find out whether their politicians are trapped in old hatreds, or up to new challenges of making Northern Ireland world class.

I have been told by some that the deadline set by the Governments is not realistic. But the truth is that four months is easily enough if the political will exists to reach agreement. If the political will is not there, then no amount of extra time will help. That is why the Governments' attachment to the 24th November is real and fixed: it is simply a reflection of the reality which is obvious to the vast majority of the public in Northern Ireland.

But I know Northern Ireland's politicians and I believe that they are up for this challenge. I believe they can reach agreement on devolution, on policing and on the relatively small number of issues which remain. I believe they want to accept the mandate of their electorate to face up to the future. By November, you and I will know whether this confidence was well placed.

Jimmy and Vincent Campbell

Members of the audience at one of the sessions

Fr Harry Bohan,
Founder and Director of Céifin

Denis Bradley
Former Vice-Chair, NI Police Authority

Marian Harkin TD, MEP

# Chapter 1

# Losing the Sense of Community

*What is Community?*
Fr Harry Bohan
Founder and Director of Céifin Centre

*Getting Rid of the Bad – Retaining the Good*
Marian Harkin TD, MEP

*The Catholic Church is Centralist and Hierarchical*
Denis Bradley
Former Vice-Chair, Northern Ireland Police Authority

# Fr Harry Bohan

Sociologist, Founder of the Céifin Centre for
Values-Led Change

*Born in Feakle, Co. Clare. Ordained in 1963 and qualified as a sociologist at
the University of Wales. He is currently Director of Pastoral Planning in the
Diocese of Killaloe. He founded the Rural Resource Organisation which has been
responsible for encouraging communities throughout Ireland to determine their
own future. In 1998 he founded Céifin to promote reflection and debate on the
direction of society in Ireland. He has written extensively and his books include:*
Ireland Green, Roots in a Changing Society, Hope Begins at Home *and*
Community and the Soul of Ireland.

## What is Community?

The simple answer is that it is a word which describes a group of
people living in one place. We know, however, that it means an
awful lot more. It's about the spirit of a people, the soul of a society,
how they relate to one another, and so on.

We have a fair idea how the economy is promoted but who
promotes community? Who promotes it in a pluralistic society? Who
promotes it in the marketplace? Where does meaning come from in
these new times outside of the soulless valve of the economic?

Family and community were two systems which held Ireland
together for generations. People lived in groups composed of
families which, more or less, had the same roots. They spoke the
same language and wore the same kinds of clothes. They lived by the
same rites, rituals and traditions, had the same code of behaviour and
accepted the same authority. There was solidarity among them born
of both their flesh and blood loyalties and their need to co-operate to
meet material needs. The sense of belonging, solidarity and identity
was etched deep in their collective subconscious.

Community cushioned the extremes of the various "isms"
that visited the people of Ireland in the nineteenth and twentieth
centuries such as colonialism and Catholicism. But its greatest test
and challenge has come in the form of the other "c-ism", capitalism.
While the other "c-isms" might have brought a certain amount of
strife, they were, at their heart, a unifying force. Capitalism attacks
the very roots of community by making the individual the centre of
everything and suggesting that once individual wants and needs are
met there is no need for other people. Contemporary society is not
the product of the market place disintegrating as it grows and testing

> Community
> cushioned the
> extremes of the
> various "isms"
> that visited
> the people of
> Ireland in the
> nineteenth
> and twentieth
> centuries such
> as colonialism
> and Catholi-
> cism. But its
> greatest test
> and challenge
> has come in
> the form of the
> other "c-ism",
> capitalism.

our powers of communication – it is the economic miracle that has made this so. While we are grateful for the fact that we are now the best housed, best schooled and best clothed generation this nation has ever seen, we must be aware of the dangers the miracle can entail for our society.

This breakdown in confidence in community pushes people into a desperate form of individualism with all the struggles this implies in order to climb the ladder of success on which they base their sense of self-worth. This is taking a terrible toll on family life and individuals alike. Stark individualism increases and a terrible loneliness sets in within which people can only find relief by working harder for more money, more success, more distraction.

No man or woman is an island. People cannot live in isolation and in such extreme forms of individualism; everybody needs friends or companions. A sense of togetherness, belonging and shared experience, be it in groups of friends, in family, in clubs, in churches or in groups of any kind, is an integral part of human nature. Community is the foundation of human society. Isolated, we curl up and die.

In one out of 20 Samaritan branches in Ireland in 2005, 29,500 contacts were made; callers confided thoughts of suicide in 1,800 calls and sadly were in the process of attempting suicide on 50 or so occasions.

But there are indications that the level of individualism is now bringing such pressures that it may be giving rise to a deeper search for tangible community, belonging, meaning and relationships.

Briefly, I want to cover *four broad areas* which I believe require serious consideration if our society is to reverse the trend and restore a natural balance in the area of human relationships.

## Spiritual Relationships

Until very recently, we defined spiritual growth purely in terms of a religious "label" which people wore – be it Christian, Muslim, Hindu or Jew – and in these times spiritual leaders were spoken of only in terms of the leaders or guides within the faiths.

In this new century, a new definition of spiritual leadership is emerging which manifests itself in ordinary people searching for spiritual inspiration both inside and outside of the established religions. Indications of a wide-spread search for meaning and of people trying desperately to connect with their own soul and the collective soul of humanity are evident in many ways. One only has to look at the "spirituality" sections of bookshops, in the new holistic centres that are springing up, in yoga, in meditation courses,

> **Stark individualism increases and a terrible loneliness sets in within which people can only find relief by working harder for more money, more success, more distraction.**

in changing food consciousness, in the exploration of alternative medicines and in a desire to be closer to nature to find evidence of this. Many of these "explorers" are practising members of other denominations, left unsatisfied by the rituals of their faith. Spiritual expression is becoming more diverse and, consequently, spiritual leadership is coming from new sources. Many people are now making a conscious choice about who they want to lead them in their spiritual quest. Religion and the established churches can only become the bedrock of community once again if they are to offer meaningful spiritual growth. Ritual, habit and tradition are no longer enough to hold people in the faith of their parents. That is the central challenge and duty facing organised religion, to regain its spiritual leadership through giving people what they need – spiritual growth. Nothing else matters – not power over others, not status in society, not the parish finances and not defending the status quo. The spiritual growth of the individual is itself a fuel to the growth of a sense of community. If people are growing spiritually then what they do as planners, business people, teachers and citizens must be enriched by this growth. The last century was about the material/external world – this century will be about the spiritual/inner world or about nothing.

**Religion and the established churches can only become the bedrock of community once again if they are to offer meaningful spiritual growth. Ritual, habit and tradition are no longer enough to hold people in the faith of their parents.**

## Building Our Future from Our Roots

There is every indication that one of the great challenges facing us is how the local will respond to the global. Already we are seeing clear indications that in the search for identity some areas of Irish life such as music, dance and language have acquired a whole new lease of life. Ireland as a nation is made up of approximately 2,000 communities of various shapes and sizes. Central to these communities would have been the former "pillars" of church and sport. People identified with these communities down through the years. Many are now expanding, some at a phenomenal rate – taking on a new shape.

Coinciding with this expansion is a renewed interest in local history, heritage, sense of place. In this context, we need to be careful to acknowledge the achievements of generations that went before us.

We are well aware of the scandals and the breaches of trust that have plagued modern Ireland with regularity in recent years. These are effectively the betrayal of the present generation by preceding generations. They call attention to the civic nature of morality.

One can only welcome the honesty which refuses to allow things to be swept under the carpet. From now on trust has to be earned, not conferred, and this is also to be welcomed.

But, as we emerge from this period of "cleansing", we need to be careful not to heap our own sins on the sins of the fathers. There is obviously a certain rejoicing in the debunking of politicians and heroes, churches and traditions, moral values and past achievements. But there is a real danger now that we are willing to delude ourselves that we are somehow better, more honest, more trustworthy, more enlightened, more moral than those who went before us. It might also suggest that we can begin from here and that we are capable of building a civilisation without roots – from scratch, almost – that we have nothing to learn from our predecessors, or that we learn only from failures not achievements. It could even lead to the suggestion that we have no past to be proud of.

We could convince ourselves that greed, for example, has no part in our world, or abuse of drink and drugs – that all the abuses of power belonged to the past and that judgmental, authoritarian people and organisations belonged only to another age. Listen to the editors of some national newspapers in recent times stand in judgement on almost everything that in their opinion does not fit the liberal agenda – an agenda that has so far not been critiqued – and one wonders is this about a search for truth or is it about selling newspapers. If we fail to think more deeply, we risk building a society that is made up, not of living people but of abstractions with a life that is lived in the shallows, without roots and without depth.

*If we fail to think more deeply, we risk building a society that is made up, not of living people but of abstractions with a life that is lived in the shallows, without roots and without depth.*

## Planning for Communities

One of the most notable features of present day Ireland is the unstoppable and rapid tide of housing and retail development in our towns, our villages and, most noticeably, our rural areas. The debate on the direction of our development is now moving on to address what I believe is a more important question – what does this type of development say about what we have become, in modern prosperous Ireland? Are we planning for houses or for communities?

There is no doubt that the rapid growth of many of our settlements has raised issues which, I think, need to be addressed urgently. Too many of our housing developments are happening in a head-long rush to facilitate the property developers and speculators.

With food and clothing, housing was always regarded as a basic necessity for life. It has now become a commodity for trading. Can we honestly say that many of the new developments are something we can truly be proud of and be admired in years to come? If we are truly honest with ourselves, I think the answer is no. Could we do it better? I think the answer is, yes we could. I believe that people should be inspired by development, should be proud of it and should benefit from it. There is much to be gained from sensitive, balanced and well designed development. But there is even more to be lost when it is insensitive, unbalanced and poorly designed – it leaves us feeling uninspired, powerless and disillusioned with progress.

We now find this necessity achieving the status of unachievable for many, particularly and most tragically for the young. To provide a solid base from which to raise a family parents are now drawn into the crushing mill of capitalism. People in their twenties are saddling themselves with crippling mortgages to buy houses that are improperly finished and worth a third of what they cost.

**People in their twenties are saddling themselves with crippling mortgages to buy houses that are improperly finished and worth a third of what they cost.**

## Coping with Cyberspace

We are all acutely aware that the great revolutions of the past 20 years are in the area of communications technology and this is having a profound effect on relationships. There has never been anything in human history like the personal computer. The impact it has made on society is probably unequalled. Computers are machines that handle information. The common use of computers by ordinary people is less than a quarter of a century old. The internet is even younger still and only began to impact on society in a big way in the early nineties.

Who could have foreseen that in a short span of years, the internet would hold more information than all the books that had been produced in the world since writing began? That is what the experts tell us. But when we try to address the concepts of community in today's world it is the manner in which computing has influenced the interaction between people that interests us.

The existence of cyberspace has made completely new forms of communication possible and, more importantly, quicker. When letter writing was the main form of distant contact there was a period of at least a couple of days before a reply arrived. With e-mails and the aptly named instant messaging services available, information can volley back and forth across the world in seconds or, in many cases, less.

The internet has become the main avenue of communication for the modern world. This development has far-reaching consequences which are only beginning to emerge. It is an unusual happening, as nobody really structured it or, for that matter, controls it.

Ironically, the machine which most clearly represents the kind of "progress" that is quoted to us by our political masters in relation to society has given people an opportunity to confront an increasingly nagging need – the need for community. The latest on-line phenomenon is that of "communities". These are virtual meeting places where people with common interests, feelings and ideals can come together to share those emotions and gain a sense of belonging that is missing from their daily and, it must be pointed out, actual lives. There is a terrible sad aspect to this expression of yearning on the part of humanity at large. There is a desperate desire to interact in a meaningful way with each other but in the modern world we can only, it seems, find it in a world that doesn't exist.

The fact that all internet communication must take place through the medium of a machine is critically important. Even with the most sophisticated web-cams or video conferencing when the interaction is over, the participants are immediately separated by perhaps thousands of miles. Even if the distance is only one mile the solitude is no less real. In this the internet achieves the remarkable feat of bringing us closer together by keeping us further apart.

## *Conclusion*

In the next generation of people, and I want to stress that word *people*, we have unlimited potential. While we have made stunning advances in recent years we must not forget that it is all made possible by people. Despite what we tell ourselves, we are very fragile animals. We are emotional, social and sentient which is a miraculous combination but also a very dangerous one. That indefinable thing that we call a soul singles us out of all creation as needing extra nourishment which, we realised very early on, we get, in the main, from each other – the shoulders to cry on and slap depending where we lie on the rollercoaster range of our emotions. We are tactile and generous and ultimately good but we need to interact with each other to enhance these attributes. In doing this we extract the very best from our human condition and this ultimately will benefit us all.

That indefinable thing that we call a soul singles us out of all creation as needing extra nourishment which, we realised very early on, we get, in the main, from each other ...

# Marian Harkin TD, MEP

*Born in Sligo and educated at the Marist Convent, Tubbercurry and UCD (BSc, HdipEd). Formerly secondary school teacher. First elected to Dáil Éireann in 2002 as an Independent for Sligo-Leitrim. Elected to the European Parliament in June, 2004 and is a member of the ALDE Group – an alliance of Liberals and Democrats. She is a member of the Parliament's Regional Development Committee and of the Disability Intergroup. She is also a member of the Delegation for Relations with Canada.*

## Getting Rid of the Bad – Retaining the Good

To suggest that we may be losing the sense of community is also to suggest that we at one time or another had a real sense of community and, furthermore, it also suggests that this particular community ethos was valuable and we are the poorer for its loss.

I am not at all sure I fully agree with this viewpoint, although I know it is widely held. I have on many occasions heard the assertion that the Ireland of the 40s, 50s and 60s and even the 70s was a much better place from a community perspective – yes we didn't have the economic prosperity and we raised our children for export, but it was a happier place, it was a safer place, older people were valued, there was a meitheal tradition, there was time – time to chat, time to visit, time to céilidh – there was respect for authority, for the institutions – and there was a sense of community, of belonging, of being rooted in time and place.

> ... but it was a happier place, it was a safer place, older people were valued, there was a meitheal tradition, there was time – time to chat, time to visit ...

That vision, that view, is often juxtaposed against Irish society in 2006 – a rat race, hours spent commuting, people glued to mobile phones, televisions, games and the internet. No respect for authority, fear stalking the streets, older people in fear of their lives, abuse of alcohol and drugs – indeed to quote the MacGill brochure: "more and more often one hears talk about greed and avarice, the vulgar flaunting of huge personal wealth, selfishness and the loss of the community spirit that was once such a characteristic of both urban and rural life in Ireland". However, as I have already said earlier, I am not convinced that it is quite so black and white.

We are of course witnessing an unprecedented level of change and part of that change is the change in the expression of community spirit. Communities are changing and community action is changing, and just because things are not the way they used to be, doesn't mean that everything is falling apart.

I would briefly like to look at the community ethos and community spirit of Ireland in the 40s, 50s and 60s, and ask the question: what did we lose? What do we need to hold on to? Looking at communities today, how can we support them and build up the community infrastructure to allow communities to manage change and not to be overwhelmed or swamped by it – as Fr. Harry Bohan has said: "we can make choices now about where we want to go with community". When we speak of the community spirit that was in Ireland, what are we referring to? – the meitheal tradition, the welcome on the mat, the genuine warmth of people, the community support at the critical times of life, particularly in times of loss, the voluntary effort in coaching the local team, organising the local festival, the community games, etc., and all of this is an accurate description, but it also leaves out a great deal. That community was often a closed community where those who towed the line and obeyed the rules survived and sometimes thrived, but what of those who strayed outside the box or those who were different, those who had a disability or those who simply refused to bow the head or bend the knee. That community ethos saw to it that those who were different, sometimes mentally ill, sometimes just plain awkward or simply an obstacle, were often dispatched to the local mental hospital or asylum. St. Columba's Hospital in Sligo at one time housed hundreds and hundreds of patients – they used to call it "The Leitrim Hotel" because the more rural areas of Leitrim were well represented there. That community ethos presided over a system whereby (i) those with a disability were consigned to the loft or the back room, (ii) any woman suffering domestic violence was quietly told, you made your bed, now lie on it, (iii) any girl who found herself pregnant outside of marriage was dispatched to places like Castlepollard or, in latter years, sent on the boat to England.

That community, sometimes unknowingly and sometimes knowingly, colluded in a system whereby children were physically abused in schools and sexually abused in their own homes and in the sacristies of churches.

That community was often a cold place for women. Women were the glue that held the family together and they were the link to the Church, but they nearly always took second place and often took last place in the greater scheme of things. The matriarchal grandmother or mother was often the power broker in the home and to placate them the phrase, "The hand that rocks the cradle rules the world" was often trotted out – but of course it's not true, not in the real sense of decision making or influencing outcomes in the outside world.

It is amazing for many younger women to learn that women did not get equal pay until the 1970s and that the marriage bar meant women had to give up work on marriage. Indeed only last night I spoke to a lady who can never have a contributory pension in her own right – she is a dependant spouse – and several times I have

> That community was often a cold place for women. Women were the glue that held the family together and they were the link to the Church, but they nearly always took second place and often took last place in the greater scheme of things.

asked the Minister for Social Welfare to change the rules at Budget time to allow those women who had to give up their jobs as a result of the marriage bar, and who started work when their families were reared, to clock up credits so that they can receive contributory pensions in their own right. I am not trying to be negative for its own sake, not standing in judgement. I am looking for balance.

First of all, we need to understand that the community ethos prevailing in that Ireland was both good and bad and we needed to lose the bad and retain the good. We needed to open up our communities to make them more inclusive and we needed to take greater care of the more vulnerable – whether we have done that or not I will come back to. Secondly, many people will say, "but that was a different time and place, you cannot judge it by today's standards" and I say, "precisely". They were different times but equally this is a different time and, while we have lost, maybe we have also gained. But the more things change the more they remain the same. One might have thought that in small communities where people had little mutual self-help that community support was crucial. In our globalised, plugged-in, always-on world we need community more than ever. Globalisation is good, globalisation is the internet, the free movement of people and services and goods – but globalisation is ruthless, it is the naked face of the market, and it scares the hell out of people – not so much because of what it is, but because we have little or no control over it. Our local politicians have no control, our Government and Ministers have no control, even the EU is just one player on a very large stage. We are constantly being challenged by rapid progress in countries such as India and China and words like outsourcing and offshoring of jobs are now part of ordinary language. Donegal, of course, was one of the first counties to feel the chill wind of globalisation with the closure of Fruit of the Loom heralding further closures and redundancies. Farmers fear for their future as the World Trade Organization (WTO) negotiations loom large and they are relying on Peter Mandelson, a man not noted for supporting agriculture, to bat for them. Parents are concerned about the global nature of the availability of drugs and the inability of our judicial system or law enforcement systems to deal with the problem – not just here but in any country.

Confronted with their own powerlessness and, in many cases, that of their Government, many individuals and communities are rudderless and feel they are being tossed like flotsam and jetsam at the mercy of the globalisation tsunami. More than ever we need some rock to cling to, we need a sense of purpose and a sense of place and, above all, we need a sense that we can regain some control over our lives and that we can influence the outcome of events.

**Globalisation is good, globalisation is the internet, the free movement of people and services and goods – but globalisation is ruthless, it is the naked face of the market, and it scares the hell out of people ...**

Community involvement, community participation allows us to influence what happens in our own local area. We move from being passive consumers to active decision makers. Community Development, Community Action underpins the very notion of citizenship. It acknowledges the role of communities in designing local responses based on local needs and, in my opinion, most crucially it is a recognition that democracy is a complex mixture of representation – your politicians and participation by yourselves.

Community Development, Community Action is alive in Ireland. It is vibrant in a few places, and growing in some areas and struggling in many parts. Volunteering is estimated to be worth between one-quarter and one-half billion euro to our economy each year. Volunteering is changing. It may be harder to get somebody to train the local team or supervise the local disco or deliver meals on wheels, but other types of community activity are gaining ground. Communities are much more active in protecting the environment.

Communities will mobilise to demand their right. Very recently in Donegal we could see where community action is alive and well when Donegal Action for Cancer mobilised 15,000 people on the streets of Letterkenny. This has achieved some success in delivering a positive outcome for the whole of Donegal. This is not just a once-off on-to-the-street protest. Donegal Action for Cancer has members and public representatives from nearly every single parish in Co. Donegal and represents community response to a community need.

People are not that interested in becoming Chair or Secretary of a local organisation because that is too open-ended and you become one of those few always called upon, but schemes whereby people give a designated half hour per week or month – let's say using your managerial skills to mentor a community company or participating for a definite period of time in fundraising, particularly if it is for a cause close to your heart – or where people come together with a common interest, say parents of children with autism, the provision of community childcare, a support group for people recovering from cancer. Many of these types of organisations are flourishing and these are real community supports.

The Leader programme in Donegal has in excess of 200 projects, Inishowen Partnership has 30 projects involving 200 groups and Inishowen Leader has 86 projects. All rely on community/voluntary effort and represent a crucial element of the new community ethos.

Finally, I mentioned earlier that, as well as losing, we have also gained. In the wider scheme of things, the vulnerable in our communities have better opportunities. It may have taken Kathy Sinnott to take the State to court, but children with disability are better cared for – we still have a very long way to go but we are on

**Community involvement, community participation allows us to influence what happens in our own local area. We move from being passive consumers to active decision makers.**

the road. As a politician, I am painfully aware of the inadequacies of our system, but it is better than it was. Older people have lost some of the respect that was automatically theirs and some live in fear, but our services are better, and there is a better quality of life for many through programmes like Active Age, Active Retirement and Rural Transport.

The banks continue to make large profits but the credit unions continue to grow and they are under the democratic control of their members. Women's lives have changed irrevocably – some of it, not all, for the better – and while women still want change, very few would go back to women's roles as they used to be.

**Women's lives have changed irrevocably – some of it, not all, for the better – and while women still want change, very few would go back to women's roles as they used to be.**

We have certain legislative safeguards in place to uphold citizens' and communities' rights. Apart from the usual appeals processes we have the Ombudsman, the Equality Tribunal, the Unfair Dismissals Board, the Freedom of Information Act. Many, though not all of these, are woefully inadequate, but it is an improvement on the stone wall that was there before.

Finally, recently, Macra na Feirme and others launched an initiative – "get to know your neighbour" – an interesting approach to facilitate people in breaking the ice. We have gone from the time when everybody knew everybody's business – valley of the squinting windows – to a time when some people do not even know their neighbours.

In some ways the pendulum has swung too far. The trick will be to slow it down on its way back and allow it settle in the middle.

# Denis Bradley

Former Vice-Chairman, Police Authority of NI

*Currently Chairman and Chief Executive of Northlands Films and Director of Treatment and Education at the Northlands Centre – a centre for the treatment of addictions. Formerly a Catholic priest. He was a member of the NI Drugs Committee and the BBC Broadcasting Council. He is a trustee of the Foyle Downs Syndrome Trust. A founder member of the Bogside Community Association, he has spent many years working with community organisations. He was appointed to the Vice-Chairmanship of the Police Authority of NI when it was set up in 2001 and stepped down in 2006. Because of his association with the Police Authority he received threats to his life from dissident republican organisations and in 2005 was subjected to a physical attack in Derry.*

## The Catholic Church is Centralist and Hierarchical

In the debate regarding the well being of community life in Ireland there are clearly different and somewhat opposing views. Some people are of the opinion that community life is healthier and more energised now than it was in olden days. Those who are of this opinion point to the multitude of groups that are to be found throughout the country. They point to the diversity of groups and societies working in every part of the country. They claim that the work that is being done and the relationships that are created are more substantive and real than what they were in the past. They certainly question the romantic notion of the past. They claim that Irish society in the past was more comfortable in avoiding and even hiding problems than it was in honestly facing up to and trying to solve them.

At the other end of the scale are those who believe that community life in Ireland is in free-fall. They regret the passing of so many of the customs and traditions that they see as having facilitated and enabled community. They point to greater isolation, people living in the same neighbourhoods in great numbers but detached and isolated from each other. They give examples of housing estates where thousands of people live but have little or no contact with each other. They are convinced that many of the institutions of Irish society have lost their authority and status and that this has led to a much less moral and caring society.

In this debate, I would probably place myself somewhere in the middle. I am very aware and, indeed, I know how much the Irish community in which I was born and reared forms me. There was

**I know how much the Irish community in which I was born and reared forms me. There was much in it that was very good. But there was also much of it that was very bad.**

– 35 –

much in it that was very good. But there was also much of it that was very bad. Isolation and detachment were probably less likely but problems and difficulties were more likely to be avoided or exported. The most concrete example in my local community was that most of my classmates went to England or further afield to earn their living. It has often been pointed out that there is no glory in exporting your youth to other countries. Most of those people have now returned to share in the riches of the Celtic Tiger and if their sons and daughters are emigrating it is to see new places and broaden their life experiences.

It is possible to argue that the new-found riches have not made us any more content or happy. If that is true there can be many explanations for it. It might be that we are not convinced that it will last, that the bubble will burst. It might even be that there is a form of Catholic guilt at work. We may be uncomfortable with riches. Riches don't get us to heaven and indeed may be an obstacle on that journey.

Personally, I am a great believer in community and its development. For most of my life I have put an amount of time and effort into community development. Way back in the seventies, I established a number of community development projects in Derry. That was the time of the beginning of the "troubles" and it seemed fairly clear to me that community needed to be developed to face and to sustain itself in the storm of political violence and death that it was heading into.

I have also been a great believer in politics and in its role of establishing and sustaining a healthy society. I think we too glibly criticise politics and politicians. We, of all people, should know the truth that politics is a substitute for civil war. Good legislation enhances society. Like many aspects of life, we only become aware of the importance of politics when things go wrong and our lives are negatively affected.

But while I am a supporter of community action and politics, I am not convinced that either or both of them scratch the spot where we are presently itching. Any analysis of the soul of Ireland will highlight unease and discontent that goes very deep. There are many manifestations to sustain that argument but among the most visible would be the amount of alcohol we consume and the damage that directly comes from that level of drinking. Report after report points to a level of consumption that outstrips most other countries in the European Community. Other reports point to the consequences of that consumption. Hospitals, courts, police, social and counselling services are all stretched dealing with the outcomes. City centres and town centres have become no-go areas for many at weekends.

The growth in suicide, particularly among young males, is another indicator of that deep unease. There is obviously deep pain that brings some to the point of taking their own lives but there is also some recognition that suicide is not something that happens in a vaccuum. It can be seen as an indicator that society and community are failing to deliver meaning and a level of contentment great enough to prevent some people from taking the extreme action of ending their lives.

This level of discontent strays into the area of belief and spirituality. It goes, indeed, to the area of what is often referred to as the soul. Soul is difficult to define but in simplistic terms it can be seen as the spark that connects meaning and human life. That connection underpins and informs not alone the individual but also the manner in which that individual lives life in relationship with fellow human beings and, indeed, with the whole of creation. Most people will define those various connections in relationship with a creative God but even those who interpret life as random and finite see the importance of soul in the affairs of humankind.

It is perhaps ironic and tragic that, at a time when this country was in great need of a spirituality that would have wrestled with the rapidity of change, the very organisation that was the customary reference and beacon of this aspect of life fell into crisis and disrepute. The crisis in the Catholic Church could probably not have come at a worst time. The sexual scandals, and more especially the way they were handled and mishandled, drove the Church into a defensive and self-protective position. The revelations of child abuse were too much for many people. Lots walked away from the Church and the majority who stayed were burdened with embarrassment and doubt as to the relevance and capability of the organisation to re-establish authenticity and proper authority.

The position has not been helped by the poor quality of the debate and discussion among both the clerical caste and what are described as the faithful. Solutions have been proposed that only amount to small adjustments that in no way address the heart of the crisis. Proposals such as greater involvement of the laity in the administration and worship of the Church, or the abolition of compulsory celibacy for priesthood, are very fine as far as they go but they go nowhere near the depth or the breadth of the problem.

Any faith worthy of the description has to have a worldview that is utterly relevant to the local. There is a similarity here with politics. It is said that all politics are local and that description rings true to those who understand politics. But its localness in no way means that politics can or should be constrained from having a world view. The expression arises from a proper understanding that there should be a harmony between the world view and the local. It is the same with faith. Faith needs to be rooted in the local and at the same time informed with a world view that forces it beyond the constraints and the preoccupations of the local.

**It is perhaps ironic and tragic that, at a time when this country was in great need of a spirituality that would have wrestled with the rapidity of change, the very organisation that was the customary reference and beacon of this aspect of life fell into crisis and disrepute.**

That harmony is impossible at the moment within the structures and the ethos of the institution that is the Catholic Church. The institution does not allow for that harmony. It is an organisation that is completely centralist in its structure. It is centralist and hierarchical. All substantive and important decisions are the prerogative of Rome or more precisely the Vatican. Nothing of import is decided at the local. At the very moment when we need a real and honest debate about issues such as faith, religion, church, community, when we need a philosophical and theological debate about matters that touch upon the soul of Ireland, the Vatican disbars us from having it. Even if such a debate were allowed, its findings and its conclusions are likely to be anathema to the Vatican.

At a time of deep, deep crisis and pain for this country, when we need space and encouragement to face difficult questions openly and honestly, we have our hands handcuffed and our legs shackled. The Vatican is strangling us. That strangulation is so great that it neutralises local leadership and it sidelines the impact of vision and insight. There is little visible leadership within the Irish Catholic Church presently but, even if there were, the possibility of it making any difference is zero. No bishop can do anything of impact that is not approved by the Vatican. No priest, good or bad, can bring any new dynamic or thinking that does not carry the imprimatur of the Vatican. That relationship between the Vatican and the local church is at the heart of the problem. Until that is changed or redefined then nothing of import can change and we are left to wallow in our distress.

If I could bestow anything on this situation it would be a declaration of UDI from the Irish church that would last at least twenty years. There would be those who would see that UDI as a miniature modern reformation. Not so. The Catholic Church is like every human institution. It is in need of continuous reform and those who claim that it is also a divine institution need to be careful that they are not harking back to olden times that developed a heretical theology according to which there was no salvation outside of this institution. The Catholic Church is, of course, a community of communities. The balance of the relationships between those communities has become distorted. The distortion is all in favour of the Vatican.

It would take something of the order of twenty years to restore confidence and authenticity and proper authority to the local church so that it could engage properly and maturely with the universal church. The call for UDI is only a symbol of the depth of the damage that has been done by a relationship that has got itself completely out of kilter.

Despite the severity of my criticism, I am not without hope. For that hope I look to the artist and to the scholar.

> No bishop can do anything of impact that is not approved by the Vatican. No priest, good or bad, can bring any new dynamic or thinking that does not carry the imprimatur of the Vatican. That relationship between the Vatican and the local church is at the heart of the problem.

It is ironic or, more accurately, prophetic that a story that had its roots in this town of Glenties identified and highlighted this very issue. It is a story that is now known around the world. It is a story that was written and developed by a man whose ancestors came from this town. I am referring to Brian Friel's play, "Dancing at Lughnasa". I would guess that the author was only semi-aware of the issue that he so dramatically captured. The muse is seldom fully aware of the questions that they raise.

One of the characters in the play, Father Jack, has been in Africa for most of his priestly life. There he has gone "native", finding joy and meaning in the rituals and customs of the native people. He has now returned home, old, physically unwell and eccentric. It is only he who brings insight, compassion and understanding to a twisted set of relationships and "mores" that have grown out of a narrow and frigid spirituality. There are passages in the play where he describes the customs and the rituals of the local African people among whom he lived and, presumably, had gone to proselytise. These passages depict an understanding of the connectedness of the secular and the sacred. And, in wonderful dramatic irony, the connection is made between the joyous and profane celebrations of Africa and the autumnal festival of the ancient Irish in thanksgiving to one of the Celtic gods, Lugh, who gives the title to the play. We are a Celtic people who, over the centuries, grew and developed a Celtic Church and then we allowed it to be latinised. We are not served well by being completely latinised in our expression and in our administrative structures.

I had believed that I would have died without seeing a fully developed theology that was appropriate to the times we live in. A number of weeks ago, a transcript of a new book arrived in my home. It will be published this autumn and it is called *The Essence of Christianity*. It is the first fully satisfying theological thesis that I have read. It is the more satisfying because an Irishman and a good friend wrote it. James Mackey is a retired professor of theology and philosophy. He has taught in some of the most eminent universities in the world. I am not certain but I suspect that the present crisis that I am trying to describe drove him to leave his retirement couch and write a wonderful and demanding treatise. It is completely and wholly based on the Bible. It tackles all the great themes that are so pertinent to all ages. Creation, original sin, Christ, church are among the themes that he tackles and it is refreshing that, as well as the Bible and the great philosophers, he also refers to Irish writers and poets for elucidation.

There is hope. The soul of Ireland may not be as healthy as you or I might desire but there are still enough Irish men and women with great soul who will face up to and will eventually face down the painfulness of the present time. Good, as always, will overcome.

> We are a Celtic people who, over the centuries, grew and developed a Celtic Church and then we allowed it to be latinised.

David Begg
General Secretary, ICTU

Michael McDowell TD
Minister for Justice, Equality
and Law Reform

Lucy Gaffney
Chairperson, National Action Plan Against Racism

*Chapter 2*

# Immigration, Integration and Cultural Identity

*Managing Migration and Social Cohesion*
DAVID BEGG
**General Secretary, ICTU**

*We Need a Range of International Policies*
LUCY GAFFNEY
**Chairperson, National Action Plan Against Racism**

*Liberal Republicanism – Reconciling Diversity*
MICHAEL MCDOWELL TD
**Minister for Justice, Equality and Law Reform**

# David Begg

## General Secretary, Irish Congress of Trade Unions

*Formerly a technologist with the ESB. General Secretary of the Communications Workers' Union 1990–1997. In 1997 became Chief Executive of the international humanitarian organisation, Concern Worldwide. Appointed General Secretary of ICTU in 2001. Has been a Director of the Central Bank since 1995. He is also a Governor of the Irish Times Trust, a member of the Government Taskforce on Active Citizenship, a member of the National Economic and Social Council and sits on the Executive Committee of the European Trade Union Confederation (ETUC).*

## Managing Migration and Social Change

The growing potency of immigration as a political issue is evidenced by the recent collapse of the Dutch Government over the disputed citizenship status of the prominent campaigner and critic of Islam, Ayaan Hirsi Ali. The past year has seen immigration-related rioting in France, a world-wide controversy over cartoons published in a Danish newspaper and a somewhat intemperate debate about illegal immigration in the United States.

It is not immediately obvious why immigration should have moved so rapidly up the political agenda. It may be in part related to globalisation and the insecurity caused by outsourcing on the one hand and large migration flows on the other. It may, in part, also be related to insecurity arising from geo-political tension in the Middle East.

For whatever reason, immigration is fuelling a debate about identity. An example of this is to be found in clashes between Samuel Huntington, author of *The Clash of Civilisations*, and Alan Wolfe, an American academic, in a recent edition of *Foreign Affairs* magazine about Huntington's latest offering entitled *Who Are We? The Challenge to Americans' National Identity*. These exchanges are worth reading on the Foreign Affairs website for they are fairly vitriolic. What I think is most significant though is that America, a country built on immigration, should be having this debate at all.

Europe, if anything, is more challenged by this phenomenon of migration. Issues of identity are probably more acute. By history, Europe has been the continent which populated the New World through emigration. Uncertainty about where the true borders of Europe should be drawn is central to the issue of enlargement. Sitting uncomfortably with these concerns is the knowledge that an unfavourable demographic, by virtue of an ageing population,

> **What I think is most significant though is that America, a country built on immigration, should be having this debate at all.**

means that some level of inward migration is unavoidable. And then there is uncertainty about what this will do to the sustainability of the European Social Model. Americans are not affected in the same way about their social model – they don't have one!

Of course it is hardly necessary to observe that Ireland has been transformed by immigration in the last couple of years. Not only have we changed from being a country of emigration to one of immigration but it has happened at breathtaking speed. When the preliminary results from the census become available later (July 2006) I expect that our population will be larger than we think and that the proportion of non-Irish born people will be over 9 per cent. This change will have happened over a timescale of two to three years whereas it took countries like Germany and Britain over 40 years to make this kind of transition.

We are fortunate, I think, that the impact of this transition has been softened by two significant factors: a booming economy and an influx of people from Europe who are culturally similar to the indigenous population.

Had these conditions not existed I doubt that such a rapid change could have been accommodated with so little social dislocation. As it was, the labour market dimension to the change was very challenging but I believe we have acted in a timely and prudent manner to anticipate and prevent problems in this area. It is this aspect of immigration that I intend to focus on.

It was naive of Government to think that employers, faced with the prospect of an abundant supply of vulnerable, and understandably compliant, labour, would not succumb to the temptation to exploit them. That, of course, is what happened. Initially, it was below the radar screen activity in horticulture, hotels and other low pay industries. But the issue burst into serious public prominence with the GAMA and Irish Ferries disputes. Parallel developments with the Laval and Viking cases in Sweden and Denmark focussed critical attention on the implications of the EU Services Directive. In Ireland on December 9 last, over 160,000 people voted with their feet to support the Congress National Day of Protest against exploitation, displacement and a race to the bottom. Very deliberately, the banner we chose to lead the main march read: "Equal Rights for All Workers".

This issue of employment standards, compliance and enforcement in the labour market was made the central demand of the unions in the new round of Social Partnership negotiations. We were somewhat sceptical about the willingness of employers and Government to seriously contemplate moving away from the extremely flexible labour market model which had been so resisted only three years earlier. For

**It was naive of Government to think that employers, faced with the prospect of an abundant supply of vulnerable, and understandably compliant, labour, would not succumb to the temptation to exploit them.**

this reason we sought certain assurances about the principles involved before entering talks and this took three months to achieve.

What, in practice, were we trying to achieve? It can be reduced to three critical areas, viz:

- We had to make a working assumption that, if not addressed, it was only a matter of time before we had another Irish Ferries situation, albeit on land. Without a robust legal and enforcement architecture to deal with it our evaluation was that such a dispute would release very damaging racial and social tensions.

- We had to factor in the experience of the Gate Gourmet dispute in the UK which allowed the employer to contrive an industrial dispute to justify a collective dismissal of the existing workforce and its replacement with a completely new group of workers. Existing Irish law would also allow this although this is not well known.

- We had to deal with large-scale abuse of employment standards, including extensive use of bogus self-employment, principally, but not exclusively, in the construction sector.

**We had to deal with large-scale abuse of employment standards, including extensive use of bogus self-employment, principally, but not exclusively, in the construction sector.**

The new agreement, *Towards 2016*, deals comprehensively with these issues. A complex series of measures detailed over 15 pages commits the Government to extensive legislation over the next year and a half. While the provisions of the agreement are technical and not easy to access for the lay reader, the following are some of the key provisions:

- The establishment of a new Office of Employment Rights Compliance (ODERC) with an increase to 90 in the number of labour inspectors backed up by 23 new positions of a legal, accounting and administrative support nature.

- ODERC will work closely with unions through agreed memoranda of understanding to tackle problems of non-compliance.

- The Revenue Commissioners, Social Welfare and ODERC will collaborate through CAB-style joint investigation units to target serious abuses of employment standards.

- The RCT1 tax system will be reformed to prevent people in the building industry and elsewhere from being forced into bogus self-employed status to allow employers to avoid pension contributions etc.

- Employers will be obliged, under pain of a fine of €250,000 or imprisonment, to keep accurate employment records in a prescribed format for inspection by the labour inspectors.

- The Minister for Enterprise, Trade and Employment will take new legislative powers to allow him to publish the outcome of investigations like the GAMA case.

- There will be a new employment rights procedure to allow easier access to Rights Commissioners, the Court and the EAT and with compensation where rights are denied. Up to now only monies owed and expenses could be awarded. Powers to award up to two years' pay by way of compensation is a very significant change and will help many migrant workers whose cases are usually about bread and butter issues like payment of correct wages.

- Penalties for non-compliance in all areas of employment will be increased as follows: on summary conviction, €5,000 in the District Court and/or imprisonment; on indictment, penalties up to €250,000 fine.

In essence, the exploitation and abuse of workers is now a de facto criminal offence. This represents a profound cultural and social shift and one which I believe will benefit this society hugely, over the long term.

> ... the exploitation and abuse of workers is now a de facto criminal offence. This represents a profound cultural and social shift ...

- New standards of compliance with labour law and requirements of certification of same in order to tender for public procurement contracts. If certification is not received payments can be withheld. In other words, the taxpayer will no longer subsidise exploitation or sharp employment practices.

- Legislation to regulate employment agencies and educational establishments to prevent them from undermining employment standards and immigration law.

- Changes to the work permits system including the right of a person to apply for and reapply for their own permit and requirement for non-EEA students to be covered by a work permit.

- Legislative changes to prevent Irish Ferries-type collective redundancies and Gate Gourmet-type unfair dismissals.

- An LRC Code of Practice to protect people working as domestic servants.

I have no hesitation in saying that these measures in their totality, and in the context of the legislation necessary to implement them, represent the single biggest leap forward in social policy initiated in this country. Other important social policy changes were inspired by the EU but this is the biggest thing we have ever done of our own volition. It is also the most difficult project Congress has ever undertaken both in terms of its complexity and in overcoming the opposition to it. The international significance of this work has already been referred to by the Taoiseach. The validity of his observation was underlined by the fact that we have already had a visit by representatives of the British Cabinet Office seeking to explore the relevance of this agreement to their immigration challenge.

In the current debate about ratification of the agreement, I cannot understand how opponents of the agreement can rationally dismiss what has been achieved. No one on our side has criticised the proposals – in fact they were unanimously endorsed by the Executive Council of Congress. There is apparently a view that Government would make these changes anyway. I have no doubt that, in a general election year, political manifestos would promise to increase the resources of the Labour Inspectorate, but I doubt if they would go much further. It is naïve to think that a comprehensive reform of the labour market would be achieved in any context other than a social partnership agreement.

> **It is naïve to think that a comprehensive reform of the labour market would be achieved in any context other than a social partnership agreement.**

I know that some of our affiliated unions who oppose the agreement have philosophical objections to the whole concept of social partnership. While respecting this outlook I have to question whether fidelity to a philosophical viewpoint should stand in the way of an agreement which offers an unprecedented level of protection to migrant and indigenous workers alike.

Indeed, it can be argued that the Irish trade union movement has successfully bucked the very debilitating and damaging global trend towards weakening and diminishing employment rights and worker protection. Admittedly, we may have started from a low base, but we have succeeded in halting a trend that, ultimately, benefits only a tiny minority and damages social cohesion.

Of course the functioning of the labour market is only one aspect of the immigration phenomenon. Integration is another important consideration and education is relevant here. A recent OECD study on immigration reveals that there is a gap in international experience between the achievements of indigenous and immigrant children. This is hardly a surprise given the barrier to education represented by poor competency in English. The agreement is not silent on this topic either. A further 550 language teachers will be appointed to assist international students to get over this barrier. It is worth observing in passing that, in the experience of teachers, international students in general are often more diligent, better motivated and better behaved than Irish students.

One further point is relevant here. The responsibility for meeting the requirements of international students should not be disproportionately focussed on one sector of education. The new agreement requires all schools to publish their admissions policy. All must play their part and I will be watching to ensure that these new developments do not cause any further elitism in education.

The approach to integration is very important. Diversity and multi-culturalism must be considered in the context of the need to preserve social cohesion. There is a danger that the doctrine of multiculturalism, if taken to extremes, could produce a group politics to trump the politics of social solidarity. If that happens, it opens the way to increasing inequality and falling social mobility such that it becomes impossible to articulate any sense of social contract or common purpose once group rights overwhelm the belief in collective effort and collective responsibility.

But this does not necessarily mean assimilation. There is no need to abandon all ties to a country of origin or to fall in with every aspect of the Irish way of life. It is, though, important that newcomers acknowledge that Ireland is not a random collection of individuals; they are joining a society which, although hard to describe, is real enough. It is not enough to point out, as many multiculturalists do, that there is no simple moral consensus anymore. Perhaps this is true but then it seems to me that the political challenge is to create and sustain a minimum degree of moral consensus and solidarity in an otherwise pluralistic society. Diversity in itself is neither good nor bad. It is fairness that matters, placed within a human rights framework.

Indeed, we do not all have to like each other or agree with each other or live like each other for the glue that holds society together to work. As the philosopher David Miller has written:

> "Liberal states do not require their citizens to believe liberal principles, since they tolerate communists, anarchists, fascists and so forth. What they require is that citizens should conform to liberal principles in practice and accept as legitimate policies that are pursued in the name of such principles, while they are left free to advocate alternative arrangements. The same must apply to immigrant groups, who can legitimately be required to abandon practices that liberalism condemns, such as the oppression of women, intolerance of other faiths and so on."

So the point is that a liberal state has the right to outlaw things that challenge its core values – such as the emergence of separate legal, political enclaves that would be implied, for example, in the acceptance of Shari law for Muslims in areas of high Muslim settlement if they existed here.

This, of course, is an extreme example. But how would we handle, say, demands for faith schools and faith-based ethics in hospitals beyond the delicate balance between Catholic and Protestant that

**Diversity and multi-culturalism must be considered in the context of the need to preserve social cohesion. There is a danger that the doctrine of multi-culturalism, if taken to extremes, could produce a group politics to trump the politics of social solidarity.**

currently exists? Our experience of immigration, and the fact that so many of the people who come here are culturally and ethnically so compatible, means that we have not yet had to confront some of these complexities.

A great deal of effort has gone into proving that immigration is a good thing for Ireland. Reports in quick succession by AIB, ESRI and the European Commission around the time we were trying to negotiate labour market reform all telling us positive news were, in my opinion, calculated to influence those negotiations.

Of course, a central problem is that this country does not yet have a coherent, joined-up, immigration strategy – to date, all moves in this area have been dictated by the requirements of business.

"Towards 2016" changes that. The employments rights provisions won by Congress represent a coherent, strategic approach to immigration and the labour market. It could well prove to be a building block for a broader social contract on the issue.

My own sense of it is that we do not have sufficient, up to date, detailed data to fully evaluate the impact of immigration. The new agreement provides for the collection of that data and for a high level group to monitor it. This will, hopefully, lead to evidence-based decision making in respect of the labour market.

In the short term, Irish business has benefited hugely from first mover advantage in opening the labour market to the 10 new EU states. In the longer run, however, we may come to regret aspects of it. The demographic profile of the Eastern European states is worse than ours. There is perhaps a seven to ten-year period, or even less, in which people of an age interested in migration will come to us. The incentive to bypass the non-active citizens here or to fail to provide the infrastructure of caring necessary to allow women to remain in the labour force or to increase our productivity through upgrading skills – in favour of drawing on immigrant labour supply as the easier option – may lose us the demographic advantage we have over the rest of Europe. In other words, the danger is that immigration will be taken as a panacea for longer-term structural problems in relation to labour supply, which it is not.

This concerns, too, our attitude to economic growth. The legacy of our high unemployment years has left us with a mantra that maximising growth is good in all circumstances. The population increase which is a consequence of this mentality will continue to overheat the housing market – with a current inflation rate of 14.2 per cent – and with a continuous loop in which Irish people invest in houses to rent to immigrants who come here to build houses!

Whatever it is, this does not look like a formula for sustainability. Would we not be better to try to optimise rather than maximise

*Of course, a central problem is that this country does not yet have a coherent, joined-up, immigration strategy – to date, all moves in this area have been dictated by the requirements of business.*

economic growth in a manner which addresses all of the foregoing issues in a more sustainable way? Should not the objective and purpose of our migration policy be that of sustainable development of our economy and society?

Let me acknowledge that it is no easy matter to achieve this desireable equilibrium. One cannot calibrate our system to a predetermined level and rate of economic growth. Neither can one easily stop immigration. The push-pull factors are too powerful. Even as this is being written, a conference of African and European leaders is taking place in Morocco to agree a joint strategy in the face of increasing alarm caused by the numbers of people seeking to reach Europe illegally from the South. In October last year, hundreds of migrants from Sub-Saharan Africa tried to storm the border fence separating Morocco from Ceuta and Melilla, Spanish enclaves in North Africa. Five people were shot dead in the attempt.

This difficulty in managing migration highlights the importance of standards. Standards can act as automatic stabilisers within the economy. Properly enforced, they can reduce the incentive to competitiveness based on the availability of large numbers of workers – cowed, undemanding and easily exploited. Standards can force business to choose instead competitiveness based on high skills, high productivity and high levels of participation. Standards can force society to choose to invest in life long learning and public services necessary to support this activity. And if we choose this model it also implies that we will invest in integration. This is crucial. We must not allow a situation to develop in which newcomers, by virtue of their circumstances, become engaged in competition for housing and public services with people who are already deprived and struggling. The tension this causes is sometimes dismissed as racism rather than as reflections of genuine problems in dealing with sudden social change.

If we take time to analyse the forces behind immigration we would have to acknowledge that it is both vital to our society and, in today's world circumstances, inevitable. But we also have to accept that its costs and benefits are very unevenly spread, and that we don't do enough to ensure that the people who are most affected by it, either as immigrants or as hosts, can manage the change being forced upon them. Upon our ability to engage with this reality will rest our future as a society.

**We must not allow a situation to develop in which newcomers, by virtue of their circumstances, become engaged in competition for housing and public services with people who are already deprived and struggling.**

# Lucy Gaffney

## Chairperson, The Strategic Monitoring Group, The National Action Plan Against Racism (NPAR)

*A graduate of the College of Marketing and Design in Dublin, she is the Chairperson of 98FM, and of Servecast, Europe's leading provider of broadband video solutions. Formerly Director and Chief Operations Officer of Esat Telecom until it was acquired by British Telecom in 2000, she is Chairperson of Communicorp Group Ltd. and a Director of Digicel Group in the Caribbean. In 2000 she was appointed to the strategic advisory board of Tesco (Ireland) and to the Government-sponsored Campus Ireland board.*

## We Need a Range of Integration Policies

The Irish demographic has changed, but so has our economy and our society. We are a small but thriving sophisticated European economy without reduced labour restrictions. The recent demographic changes stem from our success and from international citizens wanting to share in that success. The reason for migration is the same as it has been since homo sapiens left the African plains – the search for a better life. We are now privileged to offer that better life to others.

**The reason for migration is the same as it has been since homo sapiens left the African plains – the search for a better life. We are now privileged to offer that better life to others.**

As a people who are very familiar with emigration, we should perhaps view this age-old phenomenon of migration with a good sense of fellow feeling for our immigrants and what it means to leave home for pastures new. It is particularly apt to be speaking about the topic of immigration, integration and cultural identity in Donegal – a county with a long and painful history of emigration.

### Migration is Different Today

The context of migration today is, of course, very different to what it was even two decades ago and certainly very different to Patrick MacGill's time. I'd guess that if he was heading off to Scotland or the States today it would be by choice rather than necessity.

He would probably be armed with a third level qualification in engineering or the Sciences from Letterkenny Institute of Technology.

He could probably get a fairly good deal on his airfare.

He could go on the internet or text his friends to find out how Donegal did in the Ulster final.

Technology and globalisation has made the world a smaller and,

I think, a more manageable prospect for many, and in particular those far away from home.

For the Patrick, or Patricia, MacGills who come to our shores today home is never very far away. Cheap air transport means that regular return trips are a possibility (look at the departures board in Dublin Airport and see the many cities, provincial and capital, which are now accessible directly from Ireland). The internet and mobile phones provide instant communication and news of home, and satellite technology means that people can watch their national TV no matter where they are.

That is notwithstanding the negatives – there are still the hardships, particularly for people in the developing world where flight from persecution or dire economic necessity drive them to desperate measures. We all know the stories that end in tragedy such as the many migrants who never make it on their journey to what they hope will be a better life.

## *Migration: The Economic Solution to a Global Phenomenon*

Over the past 15 years the number of people crossing national borders in search of a better life has been rising steadily. At the start of the twenty-first century one in every 35 people is an international migrant. According to global estimates, in 2005 there are 191 million migrants worldwide, up from 176 million in 2000. Migrants are now estimated to comprise 3 per cent of the world's population and, if put together, would comprise the fifth largest country in the world.

Peter Sutherland, one of the most impressive and eminent Irish business and legal minds, who is now Kofi Annan's UN representative for migration, believes that migration and the environment will be the two major issues of this century at a global level. Attracting international migrants is an increasing part of global competition.

Sutherland understands clearly the positive economic impact of harnessing and managing migration. He is the driving force behind the search for a structured approach to this around the globe.

In June, the UN produced a report on international migration and development. Not only does the study address the fluidity of migration between countries, particularly the EU, and also the mobility of migration due to technology and globalisation, but most importantly, it views migration in the context of being a key economic driver.

The report showed that, just as in the past, immigrants contribute not only to their new countries but their native ones as well. Money sent by migrants to their countries of origin is an increasingly important source of outside funding for many developing countries.

**Migrants are now estimated to comprise 3 per cent of the world's population and, if put together, would comprise the fifth largest country in the world.**

Remittance funds are the second largest source, behind foreign investment by private companies, for many developing countries.

In 2005 remittance flows are estimated to have exceeded 233 billion US dollars, 167 of which went to developing countries. This would seem to reflect the Irish experiences of the past where the money sent home from the Irish abroad was very important to an ailing economy.

While acknowledging the many negative consequences of migration – political, economic and social – the UN report provides a template for countries to collectively manage migration more intelligently.

In his recent report Peter Sutherland said, and it is particularly apt to Ireland of 2006:

> "The passions migration stirs, and the perils it presents for politicians, have sent too many thoughtful people into defensive poses. We need to change this. Migration is the mother of progress and invention. The will and courage it requires to leave behind family and country are the same traits that have driven entrepreneurs and innovators throughout history. Our world today is shaped by the industry of immigrants."

**" ... Migration is the mother of progress and invention. The will and courage it requires to leave behind family and country are the same traits that have driven entrepreneurs and innovators throughout history ..."**

Ireland must be part of this sea change. Ireland, along only with the UK and Sweden (belatedly followed by Spain, Portugal, Finland and Greece), has already benefited as one of the first EU countries to open their labour markets to the EU expansion with no significant increase in unemployment and big increases in employment.

Instead of suffering from a "brain drain" as Ireland did in the eighties, we are now on the upside of that cycle, experiencing a "brain download". How we approach this influx of extra man and brain power in order to utilise and maximise it, is at the core of what I want to say.

We are a small, vibrant, open economy which is currently benefiting from migration. We are at the top of most quality of life and wealth indicators surveys, but we mustn't lose the run of ourselves. For example, if a country such as Germany opens its economy to migrant labour, some or many of our current Polish population may decide to move closer to their homeland. Without the correct structures to ensure that this new resource is tied through love, loyalty, or employment, we cannot be sure this labour and economic boon is here to stay.

We must be robust in our approach to integrating our international citizens. Anecdotes tell of international citizens with law and bar degrees digging gardens or waitressing. We need to address this issue quickly by developing "on-ramps" which allow the labour force access to roles commensurate with their qualifications, and enable us to tap into their skills.

The impact on our vital statistics as a country show the potential we have to continue our economic growth. In 2005 our population exceeded four million – the highest figure since 1871. In the coming five years it is predicted that net migration will reach up to 150,000 according to current and projected level of economic growth. Foreign nationals now account for almost 8 per cent of our workforce and almost 6 per cent of the Irish population. Some estimates show Ireland's foreign national population could be almost one million, or 18 per cent, by 2030.

Now is the time for us to develop our policies and structures effectively to ensure that our growth is a long-term success.

## The Human Approach

From a human angle and this, after all, is a very human story, we also have a responsibility to recognise how complex this subject is and in light of this provide flexible structures to deal with the needs of real people and their hopes and aspirations. Now there will be a greater variety of cultural backgrounds, more visible minorities, and more people from abroad who have made their homes here. In the future there will be second and third generations of migrant families who know Ireland as their only home.

How we integrate these new communities into Ireland is the great challenge that we now face. If handled properly we have the opportunity to see the differences and the "them and us" attitudes change. I see this moment as Ireland's tipping point when we have the chance to lay the foundations for the future integrated and balanced population of our country.

My job then is to use whatever influence I have to encourage Government, business, trade unions and NGOs to play their part in implementing the objectives of the National Action Plan Against Racism. Simply put, this is to create the conditions in which cultural and ethnic diversity can be reasonably accommodated and racism rooted out.

The NPAR is a hugely significant document; forward looking and ambitious and flexible enough to guide us through the future changes I talked about earlier. It is an example of effective Government action through partnership. The Irish Government, taking its lead from the UN Conference in Durban 2001 and seeing the importance of such a development to our domestic circumstances, developed the NPAR following a widespread consultation process that included the social partners, NGOs and representatives of cultural and ethnic minorities.

The NPAR sets out the strategic direction to develop a more inclusive, intercultural society in Ireland based on policies that

**How we integrate these new communities into Ireland is the great challenge that we now face. If handled properly we have the opportunity to see the differences and the "them and us" attitudes change.**

promote interaction, equality of opportunity, understanding and respect. The intercultural framework underpinning the NPAR consists of five key objectives:

- Effective protection and redress against racism

- Economic inclusion and equality of opportunity

- Accommodating diversity in service provision

- Recognition and awareness of diversity

- Full participation in Irish society.

**The Irish must be pragmatic in their approach to diversity – and already in some cases I'm proud to say we have an Irish solution to an Irish problem. For instance, children who want to wear head-dresses are permitted so long as they match the uniform.**

The plan is the Government's key policy statement on diversity management in Ireland and all credit to Minister McDowell and the Government for seeing this through – not many governments have produced a plan of this breadth and depth.

The Irish must be pragmatic in their approach to diversity – and already in some cases I'm proud to say we have an Irish solution to an Irish problem. For instance, children who want to wear head-dresses are permitted so long as they match the uniform. A specific sterilised head-dress is now being used by female Muslim surgeons in Ireland. There must be hundreds of examples which are simply variances of custom and belief and, one by one, we are working to find pragmatic and flexible solutions.

I believe that the NPAR provides a suitable framework to develop and implement wider integration strategies which will be required in the coming years. (Allow me a plug: www.diversityinireland.ie is well worth a visit to discover what is happening).

Let me give some brief examples of how work has been progressing to demonstrate the kind of strategies that are taking place to promote diversity:

- An Garda Síochána is targeting recruitment of members of cultural and ethnic minorities. To overcome barriers to participation adjustments were made to the application criteria (including the Irish language requirement)

- Development of intercultural strategies in health

- Intercultural guidelines for primary schools

- Study into core funding issues for groups representing ethnic minorities

- Anti–racism and diversity plans (Galway, Dublin Inner city, Fingal, Roscommon, Louth)

- Study on racism and the criminal law

- Workplace initiatives where native and newcomer are most likely to come into contact with each other.

The emphasis, as these projects show, is on tackling strategic areas to ensure equality of opportunity and accommodation of diversity in service provision.

I believe that respect for individuals should be the core of any integration policy. In an increasingly transnational world, traditional notions of migrant integration into host communities needs to be rethought. What we need to see is a range of integration policies emerging and these policies need to reflect the fluidity of movement of migrants.

## The Future

Thus I have a vision for the future, which I am laying the foundations for now. In ten years' time I want to see and know that all children at school have the same opportunities, that every child, regardless of background or ethnicity, has the same access to education, qualifications and employment. I would like every worker to be capable of securing work equal to their qualifications. I would like every woman, man and child to feel attached to and proud of the country of Ireland and its growth and development.

I can't do that alone, and all the initiatives implemented by NPAR, the Government, NGOs and citizen groups will not change a thing unless the attitude of our society moves with this tide.

I have laid out clearly that our economic and cultural prosperity relies heavily on the work and dedication of our migrant community. It's now time for Irish society to recognise this, if for nothing else but its own good.

What is the soul of Ireland? I will tell you what it is – what it has always been: it is its people. The people who live, work and love here.

Martin Luther King said: "The ultimate measure of a man is not where he stands in moments of comfort and convenience, but where he stands at times of challenge and controversy."

Ireland is standing in a time of challenge and, for some, controversy – we did not seek it, global trends have thrust it upon us. It will be a measure of the strength and breadth of our country, our people and our soul to see how we face those challenges. And what legacy we leave behind us.

> In ten years' time I want to see and know that all children at school have the same opportunities, that every child, regardless of background or ethnicity, has the same access to education, qualifications and employment.

# Michael McDowell TD

## Minister for Justice, Equality and Law Reform

*Born in Dublin and educated at Pembroke School, Gonzaga College, UCD and Kings Inns. Formerly, senior counsel. First elected to Dáil Éireann for Dublin South-East in 1987. Attorney-General 1999-2002. Minister for Justice, Equality and Law Reform since 2002. Chairman of the Progressive Democrats 1989-92 and President of the Party 2002-2006. Succeeded Mary Harney as Leader in October 2006 when he also took over Ms. Harney's position as Tánaiste.*

## Liberal Republicanism – Reconciling Diversity

When we speak of "the soul" of a country, we have to ask, what are we talking about? What do we really mean by that term? Are we talking about moral outlook and values? Or are we talking about history? Are we talking about the deep veins of prejudice on the one hand or values on the other? Or are we talking about some moral concept which allows politicians in particular to say that they resonate in some way with the soul of their country or that they speak to or on behalf of the soul of their country?

I believe that we have to be careful when talking about the "soul" of our society. It may connote a shared and monochrome personality to our society or that our society is not diverse, complex and sometimes contradictory.

### A Liberal Republican Perspective

A classical republican is prepared to build a society in which the institutions of state don't always attempt to reflect one single orthodox view, one single established religion, one established philosophy, or one established set of values, but rather seek to reconcile a diversity on some or all of those matters.

I believe in liberal republicanism, and I believe it has certain consequences. It is foolish to talk in terms of the whole issue of immigration and national identity in a naive or simplistic way.

We have to accept that at the very core of all of this debate there must be in any viable society some requirement of cohesion. A society is not simply a place where a large group of people exist at any given point, and which anybody is entitled to walk in or out of, regardless of law or consequences.

> We have to accept that at the very core of all of this debate there must be in any viable society some requirement of cohesion. A society is not simply a place where a large group of people exist at any given point ...

## A Sense of Society

Margaret Thatcher said there was no such a thing as society. I totally disagree with her. I do believe there is such a thing as society. I think it involves a shared sense of history, a shared sense of values and a shared sense of cohesion. Whether you call that "fraternity", as the French Republicans did in the late eighteenth century, or "solidarity", as it is now more politically correct to say, there must be a sense of cohesion – some sense of responsibility for one another.

Solidarity does not mean that one is "against" other societies, but rather that one believes that our society does not simply give one an economic or a social existence but also attracts one's loyalties. Without labouring the point too much there must be a sense of pride in the society, a sense of common ownership and achievement for everybody in society – a sense that you are "cheering for" that society and that you are not completely indifferent to it.

## We Have Duties to Society

Very frequently in discourse we talk about "rights" and we often talk about our "rights as against society", but very few of us ever talk about our duties to society. Article 9 of the Constitution of 1937 raises the matter of the duties of citizens and states that one of them is a fundamental duty of "loyalty" to the State. To many it may be a surprise that we actually have a duty of loyalty to our State.

One can't have a sense of loyalty to a country which is merely a staging post for people to come in and out at will, and which has no shared history or values. Nor can one say, "give me, give me, give me," on the rights front without saying, "I owe" something to this society by way of loyalty. You can't have a sense of loyalty to something which has no sense of cohesion.

So, while we live in a society and in a world in which there is huge mobility, we cannot simply throw out the notion of some form of necessary social cohesion. In some sense a spirit, or a soul, or a personality, or a shared minimum set of values is at the heart of society.

**In some sense a spirit, or a soul, or a personality, or a shared minimum set of values is at the heart of society.**

## We Are a Diverse Society

We aren't a monochrome society. We aren't simply a Celtic, a Gaelic, or a Catholic society. We have the Danes in our blood. For example, the McLaughlins and the O'Loughlins, and all the other people in Donegal who have Danish blood in them prove that. We have old English blood in our veins. We have Norman blood in our veins. We have Planters blood. We have Scots blood. We have Anglo-Irish blood.

We are a society for which there has never been a single official version of who we are or what we are about. Ireland has always benefited from migration and from infusions from outside. It is foolish to portray Ireland as a country always "done down" by the invader. That is a nonsensical view of history.

## Defining Irishness

I will come to the question of immigration but I believe that we should remember that Ireland is a complex society and that recent waves of migration make us more complex.

We have never been an uncomplicated society, and anyone who portrays Ireland as an uncomplicated society, either historically or going forward, is peddling dangerous falsehoods.

> **We have never been an uncomplicated society, and anyone who portrays Ireland as an uncomplicated society, either historically or going forward, is peddling dangerous falsehoods.**

## Diversity and Northern Ireland

Before we move on to the question of recent immigration into Ireland, there is already unfinished business on this island and in this society in relation to our definition of Irishness. Before we start talking about a threat to our identity or Irishness from the migration waves we are now dealing with, let us address one simple question, and that is whether we have yet come to terms with the proposition that Gaelic, Catholic nationalism alone is not Irishness, and that the ideals of Tone, Davis, Emmet were a higher and a more noble ideal of our identity. That belief was that people of quite diverse views could agree on a society, even though they came from very different backgrounds and came with very different values and, sometimes, very different political interests.

In Northern Ireland in particular, there is a big issue about the whole sense of Irishness. I just want to mention here the massive divide between Orange and Green. The republican ideal embodied in the tricolour flag is that those two traditions can be reconciled in one republican state; that the people who stand on one side or the other of the Orange/Green divide can be reconciled in common institutions and in a shared society.

The Provo view, by contrast, has been quite different. They have offered a view in relation to Northern Ireland which is based on the proposition that polarisation is the way to vindicate national values.

Sometimes we read criticism of President Mary McAleese and her husband Martin for the wonderful work that they do in building bridges. Sometimes we see stones thrown at them either for "naivety", or for "over-enthusiasm". But could anything be more appropriate than that the President of this State, a republican state whose flag is green, white, and orange, should, on the 12th of July, have people from the Orange tradition to Áras an Uachtaráin and say to them, " I recognise and celebrate your values".

If reconciliation is ever going to take place on this island, could anything be a more likely basis than their generosity of spirit? Could anything be less likely to accomplish those aims than the negativity which their courageous efforts sometimes encounter?

Nobody in Ireland can fairly describe himself or herself as Republican who doesn't believe in the reconciliation of orange and green. Nobody pursues "Republican policies" when they polarise orange and green. Nobody pursues "Republican policies" when they shred the centre ground in Northern Ireland, and produce over seven years the situation which we have now. The extremes have gone from having one-third of the vote in Northern Ireland shared between them to two-thirds of the vote. A recent opinion survey suggested that both communities are drifting further and further apart.

No true Republican could believe in the polarised, cantonised version of Northern Ireland society that is sadly evolving today.

In this part of Ireland, our sense of Irishness is, and has to be, much different from that manifested by some of the people who wave our flag in the forefront of the nationalist struggle, as they see it, for Irish unity. They don't believe in the unity of the Irish people. They certainly don't believe in the reconciliation of Orange and Green. They have betrayed emphatically and comprehensively the values of the Republican founder figures whom they honour at their graves every year.

**Nobody in Ireland can fairly describe himself or herself as republican who doesn't believe in the reconciliation of orange and green. Nobody pursues "republican policies" when they polarise orange and green.**

## We Have Coped Well with Immigration

Moving on to the other issue of how Ireland is changing in terms of its demographic make-up, it is true that we now have very significant migration inwards, and it is true that this is a new experience. And may I say, at the very outset in relation to this issue, that, all things considered, we have handled it quite well. We haven't had what has happened right across Europe – the emergence of immigration-based or race-based politics.

The political system has, generally speaking, been coherent and cohesive and true to republican values, and has not allowed any of its participants much leeway to exploit race-based politics or xenophobia or atavistic nationalist values as a basis for garnering electoral support.

## No Ethnic Violence on Our Streets

May I make a second point to you: we haven't had in Ireland any occasion, with one exception which I will come back to in a moment, on which violence was gratuitously offered to people of different ethnic groups by Irish citizens. Nearly every society in Europe has experienced that.

The one exception here was the "Love Ulster Rally", where some Orangemen proposed to walk down O'Connell Street and the Gardai proposed to deal with the demonstration in a light-handed way. A group of people claiming to be Republican and claiming to be nationalist and claiming to be standing up for Irish values attacked them.

**What did the perpetrators believe in? Why, when they had finished throwing stones at the police and the Orangemen, did they suddenly think that the Chinese, the Pakistanis, and the Indians were people who deserved their attention as well?**

When they were finished creating mayhem on O'Connell Street, they rampaged through the city. They pulled out Chinese and Asian workers from their workplaces and beat them up on the streets. Let that be a warning to us. It is a sobering thought that this was the one occasion in the last five or seven years since migration into Ireland has become very significant in which there was gratuitous violence on our streets against people of racial minorities. What did the perpetrators believe in? Why, when they had finished throwing stones at the police and the Orangemen, did they suddenly think that the Chinese, the Pakistanis, and the Indians were people who deserved their attention as well?

## The Migration Debate Has Been Distorted by the Extremes

The management of migration is a duty of Government. It is nonsense to say that migration should take place without anybody keeping their eye on it, or anybody trying to regulate it.

We've had, to some extent, in the media, a wholly unrealistic debate between, on the one hand, the Justin Barretts and, on the other hand, the people from the various NGOs who say that every deportation is wrong in principle. We have two groups, the Left and the Right, the Left arguing from internationalist principles that all migration is almost by definition a good thing and shouldn't be discouraged or inhibited in any way, and the Right saying that virtually all migration is a bad thing, and that it should not be tolerated in any circumstances whatsoever.

## There is a Middle Course

There is a middle course as most Irish people understand instinctively. This acknowledges that we benefit from migration, that, when Ireland is part of a prosperous European Union and is growing very fast, it is inevitable that people will want to migrate here and that, whether they come from outside the EU or inside the EU, it is not some malign intent that has them queuing at our door. On the contrary, it is what every reasonable person in their circumstances would attempt to do for themselves and for their families.

In the context of social solidarity and of the partnership approach to government, the implications should be looked at reasonably and dealt with reasonably as well. By the same token, we have to remember that there are 150,000 Poles in Ireland as well as people from Latvia, Estonia, Lithuania, the Czech Republic, Hungary and such countries working in Ireland and that they are helping immeasurably to build our society. They are not some form of threat.

Indeed, in the late 1890s and in the early 1900s, there was a similar influx into Ireland of people who were persecuted, who came to both parts of the United Kingdom, Ireland, and Britain, seeking refuge. These were our Jewish population.

I sometimes think that we should reflect on what happened to our Jewish population. They came here, they prospered. In my own Dáil constituency there might have been between 4,000 to 5,000 of them. They had Jewish TDs, they had a good and solid role in Irish society and yet, at the same time, they reached glass ceilings. They encountered prejudice and they encountered exclusion. Their numbers are now dwindling, perhaps for demographic reasons, perhaps for economic reasons, perhaps for other reasons that are more difficult to put one's finger on. We have to ask ourselves, "Were we as a society decent to our Jewish migrants. Did we as a society deal with them fairly?" I think that, compared with Britain, for instance, the answer is that we did not – which is much to our discredit.

> *... it is not some malign intent that has them queuing at our door. On the contrary, it is what every reasonable person in their circumstances would attempt to do for themselves and for their families.*

## Integration – We Shouldn't Push it Too Far

The last point I want to make is in relation to the whole question of integration. You might believe, and I don't, in the notion that there is a simple Irish soul, that there is a single definition of what it is to be an Irish citizen, that there is a single set of values which all Irish citizens must hold. If you hold this belief, then you may be attracted to the French approach to integration which is that your daughters will not wear a veil to school, your sons will not wear skull caps to school, you must learn French, you must learn to be citizens of the French republic, you must effectively go under the yoke of French republicanism to participate in French society, and diversity will be frowned upon to the extent that it conflicts with those aims.

A point of minor divergence between David Begg and myself is in relation to faith-based education. We have in this country in the past accorded to the Protestant and the Jewish faiths the right to organise their education as they see it. Whether that is wise or unwise is a matter for debate, but we cannot now withdraw that right from newer migrant groups into Irish society. I don't think we can say that the drawbridge now comes up and that everyone must conform to a single form of state secular education in pursuit of social cohesion.

## We Must Remain True to Republican Values

I believe that the French approach is unnecessarily rigid. I believe that we can, by adopting a slightly less ideological approach in Ireland, allow for diversity. But it must be based on a minimum shared set of values and here I will go back to my first invocation of republican values. One of them is, for instance, that women cannot be subjugated and, secondly, that the basic principles of our own law must be adhered to on the basis that the duty of loyalty to the Irish State does apply to everyone who would avail of Irish citizenship.

The Islamic community is at the moment somewhat semi-detached from Irish society, and for obvious reasons. Because it is a new entity in Irish society with significant numbers and growing, it doesn't entirely share some of the philosophical and political attitudes of many people in Irish society at the moment. That is a problem. But it is also a challenge. Rather than isolate them and rather than deny them the right to denominational education, I believe that we should have an engagement process which brings them into a sense of Irishness and which is open and generous rather than defensive and xenophobic in relation to their lives and beliefs. Integration is essential at a certain level, but it cannot be pushed the whole way.

## We Must Combat Racism

This is where the National Action Plan Against Racism, which is to ensure that at every level we combat unfairness arising out of diversity in our society, comes into play. The 200 or 250 action points identified in that programme take in everybody including my department, the trade union movement, employers, NGOs and so on. It is a challenging programme.

It's not some academic programme set down from the top as to how we can produce a homogenous society. It is simply a menu of actions to combat unfairness. I believe that Ireland is doing a good job so far in relation to how it addresses these issues.

> I believe that the French approach is unnecessarily rigid. I believe that we can, by adopting a slightly less ideological approach in Ireland, allow for diversity. But it must be based on a minimum shared set of values ...

## *Conclusion*

We are dealing with novel and uncharted waters from the Irish political system's point of view. We have never been here before and we could make many mistakes. But, looking across Europe to the "enlightened" states of the Netherlands, Denmark, Austria, Germany, France, and Britain, we can certainly see a catalogue of errors from which we can and should learn. Without being in any way complacent, we can see a lot of dangers that we should be careful to avoid in the future.

I believe that the glass is well over half full rather than half empty. I believe that the Irish people are generous and realistic and that they are warm and positive to the notion of change; that they don't accept a simplistic, outdated view of themselves as a Gaelic, Catholic nation in danger of being swept away. We have a much more sophisticated view of our place in Europe, our place in the world, and of what works and won't work.

It's with that sense of confidence, I think, that we, as a society, dealing with this new and uncharted phenomenon of immigration, can feel a sense that we have set out with some reasonable and fair-minded values on an adventure which should, if there is good will, end well.

**I believe that the Irish people are generous and realistic and that they are warm and positive to the notion of change; that they don't accept a simplistic, outdated view of themselves as a Gaelic, Catholic nation in danger of being swept away.**

Mary Finan
RTÉ Authority

Sr Stanislaus Kennedy
Focus Ireland

Prof John Fitzgerald
ESRI

*Chapter 3*

# Coping with Affluence

*Facilitating the Co-existence of Affluence with Values*
MARY FINAN
**Chairperson, RTÉ Authority**

*The Pursuit of Affluence Dulls Concern for Others*
Sr STANISLAUS KENNEDY
**Life President, Focus Ireland**

*In the Land of the Lotus Eaters*
PROF JOHN FITZGERALD
**Economic and Social Research Institute**

# Mary Finan

## Chairperson, RTÉ Authority, Deputy Chairperson, Ogilvy & Mather

*Born in Co. Roscommon and educated at UCD (BA degree) and Harvard Business School. Managing Director of Wilson Hartnell PR for two decades. She was the first woman to be president of the Dublin Chamber of Commerce. She is a director of Canada Life (Ireland), the AA and the Gate Theatre. She is also a council member of the Dublin Docklands Authority and of the Economic and Social Research Institute (ESRI) and was appointed to the chairmanship of the RTÉ Authority by Minister Noel Dempsey in 2006.*

## Facilitating the Co-existence of Affluence with Values

Firstly, I shall examine the concept of affluence. In doing this I shall be drawing on the work of the distinguished US social researcher, Daniel Yankelovich. Yankelovich uses a simple framework to trace the effect of affluence on society in three succinct stages.

I will then apply this theory to the Irish context and finally I will outline some ways in which I feel we can use our affluence constructively for the benefit of our society and of future generations.

**Yankelovich goes on to state that a startling discontinuity takes place between the first and second stages of affluence.**

According to Yankelovich the first stage occurs when affluence is new and people suspect that their economic well-being may not be real. Incomes may be rising but people fear it will not last. Confidence is low. Values remain conservative and traditional. The focus is on social bonds, sacrifice, hard work and saving for the future. Choices are made with the family in mind rather than the individual's personal needs. Integral to this stage of the cycle is the traditional family unit comprising a male breadwinner, a female homemaker and two or more children. The US Bureau of Census shows that in the 1950s most US households – approximately 70 per cent – conformed to this model. When the word family is used today most Americans still conjure up this image yet now a mere 8 per cent of households would fit this model.

Yankelovich goes on to state that a startling discontinuity takes place between the first and second stages of affluence. From an objective economic point of view, incomes may be rising slowly and steadily but, subjectively, the transition is abrupt. People swing from undue scepticism about their economic prospects to undue optimism. They leap from doubting the reality of their affluence to assuming that it is a permanent condition and that they and their nation can now spend freely without worrying about tomorrow. They believe they can indulge themselves and make up for lost time and their nation can address long neglected problems and fix them. Almost overnight feelings change from "it won't last" to "it will go on forever and now we can afford to do anything we want". Greatly enhanced personal choice is the hallmark of this second stage and people relish their new freedom to choose careers and lifestyles in accord with their individual bent, not in conformity to the expectation of others or as a concession to economic constraints. In this second stage the quest for self-expression grows less inhibited. People assume that only when they feel, and are, well off economically can they start to live for today and for their own self-satisfaction, on the assumption that tomorrow things will take care of themselves.

At the third stage, fear of loss of affluence, a painful adaptation to the unexpected economic reality that one can no longer take affluence for granted also arrives abruptly. People begin to feel cornered and disorientated. They grow apprehensive that career opportunities, income growth, home ownership, higher education for their children and retirement are at risk.

Having looked at these three phases of affluence, I will now attempt to map them on to the Irish experience to date.

The image of the traditional family unit as outlined by Yankelovich in phase one is easily recognisable throughout Irish history right up to the early 90s. Up to then, affluence was too tenuous and too concentrated among the elite to graduate to the second stage.

Ireland today, however, is showing familiar signs of the second stage of the affluence effect as outlined by Yankelovich. Consumerism is rampant. Spending has never been higher and over the last 20 years personal debt has increased from 30 per cent of total income in 1986 to an astonishing 130 per cent this year. The new species of property developer has been born. In fact, an American recently remarked to me, "Is Ireland looking for world domination", because of the sheer volume of property being acquired internationally by Irish investors. But nowhere has the change been more dramatic than in the size and shape of today's family units. The combined effect of greater individualism, greater independence and autonomy for women, more choice, less automatic sacrifice and more questioning of traditional roles, has been to place the family under great strain. Ireland is in the throes of phase two. The latest census figures show that in just six years the number of divorced people trebled from 9,800 in 1996 to 35,000; the proportion of cohabiting couples rose from 3.9 per cent to 8.4 per cent and some 1,300 couples described themselves as same-sex cohabiting couples. Another trend has been the dramatic growth in the increase of births outside marriage. The proportion of non-marital births rose

**Consumerism is rampant. Spending has never been higher and over the last 20 years personal debt has increased from 30 per cent of total income in 1986 to an astonishing 130 per cent this year.**

six-fold from 5 per cent in 1980 to 31 per cent in 2000.

I am now going to shift my focus to examine how we can most effectively manage our affluence for society today and future generations.

A key challenge facing us is how we can facilitate the successful co-existence of affluence with family values. Here we have an opportunity to learn from the American experience.

Gradually, as the affluence effect evolved, Americans began to shape a synthesis between expanded choice and the need for enduring commitments. People do learn from experience and as they do they modify their values. Americans learned that total freedom of choice undermines the bonds that give personal relationships meaning and stability. Important research in the US has shown that, as Americans grew twice as rich over the last 30 years, divorce rates doubled and the incidence of anxiety, depression and substance abuse increased significantly, especially among teens and young adults. Isolation from parents is not unconnected to these trends and survey after survey highlights the regret of affluent parents that they did not spend more time with their children. They learned also that their expanded life choices created mounting financial debt that suddenly grew frightening when they became concerned about their economic prospects. Many also learned that the world of work can be less satisfying and less secure than they assumed, and that giving too much time to work and career can undermine family and quality of life, especially in an economic climate in which loyalty is a one-way affair, that is, the employer expects it but does not give it in return.

**Individuals too need to learn that affluence brings with it responsibilities to put something back into the society from which that prosperity is derived.**

In asking how we can manage affluence for the benefit of society and future generations, I would contend that affluence brings with it responsibilities for all the main players in our society. For many years now Irish business has been aware of its corporate social responsibility. Ten to twenty years ago, the concept was virtually unknown, yet today it is common to see entire sections of annual reports devoted to a company's corporate responsibility programmes. Individuals too need to learn that affluence brings with it responsibilities to put something back into the society from which that prosperity is derived. Affluence is new for us. We are not familiar with how to handle it so we must learn how to do so. Our education system at all levels changes all the time to reflect new priorities, developments and thinking in our society, and it can help now to engender a sense of responsibility among children and young adults to share their good fortune with the community.

The concept of philanthropy is not yet advanced in Ireland, notwithstanding the existence of the O'Reilly Hall, the Smurfit Graduate School, the Ryan Entrepreneurial School and so on. These are the exceptions rather than the norm. You will have read last month about Warren Buffet giving a staggering $31 billion to Bill and Melinda Gates' charity. This extraordinary largesse marks the latest chapter in America's philanthropic tradition which, for more than 150 years, has encouraged the country's extremely wealthy to give away their cash. In coughing up millions he is following in the footsteps of such plutocrats as Andrew Carnegie, the Rockefeller family and Henry Ford. Now is the time for the Government to create conditions conducive to the growth of philanthropy in Ireland by introducing a progressive tax regime that encourages private giving. The private banking arms of our major banks also have a role to play in advising their affluent customers how to spend their excess millions for the good of society. Many of our multi-millionaires are finding that they have enough money for themselves and their children and they are seeking advice on what they should do with the rest. The Government, therefore, now has a golden opportunity, in partnership with business and these individuals, to create a unique world class non-profit sector by building on our exceptional history of generosity and volunteering. Of course, it is equally important that the recipients of this money are accountable for it. Churlish as it may seem to criticise those who set out to do good, many charities behave as if they were unaccountable. According to July's *Economist* magazine, one study led by Bill Bradley, a former Senator and an advisor to McKinsey's non-profit practice, has found that they waste a lot of money. They squander cash on raising funds, they horde it, they fail to oversee how efficiently they spend it. Better management, the study maintained, could save tens of billions of dollars in America alone.

**Now is the time for the Government to create conditions conducive to the growth of philanthropy in Ireland by introducing a progressive tax regime that encourages private giving.**

Radio and television, too, can play an important role in developing a sense of individual responsibility. Reliable and impartial news and information, free debate, diverse cultural self-expression, minority language rights, a sense of being connected to the life of the people watching and listening, all these values are central to public service broadcasting. Securing them is a challenge that must be met by broadcasters every day. Radio and television hold up a mirror to society and in doing so enable us to reflect on some of its traits and trends. Several major RTÉ programmes in recent times fit this model admirably. Among them I would include the States of Fear programme on institutional care, the Prime Time Investigates programmes on binge drinking among the young and Leas Cross and the current monthly news features by Charlie Bird on death on our roads. They all had, and have, an important role to play in enabling us to see ourselves, as indeed did Gay Byrne's radio and television programmes over thirty years, which today would constitute an important part of our social history.

Do we want to live in a economy or a society? I would suggest we want both. Affluence can be a powerful driver for good and it brings with it huge opportunities to narrow the poverty gap and improve standards of living for all. Already we are seeing the effects of our new found affluence all around us. Because it is a particular interest of mine, I would single out the arts in this context. Never before has there been so much funding allocated to the arts and this is manifested in the flourishing arts scene throughout the country; the increasing number of talented young people who can earn a livelihood from their art; major capital projects such as the new Abbey Theatre and the new National Concert Hall and the recognition Irish artists are receiving all around the world such as John Banville and Colm Toibin who took home the Booker and IMPAC prizes respectively; Gary Hynes whose Synge cycle of plays was recently staged in New York and the Gate Theatre which last July had three sell-out shows running in Dublin, the West End and Broadway where "Faith Healer" picked up a Tony Award the previous month. The theme of this year's Summer School is the Soul of Ireland and since art touches our soul this is probably a good place to end.

**Affluence can be a powerful driver for good and it brings with it huge opportunities to narrow the poverty gap and improve standards of living for all. Already we are seeing the effects of our new found affluence all around us.**

# Sr Stanislaus Kennedy

## Life President, Focus Ireland

*Born on the Dingle Peninsula, she joined the Religious Sisters of Charity in 1958 with the desire to devote her life to the poor. In 1964, she joined Bishop Peter Birch in Kilkenny and helped to establish the Kilkenny Social Services. In 1983, she took up a position as Senior Research Fellow at UCD and carried out groundbreaking research into homelessness among women ("But Where Can I Go?"). This led her to set up Focus Ireland in 1985. In 1995 she vacated her executive position but has continued to work in Focus Ireland. She is a member of numerous committees and has written extensively on social policy issues in Ireland and abroad. She has written several books including* Focus on Residential Care in Ireland *(1996),* Spiritual Journeys *(1997), and* Gardening the Soul *(2001). In 1999, President McAleese appointed her to the Council of State.*

## The Pursuit of Affluence Dulls Concern for Others

If affluence is an end in itself then I think we have coped very well. In fact, we've done outstandingly well. This is exactly what has happened in Ireland; we have lost sight of its connection with the common good. Our vision of the common good has become dulled during our affluent years and consumerism has filled the gap left by our over-emphasis on economic success. Many good things have happened during our affluent years. If we look around the landscape, we see new industries, new houses, new cars, new roads, new comers. New relationships have been established, new energies and synergies have been released. As a nation we look at ourselves differently and others look at us differently. We are a much more confident, competent, educated and tolerant people than ever before. There is also a downside to affluence. We see spiralling property prices, rip-off retailers, soaring personal debts, pressure to keep up, pressure of childcare and commuters' traffic, together with new forms of inequality, exclusion and marginalisation. These are not all caused by affluence. They are caused by our excessive pursuit of affluence.

During our affluent years we have created a super wealthy minority which has benefited disproportionately from our good economic years. Side by side with this minority is another minority which lives in consistent poverty and feels more excluded and marginalised than ever before. And then there is the majority in between, some doing better than others, many in the middle under huge pressures to keep up and keep going.

Does the fact that so much wealth is concentrated in the hands of the few bother them? I don't think so. Because with so much emphasis

**During our affluent years we have created a super wealthy minority, who have benefited disproportionately from our good economic years. Side by side with this is another minority, which lives in consistent poverty and feels more excluded and marginalised than ever before.**

on economic success we all aspire to more and we don't notice those left behind. That is the ultimate temptation of affluence. The pursuit of affluence dulls concern for others. It also dulls the ability to see luxury as luxuries and so the second house and the second or third holiday and the bathrooms and televisions are all the new badges of progress. These are all necessary to quench the thirst that wasn't there twenty years ago. The link between affluence and consumerism is not confined to Ireland. Ten per cent of the world population, that is, its most wealthy, consume three-quarters of the planet's resources. Unnecessary consumption is now the greatest threat to human survival. This is caused by a value system that aims to fend off insecurity by acquisitions and accumulations. Consumerism is very subtle, and also very pernicious and insidious. It infiltrates and attacks the most basic relationships and institutions in society, in the family and the community. Consumerist values deny the vital importance of relationships for a fulfilled life. Fragmentation caused by consumerism is evident right across society. Consumerism affects young people in a big way. I don't think we've helped young people to see the dangers of becoming active consumers rather than active citizens. We have neglected their civic formation which is our responsibility. Civic formation and responsibility is crucial if they are to have the courage to set their sight on higher things and take personal responsibility for their own lives, the lives of their community and society. We have not provided the kind of inspiration and leadership that they need as inheritors and creators of twenty-first century Ireland.

During our affluent years, we have not created a rights-based culture, nor have we put in place the services or supports to avail of rights. Nor have we developed a good infrastructure in terms of health, housing, education or transport. We have poor public services for poor people.

In our education during our affluent years, the gap between those who benefited from education and those who did not or could not has widened. Certainly our economic success has unlocked the huge potential of many people with thousands of people flocking to second and third level education. And yet, there is a minority for whom the education system, far from being a release of potential, has in fact been a frustration of their potential. I am thinking of the children who only attend school poorly, who drop out, who leave early, who have not managed the basics of reading and writing. Over 76,000 children under 14 years of age live in consistent poverty in Ireland today. These children simply cannot avail of our education system. Today we see more and more breakfast clubs, lunch clubs, after school clubs, schoolmate programmes. These are all signs of our unequal times, signs of people who cannot avail of the regular education system.

If we look at health services we will also see that the gap between those who can pay and who cannot pay has widened in terms of

I don't think we've helped young people to see the dangers of becoming active consumers rather than active citizens. We have neglected their civic formation which is our responsibility.

accessibility, availability and provision of services. Those who can pay get what they need, those who can't, don't. We have never recovered from the health cuts of the eighties in spite of our affluence.

If we look at housing, we will see that during our affluent years the Government has abandoned its historic commitment to provide housing for those people who cannot buy their own house. If we look at the housing stock we will see that in 1989 12.5 per cent of the housing stock was local authority. In 2005, that had declined to 6.92 per cent of the housing stock. Waiting lists have doubled during our best economic years, from 19,376 households in 1989 to 43,684 in 2005.

With the absence of housing for those who cannot afford to buy, more and more are depending on the private rented sector. People who are most vulnerable and who are the poorest end up at the bottom end of the private rented sector – some of which is not suitable for human habitation – where they lack the basic necessities and essential facilities. Here individuals and families are trapped in poverty and terrible conditions. These people may not be on the streets, they may not be roofless but they are homeless nonetheless because they do not have the very basic constituents of a home. The attitude to social housing has also worsened during our affluence years – neither developers nor local residents want to see social housing in private areas because they see it as bringing down the value of property. Right across the country there have been vigorous campaigns mounted by local residents to prevent social housing or special needs housing in their area. A project that I know has not yet been granted planning permission eight years on because of opposition to a small project for the housing of older people and people with disabilities. NIMBYism (not in my back yard) is alive and well in affluent Ireland.

Regarding immigration, immigrants are seen as essential for our economic growth. Our policies, based on temporary permission to stay, discretionary and limited family reunification policies and limited integration policies, all show that the economic interest is dictating our immigration policy. Immigrants are seen as economic units and not as human beings and part of families with the same human needs as the rest of us. Our constitution recognises the natural, primary and fundamental unit of the family in society, yet we fail to give to many of our migrant labour force the right to live a full normal family life.

The challenge for us today in affluent Ireland is to create a more humane society capable of replacing excessive individualism and consumerism with humane values. This is the goal we should strive for in an affluent society. A humane society is one that distributes the goods of society in a way that gives fair access to health, welfare, education, housing and transport. Consumerism and the common good are not compatible.

**The attitude to social housing has also worsened during our affluence years – neither developers nor local residents want to see social housing in private areas because they see it as bringing down the value of property.**

# John Fitzgerald

## Research Professor at the Economic and Social Research Institute

*Born in Dublin and educated at UCD where he studied history and economics. He began his career in the Department of Finance in 1972 responsible for economic modelling and policy analysis. He joined the ESRI in 1984 and since then has contributed extensively to a number of journals in Ireland and abroad. He is the joint author of a study of the EU Structural Funds on the Irish economy and joint author of the report in 1996 for the Department of Finance on the Economic Implications for Ireland of EMU. He is also responsible in the ESRI for the Energy Policy Research Centre. He is a member of the National Economic and Social Council and of the Northern Ireland Authority for Energy Regulation.*

## In the Land of the Lotus Eaters

"I was driven thence by foul winds for a space of nine days upon the sea, but on the tenth day we reached the land of the Lotus-eater, who live on a food that comes from a kind of flower. Here we landed to take in fresh water, and our crews got their mid-day meal on the shore near the ships. When they had eaten and drunk I sent two of my company to see what manner of men the people of the place might be, and they had a third man under them. They started at once, and went about among the Lotus-eaters, who did them no hurt, but gave them to eat of the lotus, which was so delicious that those who ate of it left off caring about home, and did not even want to go back and say what had happened to them, but were for staying and munching lotus with the Lotus-eaters without thinking further of their return; nevertheless, though they wept bitterly, I forced them back to the ships and made them fast under the benches. Then I told the rest to go on board at once, lest any of them should taste of the lotus and leave off wanting to get home, so they took their places and smote the grey sea with their oars." (Homer, *Odyssey*, Book IX, vss. 83-104.

In Homer's *Odyssey*, his sailors were distracted from their ultimate goal of reaching home by the lure of the land of the Lotus Eaters and the idleness and pleasure that it afforded. Odysseus was forced to tie his sailors down in order to continue on his journey.

In today's Ireland, are we lulled into a false sense of security by today's good times, so we fail to look to the challenges ahead? Or have the Lotus Eaters, with their emphasis on the importance of time out, got an important lesson to tell?

## *Irrational Exuberance?*

Ireland's current economic boom has been sustained for over a decade, with a minor downturn from 2001-2003 which we took in our stride. Employment has grown by 50 per cent in the last decade, and Ireland is now the destination of choice for mobile young Europeans seeking work. Many of our young people know no other economic state – the world of the 1980s with its high unemployment and emigration, let alone the world of Patrick MacGill, is literally a different country.

The pattern of behaviour by households reflects a high degree of certainty about the future. The level of gross (and net) household debt is rising rapidly; households have confidence that they will be able to service this in the future. Many companies also appear to be optimistic about the future. This is reflected in very substantial increases in employment. While some firms, especially in the tradable manufacturing sector, are facing difficulties, their woes are masked by the feel good factor elsewhere in the business sector, especially in all those businesses that depend on the building sector for their success.

It is true that the economy faces a very fortunate set of demographic circumstances over the next fifteen years. Together, these circumstances will conspire to give Ireland one of the lowest rates of economic dependency in the OECD area. The benefits of past investment in education will also continue to produce a significant boost to productivity for some time to come. In addition, the economy, including the labour market, shows considerable flexibility.

While the underlying structure of the economy is evolving in a manner that should be favourable to future growth, there are considerable dangers in the current situation. In particular, the extremely high level of dependence on the continuing success of the building industry is a serious cause for concern. This is compounded by the certainty with which many in the household sector view the future prospects for growth.

Today, one of the key issues for policy-makers is how to tackle the dangerous imbalances that are building up in the economy at a time when euphoria in the household sector is possibly clouding the judgement of individual households. Trying to get households and companies to focus on future dangers at a time when the economy is thriving is always difficult. However, the nature and dimensions of the risks that the economy is likely to face over the coming decade do

*... there are considerable dangers in the current situation. In particular, the extremely high level of dependence on the continuing success of the building industry is a serious cause for concern.*

underline the importance of commencing this task.

The confidence in our future has helped fuel a sustained boom in construction. Over 80,000 new homes were built last year, roughly ten times per head what the Germans are building. But we have now reached a stage where one in eight jobs is directly in construction, and where we are becoming seriously vulnerable to a downturn in this industry. With interest rates expected to rise further, and the peak demand for new housing associated with the peak of the baby boom in 1980 expected to tail off, it will be important to engineer a soft landing rather than a collapse in the property market and with it a collapse in a critical source of employment.

## World Class Public Services

The recent landmark report from the National Economic and Social Council, "The Developmental Welfare State", pointed out the importance, having achieved world class economic performance, of ensuring that public services are brought up to first rank. This NESC report has called for a shift in our social spending from a passive structure of income supports into programmes and services that promote participation and inclusion rather than perpetuate dependence.

**However, one in five young people still leaves school before Leaving Cert., and the figures are significantly higher for boys.**

Public services are not only an essential component of every person's standard of living, they also provide an essential underpinning for future economic progress. It is a truism that improvements in education have fuelled much of the Celtic Tiger's success, particularly as a better-educated young workforce replaced the pre-free second level education generation entering retirement. However, one in five young people still leaves school before Leaving Cert., and the figures are significantly higher for boys. Recent figures from the national Education Welfare Board show a worryingly high absenteeism trend, particularly in disadvantaged schools. Clearly better performance by our school system will feed into improved economic performance down the line. Investment in transport infrastructure, including quality public transport, can reduce congestion costs in the economy. The vision and imagination that has propelled Ireland to the front of the world's economic league should be capable of solving the problems that beset our health service.

## The Balance Sheet of Growth

Economic growth has brought about a significant reduction in the number of people in consistent poverty. The fall in the numbers of long-term unemployed and the related rise in wage rates for semiskilled and unskilled labour relative to average incomes has played a role in this change. However, if anything, the distribution of income has become more uneven. This is not because those on low incomes have done particularly badly but rather because those on high incomes have done particularly well. Lone parents and people with disabilities are today the groups at highest risk of poverty.

The rapid economic growth that Ireland has experienced has been bought at the expense of some deterioration in key features of the environment. In particular, emissions of greenhouse gases have grown rapidly and the pressure on the countryside from dispersed economic settlement, both in the immediate hinterland of urban areas and in rural areas, has increased. However, there have also been significant improvements in other aspects of the environment. The emission of air pollutants other than greenhouse gases has been reduced in urban areas with a consequent improvement in health. In addition, the enhanced treatment of waste water has achieved a remarkable improvement in water quality in the seas around Ireland. Looking to the future it is clear that some aspects of the wider environment will, on current trends, be adversely affected by economic growth. In particular, there is no sign that Ireland is serious about tackling the problem of global warming.

Ireland's economic growth has been accompanied by increased congestion on our roads, and a rising number of road deaths. These factors do not appear on the balance sheet as measured in GNP terms, but represent real human costs to our society.

I am not a sociologist, so I will leave to others to discuss whether our economic progress has brought with it a coarsening in values or a weakening of community life. I want to turn to look at how, like the Lotus Eaters, we value leisure time, and in particular to look at the implications of our changed society for families and family formation.

**Our measure of economic well-being, Gross National Product, does not take into account the value we as individuals place on our time, nor of the trade-offs we make between extra income or extra time for ourselves and our families.**

## Time and How We Value It

Our measure of economic well-being, Gross National Product, does not take into account the value we as individuals place on our time, nor of the trade-offs we make between extra income or extra time for ourselves and our families. Individuals may choose to work shorter hours or take longer holidays foregoing potential earnings. Provided that the individuals freely make this choice of more leisure rather than ever higher incomes then their welfare has increased. However, making such a choice may result in lower measured GNP. This needs to be borne in mind when comparing standards of living across different societies. Here in Europe we tend to value leisure more highly than in the US. Comparing US output with EU output, this factor needs to be taken into account.

While output per hour in France is higher than in the US, French people spend much fewer days a year at work. To the extent that this is a positive choice of longer holidays then French people are better off than if they worked for longer, although measured in money alone, the US appears to be better off.

## Choosing an Irish Model

It is possible that many of the things we may choose to do with increased affluence will involve foregoing potential future earnings. There is a range of choices that individuals themselves may make or which we as a society may choose to make which will involve trading off current or future money income for a range of measures which enhance our welfare in some broader sense.

> It is possible that many of the things we may choose to do with increased affluence will involve foregoing potential future earnings.

- Choosing to take more time out of the labour force at the cost of lower incomes.

- Investing in urban infrastructure to develop sustainable cities with lower congestion and lower commuting costs.

- Choosing a more equitable distribution of resources.

- Choosing to invest some of our resources in promoting more rapid growth in Africa.

Here I concentrate on one of these areas – the choice of time devoted to paid work.

## Time Management

Already in Ireland, the female participation rate for those under thirty-five is well above the EU average. For women in their twenties, controlling for education, our participation rate is the highest in the EU. This reflects the high level of educational attainment for women (higher than for men) and the relatively late (and rising) age of first births. For older women, the participation rate is currently much lower than for their younger sisters. However, we are likely to see significant further change over the coming decade as the cohort in their late twenties and early thirties grow older. As the current cohorts age, women will gradually come to form a majority of the best-educated segment of the population in the older age groups. This will bring significant economic and social change and society will have to adjust to the new circumstances.

With a majority of women now going on to third level education, they have the education and skills to have successful and remunerative careers. In addition, the Irish economy will seek them out and encourage them to join and remain in the work force. As a result, one can anticipate a continuing rise in participation among women in their thirties and forties.

Research has shown that while there was significant discrimination in earnings against women in the late 1980s, the discrimination against women qua women had largely disappeared by the end of the 1990s. However, the research also shows that there was a very heavy penalty paid in lost earnings for anyone who spent significant time out of the labour force. As it is nearly always women who are in this position it means that women, on average, still earn significantly less than men if they take time off to look after children.

If both parents continue to work full time, they face a heavy cash cost of paying for childcare. If one or both parents take some time out to look after the family, through working reduced hours or taking a career break, the opportunity cost in terms not only of current earnings foregone but also of reduced future earnings and career prospects is high. Whereas, a generation ago, parents thought of the cost of a child in terms of could they afford to feed or clothe an extra addition to the family, today it is the cost of child care or of time out of the workforce that is a major consideration causing people to postpone having children or to limit the size of their families.

This high cost of children faces many potential parents with a dilemma. Do both partners pursue successful full-time careers and how can they reconcile this with having a family? At present, research evidence suggests that if either or both partners take time off to look after children they are likely to be heavily penalised in their career. This not only raises the cost of having children but also, given the importance of work in society, imposes a heavy social penalty in terms of status. As a result, there is an increasing pressure on potential parents to postpone having children until their thirties, possibly their late thirties. This can allow both partners to establish their careers with the hope of paying a smaller penalty for becoming parents later in their career. It also reduces the likely number of children in the long run.

If the decision to have children at a much later age than in the past were freely made by parents without economic and social constraints placed on them by society, then there would not necessarily be any implications for public policy. However, there are strong a priori grounds for believing that this is not the case. If individuals are being seriously constrained in their choices of when and if they become parents, then there is a case for looking anew at how we organise

**This high cost of children faces many potential parents with a dilemma. Do both partners pursue successful full-time careers and how can they reconcile this with having a family?**

society and, specifically, the work place.

To some extent, in a competitive economy adjustments will be made automatically as market forces operate. With the sheer size of the cohort of women involved and the need of business to attract and hold skilled women in the labour force, employers will be forced to look anew at the penalty they are exacting for time out of the labour market. Continuing to ignore the abilities of parents who take time off to look after children may be too costly for business when so many of their potentially most productive employees are in this position.

However, there is no certainty that the market will deliver a suitable solution to this dilemma. Society has a wider interest in ensuring that, where parents want to have children, the timing of this decision is not unduly constrained by short-term economic factors.

The issue of how best to meet the needs of families in today's economy is a much broader issue than one of labour supply. Instead, it concerns the quality of life for both parents and children. If it is the case that parents are currently constrained in their choices then, just as in the choice of leisure over work, Irish society may choose more family friendly policies at the expense of some reduction in measured income. This could include the provision of greatly improved childcare facilities, as well as a wider acceptance that both parents should be free to take time off to care for their children. For example, in Sweden some of the parental leave after birth is only available to fathers.

A possible objection to increased support for families through flexible working arrangements, or increased provision of childcare facilities, is that they will place further burdens on business. Whether businesses directly fund the changes or whether they are funded through taxation may ultimately make little difference to who pays. Whichever route is chosen, in an open economy such as Ireland's, it is likely that the result of the wage bargaining process will see the bulk of the financial cost ultimately falling on employees who will, in turn, be the beneficiaries. This is not a reason for forgoing a change in policy, which improves the welfare of many citizens, but the fact that it is not costless must be recognised.

The economics of caring, both for children and the elderly, are very complex and I don't have the space to treat it in detail. However, it is clear that someone will have to pay for childcare. This payment can be made directly by parents foregoing working time at a cost in terms of lost lifetime earnings; parents can pay others to look after their children; or the state can make provision, recouping the cost from taxation. It is not a question of choosing one of these models but rather of choosing the appropriate mix.

In the United States, where there is a very wide dispersion in

**Continuing to ignore the abilities of parents who take time off to look after children may be too costly for business when so many of their potentially most productive employees are in this position.**

earnings, there is a very wide use of paid childcare. With many parents on high incomes they can afford to pay the low wages that those at the bottom of the income distribution can earn looking after their children. This arrangement is profitable for both parties. However, in Europe, with typically a much narrower dispersion of earnings, the margin between what those on high incomes earn after tax and what potential carers need to earn to make it worth their while looking after children is much narrower. Thus European families tend to spend a greater amount of time caring for their own children through time out of the work force than is the case in the US. They may also prefer this arrangement, even if the costs were identical.

In the case of Ireland over the last twenty years we have relied more than other EU countries on one parent (generally the mother) taking time off work (or on grandparents who are not working or take time off work). However, as outlined above, the economic pressures are mounting for a change in the pattern in Ireland.

While the distribution of earnings in Ireland is also quite uneven, it has narrowed in recent years. This makes the option of paying someone else to look after one's children more costly. For the future, with limited immigration of unskilled labour, this dispersion is likely to narrow – childcare will not become cheaper. While it is a possibility that society could choose to rely on an increasing number of foreign childcare workers on low incomes this could have serious labour market consequences. It also does not sound like a very caring society where "caring" jobs are increasingly contracted out to foreigners on low incomes. (The model adopted by wealthy families in pre-Norman Ireland involved having their children "fostered" by someone else – even in childcare the economic models change little over time!)

The discussion to date on this issue has centred on the increased provision of childcare services, possibly by the state. However, if European experience is anything to go by, we should also be looking at the increased use of flexible working arrangements and how these can be increased, while reducing the market penalty for time out of the labour market.

The group which probably has the biggest problems today are single parents. Previous research indicates that lone mothers in identical circumstances to married mothers had a stronger desire to participate in the labour market. However, they face much greater obstacles and it is difficult to see how they can compete with couples with two incomes in buying childcare unless there is an increase in state provision for childcare.

My own view is that until both parents are required to share the

**While it is a possibility that society could choose to rely on an increasing number of foreign childcare workers on low incomes this could have serious labour market consequences. It also does not sound like a very caring society where "caring" jobs are increasingly contracted out to foreigners on low incomes.**

time off work the penalty paid in lost future earnings for time out of the labour market will remain. It is only if all employers know that all of their employees under forty will be taking some time off work to look after children that it will be treated as normal. It may be argued that introducing compulsory paternity leave for fathers smacks of social engineering. However, will our society ever really value childcare unless it is seen to be equally a male and a female responsibility? I may be past this now myself, but I am for it.

Martin McGinley, *Derry Journal*, with Frank Galligan,
Broadcaster and Journalist and Tomás Ó Canainn

Mary Claire O'Donnell, Secretary, MacGill Summer School

John Lonergan
Governor, Mountjoy Prison

Prof John Monaghan
Vice-President, St. Vincent de Paul

Emily Logan
Ombudsman for Children

Helen Johnston
CEO, Combat Poverty Agency

*Chapter 4*

# Cherishing All the Children Equally

# Helen Johnston

## Director, Combat Poverty Agency

*Born in Ballymoney and educated at Ballymena Academy, University of Ulster (BSc.), QUB (MSc.) and DCU (MBA). Has been Director of the Combat Poverty Agency for the past five years. Prior to this she was Head of Research with the Equality Authority and National Disability Authority and for eight years with Combat Poverty. Previously, she worked in the Central Community Relations Unit in Northern Ireland and in the Policy Planning and Research Unit of the Northern Ireland Civil Service.*

## Ending Child Poverty – A Shared Responsibility

A modern twenty-first century society such as Ireland should not tolerate child poverty. We are now a rich society yet poverty still exists. There are still families in modern Ireland who have to manage on very low incomes on a day to day basis, and who have to borrow on a regular basis to make ends meet. Many families have limited educational qualifications and skills and find it difficult to get or to hold down jobs. Many families experience poor physical or mental health leaving them at risk of poverty. This experience is reflected in the comments of children themselves in a study by Combat Poverty:[1]

A modern twenty-first century society such as Ireland should not tolerate child poverty. We are now a rich society yet poverty still exists.

> "I feel kind of guilty when Mammy and Daddy leave themselves without anything and we get all the stuff."

> "With some people, whether they're your friends or not depends on what you wear. People don't like friends who don't have brand name clothes."

> "The worst thing is being bullied and being frightened of being beaten up."

### The Consequences of Child Poverty

There are a number of consequences for children who experience poverty. In the short term, poor children may experience material deprivation, exclusion from everyday activities and, in some cases, bullying, often because they do not have the same things as other children. In the longer term, the consequences of growing up in poverty are poorer health, slower physical and mental development, lower levels of educational achievement leading to reduced occupational levels, decreased life opportunities and reduced life expectancy.

Children from poor households are at a higher risk of doing poorly in school, becoming teenage parents, not finding good jobs, child abuse, youth homelessness and spending time in prison.

## How Many Children Are Poor?

There are two measures of child poverty in Ireland. The Irish Government measure of consistent poverty is where an individual is below the poverty line and experiences an enforced lack of one or more items on a basic deprivation index, such as a lack of food, clothing, heating or not being able to pay everyday expenses without going into debt.[2] The latest CSO data for 2004 indicate that children in Ireland are more likely to be poor than adults. Some 109,000 children under 16 years of age are found to be in "consistently poor" homes. This represents 9.9 per cent of all children (CSO, 2005).[3] Many of these children are in lone parent households, in families where the head of household is ill or disabled or in larger families. Nearly one-third (31.1 per cent) of lone parent households are in consistent poverty.

A second measure of child poverty is relative income poverty, which measures the proportion of children under 16 in families falling below the poverty line (€185.51 per week). This measure, sometimes referred to as "at risk of poverty", does not include deprivation, and is used across Europe. Using the relative poverty measure, 21.9 per cent of Ireland's children (241,000 children) are living in families "at risk of poverty".[4]

The poverty line (60 per cent median income) is €185.51 per person per week, which is €9,680 per annum. For a family of two adults and two children you are at risk of poverty if you are living on less than €430 per week and for a lone parent family with one child if you are living on less than €246 per week. The basic social welfare payment is currently €165.80 per week.

> Some 109,000 children under 16 years of age are found to be in "consistently poor" homes. This represents 9.9 per cent of all children. Many of these children are in lone parent households, in families where the head of household is ill or disabled or in larger families.

## Extent of Child Poverty over Time

Figure 1 shows trends in child poverty since 1973. Relative income poverty increased up to the early 1990s (1994) and has since fallen slightly in the last decade. It still remains high in European terms. This relatively high rate of income poverty in Ireland has been attributed to increases in income overall and the high level of income inequality in Ireland. Living standards across the population, however, have in general risen and far fewer households are now experiencing deprivation than 20 years ago. The level of consistent poverty for children has shown a substantial decline from 25 per cent in 1987 to a low of just over 6.5 per cent in 2001. The increase since then has been attributed to a methodological change in data collection rather than an actual increase in deprivation, which is seen to decline between 2003 and 2004, when a similar method was used.

*Figure 1: Extent of Child Poverty, 1973-2004*

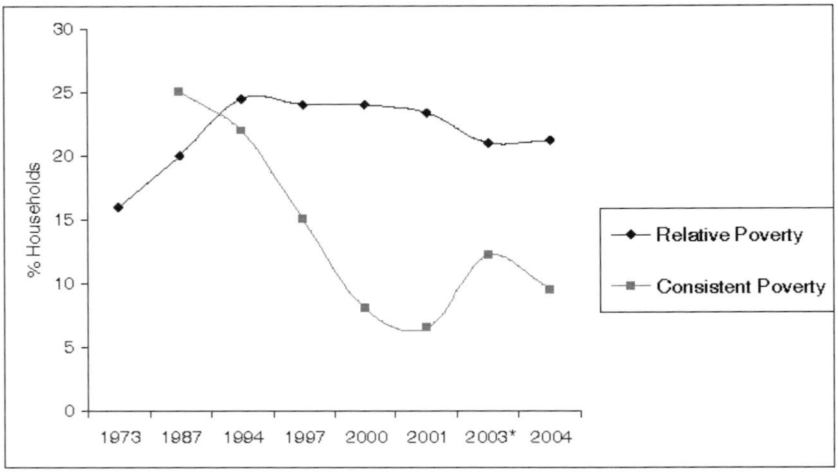

## Why Children are Poor

High poverty rates at a given point in time can come about because the number of children entering poverty is rising or because the number of poor children who leave poverty is falling. The households children live in influence the amount of time spent in childhood poverty. Children influence the household's risk of poverty because of their impact on household expenses and on the labour force status of the parents, particularly the mother.

In addition to the number and age of children in a household, the duration of child poverty is also affected by the educational levels and health of the adults in the household, as well as their dependence on social welfare. Lone parent households and workless households have a particularly high risk of poverty.

The chances of experiencing sustained poverty in adulthood are related to childhood economic circumstances and children's educational opportunities, in particular. A person whose parents have no educational qualifications beyond primary level is 23 times more likely to have no formal qualification himself or herself compared to someone whose parents have third level education.

**The chances of experiencing sustained poverty in adulthood are related to childhood economic circumstances and children's educational opportunities, in particular.**

## Policy Landscape

Ireland has signed up to the UN Convention on the Rights of the Child. This includes survival rights, developmental rights, protection rights and participation rights. Under this commitment Ireland is obliged to address child poverty. Ireland has a National Children's Strategy and a National Children's Office, now re-organised as the Office of the Minister for Children and an Ombudsman for Children. These initiatives contain a commitment for children to be provided with the financial supports necessary to eliminate child poverty.

The recent Social Partnership Agreement, "Towards 2016", sets out a ten-year framework for economic and social development. It adopts a life cycle approach, with a specific focus on children and young people, and contains a number of commitments in this regard on early childhood development and care, education, health, income support, recreation, sport, arts and culture as well as a focus on families and integrating delivery at the local level.

"Towards 2016" takes an integrated approach to social inclusion, dovetailing with a number of other important social inclusion policy documents such as the National Action Plan against Poverty and Social Exclusion and the National Development Plan. The National Action Plan against Poverty and Social Exclusion 2006-2008 is currently being prepared. The previous plan was committed to reducing consistent child poverty (currently at 9.9 per cent) to less than 2 per cent, and to move to a situation of greater equality for all children in terms of access to appropriate education, health and housing.

The next National Development Plan is also currently being prepared for 2007-2013. This will contain a social inclusion pillar and will include significant financial resources. It will be important that these are targeted at the most disadvantaged areas and populations. In the Border region the new Peace and Interreg programmes will continue to have a critical role to play in addressing the legacy of the conflict and its impact on families.

## Child Support

There are currently a number of supports in place to move children out of poverty and improve their well-being.[5] There has been a significant increase in expenditure, particularly since 2000, mainly due to an increase in the rates of Child Benefit from €49.60 per month in 2000 to €131.60 per month in 2004, now €150 in 2006 (for the first and second child; the third and subsequent children receive higher rates). The numbers of families and children receiving Child Benefit has remained fairly stable.

The next National Development Plan is also currently being prepared for 2007–2013. This will contain a social inclusion pillar and will include significant financial resources. It will be important that these are targeted at the most disadvantaged areas and populations.

However, when we examine Ireland's expenditure on public services, such as childcare, education, healthcare and housing, we do less well, spending less than many other European countries.[6]

## Proposals to Address Child Poverty

Given this situation, Combat Poverty has suggested the following actions to further reduce child poverty in Ireland:

- Continue to increase Child Benefit, at least in line with inflation.

- Increase the Child Dependant Allowances (paid to families on welfare) and link with the Family Income Supplement (paid to low income families), through a tapered Child Benefit Supplement.

- Increase social expenditure in a number of areas, specifically:

  o Contributing to the cost of childcare for low income families and extending the early childcare supplement to 6- to 12-year-olds

  o On tackling educational disadvantage especially through the provision of pre-school education to all three- and four-year-olds from low income families

  o Increasing provision of social housing, and

  o Increasing the thresholds for medical cards and funding community-led interventions to tackle health inequalities.

- Delivering integrated and targeted interventions, especially at a local level.

- Supporting family policies through:

  o Introduction of a Parental Allowance

  o Supports to ease the transition from welfare to work, and

  o Adequate supports for vulnerable families.

## Political Leadership

To be serious about ending child poverty requires that it is a clear political priority articulated by key politicians, who would put forward a positive vision of a society free of child poverty. This will require tempering the current market-oriented model of society with a stronger developmental welfare state, as articulated by the National Economic and Social Council.[7] This approach advocates a greater emphasis on services supported by adequate income supports and innovative measures to support a modern society.

*To be serious about ending child poverty requires that it is a clear political priority articulated by key politicians, who would put forward a positive vision of a society free of child poverty.*

## Institutional Leadership

The State and public authorities also have a key leadership role in the areas of social expenditure. This role has two dimensions: a leadership role through direct provision, and an indirect role through the encouragement of measures to end child poverty. The State and public authorities can directly tackle child poverty through their policies and programmes – the elimination of child poverty needs to be central to these and co-ordinated across the public sector.

State agencies such as the Combat Poverty Agency, along with organisations such as the Office of the Minister for Children and the Family Support Agency, have specific leadership roles to play in supporting the end of child poverty.

At local level, the local authorities have responsibility for the provision of adequate housing facilities, playgrounds and libraries. Through the County and City Development Boards a focus can be maintained on addressing child poverty at local level. The local authority initiatives can be complemented by local area-based initiatives through the area partnerships and by community groups.

A specific example in this regard is the work of the EU-funded Peace Programme in the Border Region. The Peace Programme funds projects which support the development of children and young people in various ways, for example through community-based education projects, in both school and out of school settings.

**The employment of women contributes significantly to reductions in child poverty. This requires the adoption of family-friendly work policies and flexible working arrangements for parents.**

## Trade Unions

The social partners also have an important role to play. The trade union movement has traditionally been supportive of initiatives to reduce child poverty, particularly among the working population. The trade unions have a role in putting the ending of child poverty at the centre of national policy concerns.

## Business

The business sector, too, can promote measures to abolish child poverty in a number of ways. The employment of women contributes significantly to reductions in child poverty. This requires the adoption of family-friendly work policies and flexible working arrangements for parents. In the area of corporate social responsibility there are many initiatives which employers can take at local level.

## Civil Society

The community and voluntary sector clearly have a key role to play. Many community and voluntary groups represent either the needs of children and/or of people at risk of poverty. They make an important contribution in raising issues of child poverty and also in promoting measures to address it. In particular, they can support the voice of children, the rights of children and promote innovative local actions. They should be supported to do so.

There are a range of other civil society organisations which can all contribute to the ending of child poverty in Ireland. The church and faith-based organisations have historically had a range of roles in this area. Opinion formers, such as academia and the media, can assist in making this a national issue and provide and promote the evidence base on which to take forward appropriate policy initiatives.

**The family, schools and the local community are key partners in tackling child poverty. They all have a role to play in supporting children, and seeing child poverty as unacceptable.**

The family, schools and the local community are key partners in tackling child poverty. They all have a role to play in supporting children, and seeing child poverty as unacceptable.

Finally, a national strategy to end child poverty needs to be promoted so that there is an understanding of the scale and nature of the problem and what needs to be done, to gain support and empathy from the general public.

## Conclusion

Child poverty is unacceptable in a modern society. We need to make the elimination of child poverty a national priority and all the relevant institutions in our society need to do all they can to work towards this end.

To cherish all the children equally we need to end child poverty and ending child poverty in Ireland is everybody's business!

### Endnotes

[1] Daly, M. and Leonard, M. (2002) *Against All Odds: Family Life on a Low Income in Ireland*. Combat Poverty Agency/Institute of Public Administration: Dublin.

[2] The most recent data available are for 2004 (Central Statistics Office (2005) "EU Survey on Income and Living Conditions" (EU-SILC). The poverty line (60 per cent of median equivalised disposable income) was €185.51 per week (€9,680 per annum). The basic deprivation index consists of:

- No substantial meal on at least one day in the last two weeks
- Without heating at some stage in the past year
- Experienced debt problems arising from ordinary living expenses
- Unable to afford two pairs of strong shoes
- Unable to afford a roast once a week

- Unable to afford a meal with meat, chicken or fish every second day
- Unable to afford new (not second hand) clothes
- Unable to afford a warm waterproof coat.

[3] Central Statistics Office (2005) "EU Survey on Income and Living Conditions" (EU-SILC).

[4] Ibid.

[5] Combat Poverty Agency (2005) "Ending Child Poverty: Policy Statement." Dublin: Combat Poverty Agency

[6] Ibid.

[7] National Economic and Social Council (2005) *The Developmental Welfare State.* National Economic and Social Development Office: Dublin.

# Prof John Monaghan

## National Vice-President, Society of St. Vincent de Paul

*A mechanical engineer, is Head of the Department of Mechanical and Manufacturing Engineering at TCD. He has been a volunteer member of the Society of St. Vincent de Paul for for more than twenty years. He is a member of the Board of SVP and is National Vice-President with responsibility for social policy.*

## Cherishing *All* the Children – Whoever the *"All"* Are

### The Proclamation of 1916

While the entire Proclamation of 1916 is an inspiring document there are two short passages that hold particular significance for the work of the SVP. These are both contained in the section that reads:

> The Republic *guarantees* religious and civil liberty,
> *equal rights and equal opportunities to all its citizens,*
> and declares its *resolve* to pursue the happiness and prosperity
> of the *whole nation* and all its parts, *cherishing all the children of
> the nation equally* ...

**... how far as a nation have we progressed towards the realisation of that guarantee and resolve over the past 90 years and, indeed, what was meant by all the children of the nation?**

The question is, how far as a nation have we progressed towards the realisation of that guarantee and resolve over the past 90 years and, indeed, what was meant by all the children of the nation?

### Ireland of 1916

There is no doubt that the Ireland of 1916 was a very different place compared to modern Ireland. The Proclamation was written at a time of widespread poverty, considerable hunger and under-nourishment among the poor, a poor health service with the consequent effects of high child mortality and low life expectancy. All of this was made more intolerable by having some of the worst slums and housing throughout Europe. Unemployment was high and so emigration to England and the US was the only alternative to destitution for many people. This was certainly so for young people brought up in the city slums or on small farms throughout the country, and particularly so for people from the west of Ireland. Coupled with this, the overall standard of education of the majority of the population was low which meant that when they did emigrate they did so to poorly paid and low-skilled jobs.

## Ireland 2006

When the Ireland of 1916 is compared to that of 2006 it is clear that considerable progress has been made in many areas. We currently have exceptional economic growth with consequent high GDP and GNP. We have reduced unemployment and, significantly indeed, to sustain our economic growth we have to rely on the immigration of approximately 70,000 people each year. In general, our health has improved and we can look forward to an increased life expectancy. Thankfully, the overall standard of education and level of qualifications within the population is now very high. So we are *all* doing very well – or are we!

## It's Party Time – We Are All Doing Great – So Ignore the Begrudgers!

Consumer spending is now at an all time high, amounting to over €70 billion per year, while consumer borrowing is now estimated to be over €130 billion, that's over €32,000 for every man, woman and child in the country. So with economic growth predicted to continue into the future, and even more billions due shortly from maturing SSIA accounts, a sense of invincibility and a "party time" attitude appears to have engulfed the country. For example, in 2004 we spent over €6.5 billion on drink and over €720 million on fizzy drinks celebrating our new-found prosperity and then we went home and spent over €125 million feeding our pets.

> It's official then – we have no problems.
>
> Ireland 2006 does not "do poverty".
>
> Consequently the SVP, and the rest of the "whingers" in the so-called "poverty industry", can just shut up and go away.

If we are all doing so well economically – have guaranteed equal rights and opportunities, we're all cherished and there is no poverty in modern Ireland – then how come each year SVP volunteers have to make over 300,000 visits to these non-existent poor and manage to spend over €33 million on a non-existent problem?

## SVP Spending on "Basic Necessities"

- Financial assistance: €7.0 million – general bills, e.g. rent/mortgage, medical expenses, etc.

- Food: €4.1 million – in one of the wealthiest countries in the world!

- Education: €3.0 million – so much for "free education"!

- Fuel and ESB: €2.8 million – keeping the house warm and the lights on

- Clothing and furniture: €1.0 million – tables and chairs, beds, fridges and washing machines

- Total = €17.9 million. This amounts to over €1.5 million per month or €640,000 per week on "basic necessities".

**These numbers suggest that we might still have a "bit" of a problem "cherishing all equally". Unfortunately it's the daily experience of those 9,000 members of the SVP that under four main headings this lack of "equality and cherishing" is all too obvious.**

These numbers suggest that we might still have a "bit" of a problem "cherishing all equally". Unfortunately, it's the daily experience of those 9,000 members of the SVP that under four main headings this lack of "equality and cherishing" is all too obvious.

- The lack of an adequate income to live, let alone live with dignity and participate in society.

- Poor access to appropriate health care – it's a sad fact that poorer people get sick more often and die earlier than better off people.

- Access to affordable and appropriate housing – we boast about building over 80,000 houses each year so why are approximately 50,000 children in households on waiting lists for social housing, and why did the SVP have to build three new hostels in recent years?

- The scandal of educational disadvantage, which continues to blight the lives and prospects of not only children but their parents and indeed entire communities.

## Our Battle with "Equality" – Income Adequacy

- In 2004 we spent over €125 million on pet food.

- Sales and waiting lists for BMWs, Mercs and SUVs have doubled in four years.

- Bulging property supplements with ads for overseas properties

- In 2002, 43 high earners paid less than 5 per cent in tax.

- Children are still going to school hungry each day.

- 400,000 people are still living in consistent poverty – 800,000 are at risk of poverty.

- Poorer people spend a large percentage of their small disposable income on food

- Increases in ESB and gas charges are causing intolerable problems.

## Accessing Health Care

We have all heard the saying, "your health is your wealth". Unfortunately, for so many people assisted by the SVP, their "health poverty" is all too obvious. There is no doubt that spending on health has increased significantly over the past decade. In fact, there has been an 80 per cent increase in non-capital health expenditure since 1994. Yet, so much of this has been for "catch-up" and still as a proportion of GDP our health spending is currently at 7.3 per cent while the EU average is 8.7 per cent.

In 1997 over 37 per cent of the population was covered by the full medical card, but this is now down to 27 per cent. Why? It's not that we have all suddenly become that much healthier or so much better off that we don't need a full medical card. In fact, it's because the income eligibility threshold has until recently remained so ludicrously low that even a modest rise in earnings meant that many people in work on low pay no longer qualified. While the recent introduction of the "Doctor Visit" card is welcome, in the sense that anything that reduces the burden of medical expenses on low income households is to be welcomed, it is an inadequate response. It does not cover visits to hospital, drugs, consultants' fees, x-rays and other tests. The government really does need to honour its commitment to provide 200,000 *full* medical cards. Indeed, the evidence supporting this argument is clear from a recent report that showed that in the past year 45 per cent of low-income households were prevented from seeking medical attention because of a lack of money. Another area of significant inequality is in the provision of mental health services. It is a sad fact that mental health problems are highest in those areas having the greatest number of full medical cards – so why are most of the mental health facilities located in better off areas? In the case of children the provision of adequate and appropriate services is an ongoing problem.

**In 1997 over 37 per cent of the population was covered by the full medical card, but this is now down to 27 per cent. Why? It's not that we have all suddenly become that much healthier or so much better off that we don't need a full medical card.**

As long as the SVP has to assist people with their medical expenses, and private tests for school going children because of long waiting lists for public services, then we still have some distance to go to fulfill the guarantee of "equality and cherishing" the sick and the poor.

## Education – The Path Out of Poverty

Unquestionably, Ireland has made enormous progress, particularly in recent years, across the complete spectrum of education. Yet we still have problems and the educational landscape of Ireland 2006 still contains some enormous holes that poorer children and adults fall into. For example:

- Each year at least 1,000 children never make the transition from primary to second level schools – *why?*

- Over 50 per cent of children in some disadvantaged areas have severe problems with literacy and numeracy – and it's estimated that up to 30 per cent of all children leave primary school with similar problems - *why?*

- 14 per cent of secondary school students leave each year without any formal qualification – *why?*

**... the debate and energy in education circles, in the media and among parents, should be around ending educational disadvantage not whether we should or should not publish school league tables.**

Undoubtedly, the underlying reasons for these dreadful statistics, and the answer to the questions, are a complex mix of many factors, but one thing we can be certain of is that the problem will be found predominantly among children from poorer households. Figures like these should make it abundantly clear that the debate and energy in education circles, in the media and among parents, should be around ending educational disadvantage not whether we should or should not publish school league tables.

To seriously tackle educational disadvantage there are things we can, and should, be doing. For example, it is well known that a good start in education is vital for all children but is essential for children from disadvantaged households. There is conclusive evidence to show that such children benefit greatly from access to pre-school facilities in the two years immediately prior to starting primary school. If this can be achieved then their progress on entering primary school is then as good as the other children in their class. However, prohibitive crèche/pre-school costs make this impossible for low-income families who do not have access to low-cost community-based facilities in their areas.

Another issue: children cannot progress in school without school books, but the ever spiralling cost and frequent change in recommended books puts an intolerable strain on low-income households each summer. Indeed, support with the cost of school books comprises a major proportion of the educational expenditure of the SVP. The question has to be asked why Ireland is nearly unique in Europe in not providing free school books to all children, or at least to all children in low-income households.

## The Ongoing Housing Crisis – And We Don't Mean Holiday Homes in Bulgaria

For many years now in our pre-budget submissions we have been asking for the building of at least 10-12,000 social housing units per year. Consequently, the SVP welcomes the recent announcement as part of the new social partnership agreement that 27,000 social housing units are to be built over the next three years. However, promises and delivery are two very different things and previous promises and commitments have not been met.

One of the biggest conundrums in all this is determining the exact number of households currently on local authority waiting lists for social housing. The latest official figures show it to be 43,000, but how can this be correct given that rent supplement is currently been paid to over 60,000 people and you cannot receive a rent supplement unless you are on a housing waiting list? Furthermore, the state is currently spending over €375 million each year on these rent supplements, most of which goes to private landlords and in the experience of the SVP often for poor and inappropriate accommodation. The ongoing scandal in the provision of all housing is the level of market manipulation and speculation around the cost of building land, and it is about time that the recommendations contained in the Kenny report are again considered. Kenny suggested that the price of building land should be capped at current unzoned market value plus 25 per cent. However, successive Governments have shied away from tackling this particular issue for obvious political reasons.

Clearly, in the current climate of spiralling housing costs, the guarantee of equality of opportunity to appropriate accommodation is a very long way off for many people, but particularly for those on low income. That's why, in a housing boom, the SVP is still one of the largest providers of social housing and now has to operate 19 hostels.

*The ongoing scandal in the provision of all housing is the level of market manipulation and speculation around the cost of building land, and it is about time that the recommendations contained in the Kenny report are again considered.*

## The Continuing Work of the SVP

There is abundant evidence that if we can reduce inequality, move people from welfare to work, eliminate educational disadvantage and give some hope to people, especially young people from disadvantaged backgrounds, then the benefits to the economy and the entire community are immense. Our spending on welfare, health, prisons and so much more can then be reduced or, at the very least, spent in a more targeted and effective way.

However, to achieve this, SVP and others working for social justice have some convincing to do. We need to bring about a change in commitment and attitude not only within Government and policy makers, but also within the wider population. However, before Irish society can successfully tackle the problem of poverty and social exclusion it must at the very least acknowledge that we do still have a problem, and the evidence so far is that we are some way off such an acknowledgement.

**However, before Irish society can successfully tackle the problem of poverty and social exclusion it must at the very least acknowledge that we do still have a problem ...**

## Changing the Attitude of the Irish Public

The combined effects of the improving economy, reductions in direct taxation and reasonable increases in wages have tended to create the impression that everyone in the country is doing fine, so there are no real problems. Indeed, when we come face to face with inadequate public services in health, education or transport and so on, we might grumble, but don't seriously question why this should be so. Recent surveys concluded that we most certainly do not want to see tax increases to fund improvement in social services, even where they might affect our own children, such as in education or health. It is this attitude that allows the following anomalies and contradictions to arise in the Ireland of 2006. For example:

- We spend more than €115 million each year on Coca Cola – this is more than the spending on the entire school transport system!

- Each year we spend more than €1.6 billion on stout – this is more than the entire budget for primary education!

- We spend €18 million on hair dyes – but only €12 million on school meals for poor children!

- More is spent on crisps than on free book schemes for poorer children!

- Our spending on mobile phones per quarter is greater than our total contribution to international aid in a year!

## *Changing the Mind of "Official Ireland"*

To effect real change, the state must get away from the idea that improvements in social provision must always be reliant on economic growth. For many years now the underlying philosophy for improvements in social provision has been based on the dubious theory that the "rising economic tide lifts all boats", a theory that has manifestly failed given that many of the boats of those assisted daily by the SVP have been anchored for years.

It is also vital to remove the thinking behind the phraseology contained in so many Government budgets and statements to the effect that improvements will be made to a given service "as resources permit" or changes will be made "within the limit of existing resources". This frame of mind, and the attitude underlying it, in effect means that many nice sounding Government statements are only aspirations with no real commitment to deliver. If we are to make any progress in the elimination of poverty and social exclusion then they must be replaced by comments such as, "we are going to do … and we will find the resources necessary to do so". However to get rid of the rising tide theory and the behaviour arising from it requires a simultaneous change in both political will and attitude and, frankly, on past evidence the chances of achieving either is doubtful.

> For many years now the underlying philosophy for improvements in social provision has been based on the dubious theory that the "rising economic tide lifts all boats", a theory that has manifestly failed given that many of the boats of those assisted daily by the SVP have been anchored for years.

# Emily Logan

## Ombudsman for Children

*Holds an MBA, an M.Sc in psychology and a Diploma in mediation. Originally trained as a paediatric nurse in Dublin, she spent ten years working at Great Ormond Street Hospital and Guy's Hospital in London. On returning to Ireland she held two senior administrative posts, Director of Nursing in Our Lady's Hospital for Sick Children in Crumlin and Director of Nursing at Tallaght Hospital. She was appointed Ireland's first Ombudsman for Children in 2003.*

## We Still Lack the Capacity to Protect Children

An Ombudsman with a human rights brief is a new concept in Ireland. It is new because, in addition to providing the well understood complaints handling service, I am also charged with a statutory mandate to promote the rights and welfare of children. This second, far more wide-reaching, function of the Office is the promotion of children's rights, including the UN Convention on the Rights of the Child (UNCRC). In 1989, the United Nations Assembly adopted the UN Convention on the Rights of the Child, a unique document in terms of international consensus on how children should be treated and respected.

My comments this evening are based on direct contact with more than 600 children, young people and their families through our complaints function, and contact made with thousands through our promotional role.

### Child Protection

> We have a system and a State that, I believe, continue to lack capacity to provide adequate child protection services.

We have a system and a State that, I believe, continue to lack capacity to provide adequate child protection services.

In January 2006, I made a submission to the Oireachtas Committee on Health and Children. It contained a summary and analysis of 61 complaints affecting 94 children made to my Office by members of the public up to December of last year. The complaints indicate concerns about the capacity of the system to respond to reports of child abuse in all its forms.

The complaints indicated concerns about the way in which reports of child abuse were handled by the relevant authorities. The main issues highlighted were:

- Difficulties in accessing services

- A lack of information and awareness about child protection services

- Delays in intervention

- A lack of adequate support after the disclosure of abuse had been made

- A lack of respect for the voice of the child, and

- A reluctance to intervene in family contexts.

My role, as Ombudsman for Children, is to give a voice to those children and young people who have experienced or who are experiencing abuse. While the role of investigating the substantive issue of child abuse lies with the other agencies, the Ombudsman for Children's Office has a role in making sure that these agencies respond to children in an appropriate way. Many families have contacted my Office because they do not know where else to go for help. I believe that the experience of the children and families contacting my Office had to be put into the public domain so that measures could be taken to give them and other families like them the support they deserve.

Children who have been through this process have told me that they do not trust the system. They feel that they were not believed, that people did not take them seriously. Children have been saying this for years and they are still saying it to me in 2006.

It is imperative that we create a culture where it is safe for a child to disclose abuse and where adults they tell are empowered to respond. The current system is not child-focused. Much of the responsibility to disclose is placed on the child, who has already suffered dreadful trauma.

In the aftermath of Ferns, the Government announced a review of Children First – the National Guidelines for the Protection and Welfare of Children. It is important to realise that reviews of these guidelines have already been undertaken. Anything less than a comprehensive review of child protection policy, practice and procedure will fall short of what is required to put things right. In my submission to the Minister for Children's Office, I have suggested that time must be given to ask children and families who have been through this system about their experience. What was it like? Could it have been better? What could we do to improve the service and support you through this process?

**It is imperative that we create a culture where it is safe for a child to disclose abuse and where adults they tell are empowered to respond. The current system is not child-focused.**

As always, I received a polite response which informed me that this is a "delicate matter" – inferring that they have no intention of asking children and families what or how things could be better. I am suggesting that we ask those in the midst of this trauma, those for whom this experience is very real.

In May of this year, we heard evidence given at the Child Abuse Commission that, as far back as 1954, nine children were being transferred from St. Joseph's in Kilkenny to a reformatory in Limerick because of their "misbehaviour". To one Department of Education inspector, Anna McCabe, this seemed strange. In the absence of child protection policies or guidelines, she took responsibility and she took time to talk with the children and discovered that they had been sexually assaulted.

So why is it that a suggestion in 2006 that we ask children about their experience is met with resistance, when as far back as 1954 someone who was willing to take responsibility took time to talk with them? Is it because the system of child protection is there above all to protect itself?

As Ombudsman for Children I have been given statutory responsibility for monitoring how the State treats children and young people. As part of this monitoring process, my Office submitted an independent report to the UN Committee on the Rights of the Child on our experiences so far. We presented these experiences to the Committee in Geneva in June. The Ombudsman for Children's Act, 2002 states that "the Ombudsman must highlight issues relating to the rights and welfare of children that are of concern to children".

**Many of the areas of deprivation are rooted in the reality that we do not think of children as individuals with rights. They are treated as either possessions of families or of the State.**

Many of the areas of deprivation are rooted in the reality that we do not think of children as individuals with rights. They are treated as either possessions of families or of the State. And it appears to me just now that it is the State who is the worst parent. Children are not recognised as individual rights holders in the Irish Constitution. Their rights remain subordinate to those of their parents and the family unit as a whole.

What is problematic in Ireland is that the threshold for State intervention in the interests of the child is extremely high because of the protections afforded to the family as a unit. And while this may not affect the average child it is certainly not the case for the more vulnerable.

The State has not implemented the recommendation of the 1996 All Party Constitution Review Group that a statement of express rights for children be inserted into the Constitution. Worse still, a recent report of an Oireachtas Committee has proposed to roll back on the recommendations of the Review Group.

I consider that express recognition of the child as a full subject of rights in the Constitution would enhance protection for the rights and welfare of children, for those who most need protection in Ireland, and I would encourage the Committee to again raise this matter with the State later this year.

The experience of our Office in dealing with complaints is that administrative systems are overly bureaucratic and highly centralised. It is very difficult to say to complainants that they have to exhaust local procedures before we can help. By the time they get to us they are already frustrated and reluctant to return to local procedures.

There is often inflexibility in decision making which suggests that the best interests of the child are not at the core of decision making.

Many of those who contact my Office are not aware of internal complaints systems. Others have tried to secure their entitlements but have endured long delays in the delivery of services or have had no success at all. Persons working with some of the most vulnerable children in the State, such as separated children seeking asylum and children in detention, often have not received appropriate training relevant to their role.

## Child Deprivation

The concept of deprivation sounds outdated but it is very real. I prefer to conceptualise deprivation as the lack of achievement of rights.

People tend to equate deprivation with material deprivation but modern concepts of poverty focus not just on material indicators but also on issues of perceived well-being, exclusion and marginalisation. On all of these counts, children are probably the most vulnerable citizens of the state.

Thinking of deprivation as the denial of rights fundamentally alters our perceptions and it should alter our response.

> Thinking of deprivation as the denial of rights fundamentally alters our perceptions and it should alter our response.

In times of such economic confidence, many of our children have, perhaps, experienced improved material well-being (certainly not all!) but, for many, the same old issues persist – issues of bullying, abuse in all its forms and exclusion through not being listened to or heard remains as terrifying or frustrating as ever.

One of the most fundamental rights set out in the Convention on the Rights of the Child is the right to have a say in decisions that affect you, the right to participate. This right to participate places no obligation on the child to participate. It moves away from a paternalistic model to one that accepts the differing capacities of children and their families to become actively involved on issues of their own rights. From this perspective, it is important that the state and its systems should recognise that some children and families do not have the capacity to easily participate.

The State appears to be afraid of the economic repercussions of recognising rights but, in all the complaints I have heard, I have only once come across someone who was seeking compensation. In fact, I would like to point out that in many, many cases children and their parents just want a simple apology. They want someone to accept or acknowledge that what happened to them was unfair or wrong. In the case of abuse, it is only the acknowledgement or recognition of the abuse which can set the foundation for them getting on with the rest of their lives. Not only have they been abused, but they go on to find that they are also denied the simple act of acknowledgement which could start their healing. Can we really accept systems which double the impact of child abuse by denying people the basis of living and loving, self-esteem and self-respect? To me, this is deprivation at its deepest – children ignored, not listened to, made to feel like ghosts living some separate life from others.

**Many children want things to be better for other children. It is incredible to hear a 16-year-old say that they know it is too late for them but they would like things to change for other children.**

But I also hear many things which hearten me greatly. I have often been struck by the altruistic nature of complaints. Many children want things to be better for other children. It is incredible to hear a 16-year-old say that they know it is too late for them but they would like things to change for other children.

It is also striking that 30 per cent of all complaints received by my Office relate to children with special needs. Children with disabilities are finding it very difficult to attain the support they are entitled to and will no doubt continue to do so unless action is taken to redress the accountability deficit which persists in Ireland.

To summarise I wish to make three main points:

1. All the policies, strategies and guidelines in the Government Publications Office in Molesworth Street are worth nothing if they do not result in changed behaviour by individuals who operate services.

2. People in services need to be trained and empowered to make decisions that provide flexibility and responsiveness to people. The systems are there to serve, not to exclude.

3. Children are not mini-adults; they are individuals in their own right who need not just to be listened to but heard.

# John Lonergan

## Governor, Mountjoy Prison

*Born in Bansha, Co. Tipperary, he joined the Irish Prison Service in 1968. He has been Governor of Mountjoy Prison since 1984 and also served as Governor of Porlaoise Prison 1988 to 1992. He has lectured extensively on the link between crime and economic and social deprivation and on the need to create a just, inclusive and cohesive society.*

## The Loneliness of Poverty and Social Deprivation

One of the most depressing consequences of our recently found wealth and affluence has been our neglect of children born into social and economic deprivation. Indeed, we appear to have deliberately orchestrated their removal from mainstream society by placing them on the very periphery. Have we developed a sub-conscious philosophy of "out of sight, out of mind"? We build and sustain ghetto-like housing estates, located well away from our more affluent areas, we provide inadequate social, educational and recreational facilities and supports. We totally neglect their cries for help and, worst of all, we ignore their human suffering. I am not unconscious of efforts made by both religious and state bodies in certain areas, but they have proved to be hopelessly inadequate.

It is impossible to even remotely convey in this short reflection the pain and misery suffered by children living in poverty. For most of these children basic human needs are no more than innocent dreams – dreams unlikely to be fulfilled. Most of their basic human rights are not being met – the right to have parents, a proper home, regular food, warm clothing, adequate medical care, a broad education, protection from abuse and the other evil influences associated with poverty. Above all, they are deprived of a nurturing family environment so essential for their growth and development. And I'm not referring here to a third world country – child poverty, with all its most destructive consequences, is in our very midst. If we are to retain any credibility as a caring and compassionate people we must seriously tackle the elimination of child poverty in Ireland. It must be put at the very top of our economic, social and political agenda. The problem will not go away; it requires planned intervention at all levels.

Our educational system has also failed many thousands of our children, mostly, but not exclusively, those at the bottom of our social status ladder. We hate to hear this but our formal educational system

**If we are to retain any credibility as a caring and compassionate people we must seriously tackle the elimination of child poverty in Ireland. It must be put at the very top of our economic, social and political agenda.**

is very much a two-tier system and (fees or no fees) money still plays a significant role in the quality of education available to our children. In our most disadvantaged areas second level education is still out of the reach of many children. Indeed, many do not even complete primary level. In addition, a recent survey covering access to third level education highlighted appalling discrepancies between affluent and disadvantaged areas in Dublin. In many instances, the discrepancy was as high as 70 per cent. Social circumstances rather than academic ability is too often the deciding factor. It is not that everyone must go to third level, it is about choice. Education is not the be all and end all in terms of justice but it is one of the most significant factors. Children who miss out on formal education are at a huge disadvantage in modern Ireland and one of the most serious repercussions is that it greatly reduces their job prospects. As a society, we have an obligation to ensure that every child has free and equal access to all levels of education. In particular, we must ensure that money is not the deciding factor.

The booming economy is presenting us with a wonderful opportunity but also with a huge challenge. We must decide our priorities – people and their needs or the economy. This requires much soul searching for all of us. Put bluntly, the economy must be managed to serve our society and not the other way around. Of course, we should rejoice in our successful economy but we must reassess the priorities we give to human needs. We must ensure that the economy does not become a monster and, above all, we must make sure that people are not forced to become slaves to it.

*Space for Human Needs*

On reflection, therefore, it is not surprising that many young people feel under great pressure to meet the very high expectations we demand of them. Those who fail to measure up often feel isolated, unwanted and rejected. Do we hear their cry for help or are we completely out of touch? Are we much too busy to even think about their human needs, or worse, do we really care anymore? Loneliness and rejection are two of the most hurtful and traumatic of all the human experiences. Young people are particularly vulnerable when they experience rejection. Their self-esteem takes a battering and they are convinced that they are no-hopers. As adults, we must be very sensitive during such crisis periods and we must be most generous in giving our time to help them cope and overcome these negative experiences. I cannot over-emphasise the importance of this and we have a real responsibility not to be found wanting at such times. One of the most disturbing and negative consequences of our modern materialistically obsessed society is that we all feel too busy to spend time with those in need.

We may be very generous financially, but money, which is usually the soft option, is definitely no substitute for personal attention. In our pursuit of materialism we have developed a hardness of heart which is preventing us from even noticing the pain around us.

Poverty and social deprivation have many consequences for children, and a one-dimensional materialistic-based response is not the answer. Of course, a financial and material response is part of the solution but it must not be seen as the whole answer. Children in poverty experience physical, psychological and emotional difficulties and we must respond on all three fronts. The RTE Primetime programme "Cradle to the Grave", broadcast last year, really highlighted this reality.

Finally, we must also focus on our own attitudes towards children from deprived areas – how do we see them? A child develops self-esteem mostly based on how they are accepted and treated by other human beings. Children living in deprived areas soon learn that they live on their own cut off from mainstream society. In their areas all the professionals come in, deliver services and quickly leave. It is we – main stream society – who stigmatise these children and as a result directly contribute to their difficulties in life. All elements of child neglect and abuse must concern each one of us and we must not focus exclusively on sexual abuse. Talking the talk is useless unless we walk the walk as well.

**It is we – mainstream society – who stigmatise these children and as a result directly contribute to their difficulties in life.**

Prof Dermot Keogh
Department of History, UCC

Senator Martin Mansergh

Mary Clancy
Women's Studies, UCG

*Chapter 5*

# The Relevance of 1916

*The Legacy of 1916 – A Stable Constitutional Democracy*
PROF DERMOT KEOGH
**Department of History, UCC**

*Equal Rights Still Need to be Asserted*
MARY CLANCY
**Women's Studies, UCG**

*We Are Reaping the Harvest of Our Soverignty*
SENATOR MARTIN MANSERGH
**Fianna Fáil Senator and Columnist**

# Dr Dermot Keogh

## Professor of Irish History, UCC

*He is Head of the History Department of University College Cork. He has written extensively in Irish and foreign journals and is a frequent contributor to the media. He has published many works on Irish and European history including*: The Catholic Church 1950-2004 *and* Twentieth Century Ireland *which has recently been reissued. Forthcoming publications include* The Making of the 1937 Constitution *and* Jack Lynch: His Life and Times.

## The Legacy of 1916 is a Stable Constitutional Democracy

The scholarly world has been quite slow to respond to the need to study the leaders of 1916. This is now being done by a new generation of scholars, freed by the success of the peace process in Northern Ireland from the professional preoccupations of the 1970s and 1980s. There is also a pressing need to examine the role of the rank and file. Happily the central place played by women has been receiving attention by scholars. The international context of the Rising requires, however, major work in continental and US archives. Specifically, the events of 1916 urgently need to be studied in the broader context of political, social and cultural movements in the first two decades of the twentieth century.

Despite the flourishing scholarship surrounding the commemorations in 2006, much has yet to be discovered about the men and women – their ideas and their ideals – who were responsible for the central event that brought the Rising and the creation of the Irish state in 1921–22. Therefore, the answer to the question posed by Dr Joe Mulholland and the organisers of the MacGill Summer School is difficult to answer with precision. To give a response, albeit at a very simple level, would be to state that, unless one studies the complexities of the ideas and the processes that led to the 1916 Rising, it is difficult to understand the values and the ideals that propelled the generation of revolutionaries who founded the Irish State in 1922. William T. Cosgrave and Eamon de Valera, Michael Collins and Sean Lemass, Desmond Fitzgerald and Sean MacEntee – these, and many others, took their ideas in part from that 1916 generation. The political ideas of one man – Arthur Griffith – did more than anyone else to shape the founding philosophy of that state. He was not "out" in the Rising but that did not make him an alien. His books and articles had an enduring

> The political ideas of one man – Arthur Griffith – did more than anyone else to shape the founding philosophy of that state.

influence on his generation. That cannot be gainsaid. Therefore, the question posed by the organisers of the Summer School ought to embrace more than those who were shot as insurgents.

In reviewing the ideas and ideals of 1916, I will refer to two personalities who, in the end, did everything possible to halt the mobilisation of volunteers that Easter weekend. Both were radical nationalists and revolutionaries, and were personalities of considerable influence. Yet, both opposed the timing of the Rising and did everything possible to prevent it. Eoin MacNeill was Chief of Staff of the Irish Volunteers. A Professor of Early Irish History at University College Dublin since 1908, he was a founder member of the Gaelic League in 1893. His article, "The North Began," in *An Claidheamh Soluis,* had advocated the setting up of a volunteer force. He became Chief of Staff of the Irish Volunteers in 1913. A strong nationalist from Glenarm, County Antrim, he has been all-too-often viewed in a negative light in the early decades of the history of the state. His ideas ought to form part of the question framed.

Another Northerner, Bulmer Hobson, was a founder member of the Irish Volunteers. He was also a member of the Irish Republican Brotherhood, the organisation most responsible for the planning and execution of the Rising. But Hobson had been marginalised in the IRB by leadership intent on insurrection. A small group within the IRB planned the Rising while shutting out many of those likely to oppose what they saw as recklessness. This required the use of methods of conspiracy, deception and subterfuge. Yet, the actions of MacNeill and Hobson did much indirectly to shape the course of events that led to the uprising in April 1916.

Before dealing with the questions of difference and division, I will spend a little time on the vision that bound radical nationalists together in the lead up to the Rising. There was a common belief that the twentieth century had sounded the death knell of empires and competing imperialisms. Arthur Griffith, one of the founding fathers of twentieth century Irish nationalism, sensed that the British Empire was under threat. The Boer War signalled a crack in the colonial structure and in the imperial balance of power. By the end of the first decade of the new century, Griffith had a range of both followers and competitors for the leadership of radical nationalism. But all had come to realise that there was something very radical changing in Europe in those early years of a century that was ushered in by the motor car, by the aeroplane and by newly-generated weapons of mass destruction. Technology was going to be put to a most destructive use in World War One. But the generation of 1916, to coin a phrase, were bound together by a sense that the British Empire was weak and vulnerable to a demand for national self-determination. However diverse in

**A small group within the IRB planned the Rising while shutting out many of those likely to oppose what they saw as recklessness. This required the use of methods of conspiracy, deception and subterfuge.**

background and thinking, those who entered the GPO in 1916 believed that their actions would set in train an irreversible series of events that would lead to national independence. The signatories of the Proclamation, Eamon de Valera and other leaders of Sinn Féin in the post-rising period, believed that independence was attainable.

The coalition for self-determination stood in growing contrast to the once radical Irish Parliamentary Party whose leader, John Redmond, continued to believe that the defence of the British Empire would ultimately lead to Home Rule and to a modicum of independence. So, conditioned by the institutionalising influence of membership of the British Parliament, Redmond supported the Irish defending the British empire in 1914 by joining up and fighting for a noble cause, a call nobly followed by Tom Kettle MP, Willie Redmond MP and many others. What Redmond failed to realise was that the British Empire was on the wane together with other empires in Europe. A new international alignment was emerging and the leadership of 1916, and not the Irish Parliamentary Party, had correctly diagnosed that change. There were discordant voices in the Irish Parliamentary Party, that of John Dillon being uppermost among them. He was a man of great courage, as were many of his fellow MPs, a number of whom were veterans of the land war of the 1880s. They had been jailed for their resistance to landlordism. They had stood courageously in the House of Commons, with Parnell and with Redmond as their leaders, demanding good government for Ireland. They did not get it. With the outbreak of World War I and the suspension of Home Rule, they lost their opportunity to continue to lead. They could not see that the political world in which they had operated was changed, changed utterly by World War I and by the clash of competing empires.

The nature and the profundity of that political change were not immediately evident to those who witnessed the events of the Rising. On 3 April 1916, Padraig Pearse issued orders for a three-day march and field manoeuvres throughout Ireland beginning on Easter Sunday 1916 (23 April). On 20 April, a German arms consignment on the *Aud* was intercepted in Tralee Bay by the British navy. Its captain scuttled his ship on 21 April.

Sir Roger Casement landed on the same day from a U-boat at Banna strand, near Tralee. He had news that the promised German support would not be sufficient to launch a rising. Shortly afterwards he was arrested.

On 22 April, Eoin MacNeill issued a countermanding order, cancelling manoeuvres for the following day. This appeared in the *Sunday Independent*. The inner core of the IRB, led by Thomas Clarke, Padraig and Willie Pearse, Seán MacDermott, Thomas MacDonagh, Joseph Mary Plunkett, Eamonn Ceannt and others, ignored Eoin

**What Redmond failed to realise was that the British Empire was on the wane together with other empires in Europe. A new international alignment was emerging and the leadership of 1916, and not the Irish Parliamentary Party, had correctly diagnosed that change.**

MacNeill's countermanding orders. Bulmer Hobson was kidnapped by his fellow members of the IRB and held under house arrest in order to prevent him from trying to stop the Rising.

Here is one contemporary eye-witness account to the Rising, written in the heat of the moment. The extracts from these letters offer a surprising perspective on the Rising of a person who, by 1921, was a strong supporter of national independence. Progressive nationalists may have identified with the views expressed below during Easter week. The letters were critical of the Rising and of its leadership, the unnecessary loss of life and the destruction to property and to commerce. But the draconian nature of the repression which followed, the executions, the mass arrests and the trial and hanging of Roger Casement, pressed many people initially hostile to the Rising to shift their opinion towards support for Sinn Féin.

Mgr Michael Curran, secretary to Archbishop William Walsh of Dublin, had a unique vantage point from which to observe the run up to the 1916 Rising and its execution. He wrote to a close friend on Saturday, 22 April 1916:

> "Things are even more serious here. Yesterday (Good Friday) the leaders of the Volunteers received serious news. I don't know what it was except that they are convinced on what they regard as absolutely reliable authority that preparations to disarm them are in progress. The Volunteers will resist if this is attempted and are taking steps not to be surprised unawares. A rash step by a fool on either side will precipitate an outburst. Frankly I do not see how the thing can end without a blaze sooner or later."

Curran identified the extremists, as he described them, within the nationalist ranks: "But the military people form the dangerous element on one side and Liberty Hall, the Secret Societies, and some of the more extreme Irish Volunteers form the dangerous elements on the other".

Curran wrote again on Sunday 23 April 1916:

> "Things passed off quietly here today. John MacNeill issued an order countermanding the mobilisation of the Volunteers. It was published in the Irish Independent and by messenger. The more extreme party (Liberty Hall and Pearse) tried to suppress it and declare that it was bogus. Result – a new scare. Miss MacNeill [Eoin MacNeill's sister] came here [Archibishop's House] towards 3 p.m. to obtain help to stop the mobilisation and to declare the MacNeill order authentic. According to John MacNeill the carrying out of the mobilisation would end in a catastrophe and bloodshed. The order was obeyed, though there were small gatherings of Volunteers. A crisis has evidently come. I fear today's change

... the draconian nature of the repression which followed, the executions, the mass arrests and the trial and hanging of Roger Casement pressed many people initially hostile to the Rising to shift their opinion towards support for Sinn Féin.

of procedure will lead to a split between the moderate and more extreme Volunteers."

The IRB, or those in the organisation in the confidence of the conspirators, met all day on Sunday, 23 April, and together with James Connolly and the Irish Citizen Army determined to begin the Rising the following day. On 8 May 1916, Mgr Curran wrote to his friend:

> "We have had a terrible fortnight since and we have tasted of the horrors of war and don't want any more. It is all a nightmare and I can hardly bear to [think] about it. The whole thing was terribly foolish and tragic! I told you in my last letter (Easter Sunday) that the danger of a collision with the police (and) troops seemed to be at an end, as on that day MacNeill ordered the Easter meeting of the Volunteers should not take place. An attempt to nullify the orders by the extremists was met by a second order from MacNeill authenticating his previous orders, and these orders were obeyed."

**"We have had a terrible fortnight since and we have tasted of the horrors of war and don't want any more. It is all a nightmare and I can hardly bear to [think] about it. The whole thing was terribly foolish and tragic!"**

Mgr Curran then described what happened next:

> "What was our dismay on Easter Monday to hear about 12.20 that the G.P.O. was taken by the Volunteers and that the Castle was attacked! It was hard to realise that here in the year 1916 we were back in 1798 and that the Rising was at our very doors, largely by people known to every Dublin man. It would appear that the Larkin crowd leader, James Connolly, the Secret Soc. Men headed by T[om] Clarke and an extreme fanatical section of the Volunteers headed by Padraic Pearse, [Thomas] MacDonagh and [Eamonn] Kent, determined on Sunday evening to rise! There seems to be all too convincing evidence that they had conspired with the Germans through the Clan na Gael, or directly, for such a rising and that they used the Irish Volunteers for their own purposes. MacNeill was latterly a mere figure-head in their hands. I fancy MacNeill must have got wind of what was on late on Good Friday or on Holy Thursday. Many say he cancelled the orders for the Easter assembly of the Vounteers – probably on hearing of Casement's appearance in Kerry."

Mgr Curran continued:

> "At any rate the Connolly-Clarke-Pearse section summoned their men. I have no doubt whatever that very few knew what really was on. The rank and file were composed of young men, very many only 15-17, who formed the Volunteers (1) to counteract Carson's, (2) to be prepared against Conscription. These did not want rebellion, though they were prepared, as I warned you, to resist disarmament. Some believed that disarmament was immediately at hand and were quite prepared

for resistance, but very very many only thought that it was one of the usual route marches. You need have no doubt about these facts for we have all met several instances of such cases during the terrible crises. Rebellion was the last thing they dreamed of."

Mgr Curran was convinced that:

"... it was the strong men of extreme views that stampeded the whole thing and compromised all. MacNeill was no match for such men and the only strong thing he did was resolutely to refuse countenance to them and he certainly saved a general rising all over the country. His words were everywhere obeyed, except to a small extent in Cork City. The risings in the country were due to the news from Dublin on Wednesday and Thursday. We were saved the prospect of a German invasion."

Mgr Curran wrote:

"The rising was very nearly being a terribly serious one. Had John MacNeill's orders not been sent and obeyed, we would have had a score of Dublin's over the country. The rising would not be over yet and the entire country would have had to be [deployed] with soldiers and starved and burned."

Mgr Curran was convinced:

"... not that the country wanted revolution any more than Dublin, but a few strong madmen in each district had it in their power to shoot a policeman or seize a barracks or post office. All would have been involved, and all would have thrown in their lot as the young fellows in Dublin did."

Mgr Curran observed: "the material damage done in Dublin is immense." He added:

"O'Connell Street is a smoking ruin from Cathedral Street to Eden Quay and from Henry Street to Elvery's. Other houses, though standing, are shattered and torn. I suppose 500 civilians and more soliders have been killed or wounded. The Volunteers did not lose so many. One redeeming feature was their conduct. They fought courageously against numbers and equipment. They fought cleanly – no drink, no looting, no personal vengeance and no unnecessary destruction of property. The soldiers, too, seemed a decent lot – there was no signs of racial hatred and no unnecessary violence."

He also described what it was like to live under martial law:

"We must be indoors at 8.30. Houses are searched for arms and papers. Letters are opened and afford abundant material for prosecution and arrests are being made wholesale."

**"... it was the strong men of extreme views that stampeded the whole thing and compromised all. MacNeill was no match for such men and the only strong thing he did was resolutely to refuse countenance to them and he certainly saved a general rising all over the country."**

The tide was turning in favour of those who had rebelled. On 26 April, Francis Sheehy-Skeffington and two others were summarily executed on orders of a Capt. J. C. Bowen-Colthurst. It was an extra-judicial killing. There had been a proclamation of martial law in Dublin on 25 April. General Sir John Maxwell, a newly appointed Commander in Chief, arrived in Ireland to take charge of the quelling of the Rising. The rebels agreed to an unconditional surrender on 29 April. The rising had caused 3,000 casualties and over 450 dead. Mass arrests began almost immediately. On 1 May, some 400 "insurgents" were sent to Britain for internment.

Paradoxically, Eoin MacNeill was among those to be arrested in the swoops that followed the Rising. He was sentenced to penal servitude for life only to be amnestied the following year. However, the military leaders of the Rising were found guilty of treason at court martial and sentenced to death. On 3 May, Pearse, Clarke and MacDonagh were shot. The executions ended on 12 May with the deaths of Connolly and MacDermott, if one excludes the later hanging of Roger Casement. Curran and Archbishop Walsh quickly became strong supporters of the Sinn Féin movement that emerged in the wake of the 1916 Rising. Their conversion to radical nationalism provides a partial explanation of the evolution of Irish constitutional politics leading up to the foundation of the state in 1922.

Men like Curran and Archbishop Walsh watched with incredulity as the Rising unfolded. Their frame of reference had, you will recall, been 1798. They explained the present in terms of the not so remote revolutionary past. But, within two years of 1916, Arthur Griffith, Eamon de Valera and the new Sinn Féin leadership were representative of radical independence movements in many parts of Europe, Africa and Asia. The First World War had toppled the *ancien régime* as the historian Mark Mazower argues:

> "In that moment of 'bourgeois triumph,' the *ancien régime* was finally toppled – sultans, pashas, emperors and dukes reduced to impotence. Before the First World War there had been just three republics in Europe; by the end of 1918 there were thirteen."

He continues:

> "Following the whole unforeseen collapse of of the great autocratic empires of Russia, Austria-Hungary, Hohenzollern Germany and Ottoman Turkey, the Paris peace settlement saw parliamentary democracy enthroned across Europe. A belt of democracies – stretching from the Baltic sea down through Germany and Poland to the Balkans – was equipped with new constitutions drawn up according to the most up-to-date principles."

**The rebels agreed to an unconditional surrender on 29 April. The rising had caused 3,000 casualties and over 450 dead. Mass arrests began almost immediately. On 1 May, some 400 "insurgents" were sent to Britain for internment.**

But change was not in a single direction. The Russian Revolution brought into being one of the most repressive regimes in modern times. Italy succumbed to fascism and over 20 years of Mussolini in power. Spain threw up the dictator Primo de Rivera, Portugal Salazar, and Hungary Admiral Horthy. After 1926, Poland moved to the right. Hitler came to power in Germany in 1933 and Petain in France in 1940.

In that world of crumbling empires, fragile democracies and burgeoning fascisms, Ireland proved an interesting case study in the attainment of a stable constitutional democracy. The fundamental rights of every citizen were protected. There was a professional army and an unarmed police force. Despite a civil war, a world war and cyclical attempts at subversion from within, the state never deviated from that democratic path between 1922 and 2006.

The role played by the leadership of 1916 in the process leading to the foundation of the state remains paradoxical, complex and ambivalent. Those who took part defy simplistic categorisation. The 1916 rising is an integral part of the history of modern Ireland. It still awaits a definitive study.

This session is entitled: "Have the ideals of the men and women of 1916 any relevance in 2006?" My answer is as follows: Firstly, the ideals of those who took part in the 1916 Rising need to be studied. They made history. They were the agents of change and not the subjects of swirling historical forces over which they might have claimed they had no control. Their diagnosis was accurate and it anticipated the crash of "civilisation" as it was then known – a world dominated by grand alliances and competing imperialisms. They helped found the Irish state in accordance with democratic principles and there has been no deviation from that path. Besides the study of those 1916 ideas, this generation of politicians might review the state's past and recognise the need to read historical trends correctly. That means taking control of those historical forces and moulding society in an active way according to certain ideals. The alternative is to allow historical forces to sweep a country down stream. It may be that the country enjoys a wave of affluence thanks primarily to international forces. All may appear to be going well – we never had it so good. The example of the men and women of 1916 is of value in 2006 in the manner in which they read international political and economic trends, and acted accordingly. There is a danger today that Irish political leaders of all parties may find themselves the prisoners of their present in much the same way as John Redmond in 1914 when he continued to place his faith in the good will of the British Empire. Therefore, the ideals of the men and women of 1916 – contrary to prevailing political correctness – have an enduring relevance which may only be ignored at an incalculable cost to Ireland's future.

**The example of the men and women of 1916 is of value in 2006 in the manner in which they read international political and economic trends, and acted accordingly.**

# Mary Clancy

## Historian and Teacher

*Teaches, researches and publishes on women's history and has extensive experience lecturing in adult education, including access and community education. A long time member of the Irish Labour Society and a founder member of the Galway branch. With a particular interest in women's political history, has published on women in post-revolutionary Ireland and on women in the life of County Galway and is currently researching the decades 1880-1920. Her most recent publication is a contribution to Teaching with Memories (a European text).*

## Equal Rights Still Need to be Asserted

This paper will refer, in particular, to the ideal of equality and the situation of women in Ireland. It will examine the significance of the 1916 Proclamation as a guide to formal revolutionary thinking in the context of women's public effort during the preceding decades and the legislative conservatism of post-Proclamation political leaders. Women's political history in Ireland is different to that of men; the question of citizenship, its definition, requirements and objectives, was an integral and contentious part of that history in a way that it was not for the male electorate. It is a story of loss of rights, as it is of campaigning for rights and of revolutionary conservatism and of imperial obstinacy. The main outline of this history is familiar at this stage, especially the efforts of the first generations of elected women who held out, as best they could, against the diminution of the civic status. Does any of this matter now? Ireland, South and North, is taken up with the local and global concerns of the twenty-first century, the questions of the moment. Europe is well established as an influence in national and regional life. Yet are there not continuing uncertainties and threats, even to the basic question of equality, that still require women to be vigilant – watching, monitoring, campaigning?

As this short paper hopes to show, the story is as much about what happened to the promise of equality as it is about the context of that promise. There are questions to be answered as to why the principle of equality became such a burden in the new state. Such history is relevant, especially at a time when there is an impression of such scope, freedom, fairness, openness. The act of remembering becomes an important political act with implications for the future, not the past.

> Women's political history in Ireland is different to that of men; the question of citizenship, its definition, requirements and objectives, was an integral and contentious part of that history in a way that it was not for the male electorate.

## A Context of Expanding Rights

The decades leading up to 1916 were notable for the ability of women campaigners to achieve civic rights – notably, access to formal education, legal rights, the professions and, in the political sphere, local government. Debates and campaigning on equality and the role of the woman citizen constituted, then, an important part of political and public discourse up until the outbreak of war in 1914. Even the county councils, recently established and politically valuable, were forced to accept women candidates. So, although Westminster remained determinedly rigid and devious in preventing the introduction of parliamentary legislation on votes for women – petitions, resolutions, amendments and bills since 1866 – women were prominent in other spheres such as medicine, nursing, teaching, asylums, local government and poor law work. The thousands of women religious, though guided by different criteria and not always visible, augmented the numbers of professional women. It was the era of the professional pioneer – the new woman creating social and political spaces in rural Ireland (as instructress or relieving officer or district nurse) and in urban Ireland (as university lecturer or hospital matron). To take the example of county Galway: in 1906, the teenage Alice Perry qualified as the country's first civil engineer; Aleen Cust was already a county veterinary officer (though barred from taking her qualifying examination) while Dr Ada English was at the start of her long career as medical officer in Ballinasloe Asylum. As the latter name reminds us, this, too, was the intellectual and professional context of those women who were prominent later in Sinn Féin and the separatist movement, especially at leadership level. Of the six women returned to the Second Dáil in 1921, Ada English and Kathleen Lynn were medical doctors and Mary McSwiney and Kate O'Callaghan had received formal, university level education. The decades leading up to 1916, then, were ones of encouraging scope, especially for educated, middle-class women – working-class women, like indeed their upper-class peers, were more free to do whatever work that they could find. Essentially, those living in the period from (roughly) the late 1890s to the early 1920s had experience of women working on public or on local boards and councils to a far, far greater extent than did later generations in Ireland.

> The decades leading up to 1916 were notable for the ability of women campaigners to achieve civic rights – notably, access to formal education, legal rights, the professions and, in the political sphere, local government.

## The Proclamation

The most obvious comment about the Proclamation, in light of this discussion, is that there were no women signatories and there was no mention of Cumann na mBan among the list of relevant organisations. Typically and ambiguously, Ireland is symbolised as a woman and a mother in parts of the text. Otherwise, the text gives valuable attention to the woman citizen, by addressing itself to Irishwomen as well as Irishmen and by its promise of civil rights, including equal rights to "all" its citizens. Importantly, the text aspired towards representative government to be elected by "the suffrages of all her men and women" (though not, it seems, necessarily in relation to the Provisional Government). The reference to "women" gave added value to the aspiration for, as emerged time and again during later decades, politicians were inclined to delete specific mention of women, something that diluted the various guarantees under discussion. The other obvious point about these declarations of equality found in the Proclamation, as they affected women, is the timing – 1916 is an unusual moment to find a reference to women's franchise given that, since the outbreak of war in late 1914, the women's suffrage campaign was, for the most part, put to one side. There was important pacifist-suffragist activity, including in Ireland, during the war years but at formal level the resolutions, amendments and bills, so frequent for so long, were displaced by the engulfing matter of war. The promise written into the Proclamation, then, is a rare enough instance of formal suffrage visibility at this time. It is also interesting evidence of how women suffragists, a small though well-organised strand in the Ireland of the day, were able to exert political influence. It was in tune with the traditional manner of exerting influence on parliamentary legislation, that of working through the sympathetic male; as noted above, there were no women signatories of the Proclamation. The likely source was James Connolly, whose socialist-feminist perspective and beliefs made for contact with leading suffrage campaigners like Hannah Sheehy-Skeffington. The organised Irish-Ireland cultural strand – the dominant political influence – with its emphasis on customs, dress, language, music, sport, did not noticeably engage in arguments about women's citizenship. However, the scope of middle-class cultural and intellectual effort – university, theatre, publishing, conferences, summer-schools, philanthropy, holidaying in the west of Ireland – provided a space for people of sometimes differing views to meet. In such manner, for instance, Padraig Pearse, though not ordinarily associated with women's political history or equality, had contact with suffrage organisers James and Gretta Cousins. He would not have found reference to women's suffrage or equality either objectionable or unintelligible.

**The reference to "women" gave added value to the aspiration for, as emerged time and again during later decades, politicians were inclined to delete specific mention of women, something that diluted the various guarantees under discussion.**

## Suffragists, Politicians and Legislation

The Unionist suffragist, a long-standing activist in the Irishwomen's suffrage campaign, should have noticed the promise of equality in 1916 even if the purpose of the Proclamation negated any welcome. The Unionist party's promise to enfranchise women under its proposed provisional government was already (though perhaps sparingly) acknowledged by the broad suffrage body. Women's suffrage, after all, was a political objective that affected women irrespective of party and usually operated on the principle of favouring politicians who supported suffrage legislation and working against those who did not. Unionist women, for instance, already had to deal with the Home Rule legislation during the busy period when Irish suffragists united in the fight to have votes for women included in the third Home Rule bill. Indeed, the suffrage campaign offered overall an interesting political space where women throughout Ireland had occasion to meet and to organise on the question of how to achieve a democratic role for the woman citizen.

An important aspect of this political context, too, is the negative reputation that Irish nationalist parliamentarians (the Home Rule party) earned themselves when their appeasement of the anti-suffragist Asquith led them to neglect the suffrage campaigners. The Irish Party cannot be regarded as principled anti-suffrage in the formal sense, as embodied by Conservative activists in England (and Ireland to a less obvious extent), and they had greater experience of women's equality campaigns and legislation than did the political men of later generations. This, in a sense, was their testing time. The party's crucial mistake was to ignore the strategic value of the woman citizen – mostly because they had sufficient men and priests to make up the numbers and because Home Rule was the defining objective – and it may, indeed, have cost them votes in the defining election of 1918, now that qualified women over the age of thirty were able to award and to avenge at the ballot box at last.

For the alienated Unionists, aware that Home Rule was a matter of time, women proved to be an important addition to their campaigning in what was a remarkable show of political power by women, well skilled organisationally through their long-standing effort in charity, landed or church-related activism. Northern unionists in the early days had sponsored and supported equality legislation (in education and local franchises) and Northern women were among the first in Ireland to be elected to local politics though the long-term political value of their anti-Home Rule effort is more complex. Like their southern sisters, it is the silences and lack of visibility that seems to mark out their public roles, too, after c. 1920.

... the suffrage campaign offered overall an interesting political space where women throughout Ireland had occasion to meet and to organise on the question of how to achieve a democratic role for the woman citizen.

## Today

To monitor, to advise, to recommend and to lobby are among the tasks that women or women's organisations continue to do today. The infrastructure and the expertise, as well as the achievements, are sophisticated; there is greater scope for consultation and international networking. The contemporary context is quite, quite different in that now women are operating as enfranchised citizens as, also, are working-class citizens. The influence of women ensured that the Proclamation was a modern document, one that took a position on a question of international significance, a question for which the imperial parliament felt unable to formulate legislation. This is one way to interpret relevance – to ensure that policy or constitutional documents reflect the questions of the day. What is so remarkable is that the issues identified by women suffragists – childcare, equal pay, sexually transmitted diseases, sexual assault, poverty, homelessness and public health – are as familiar and relevant today as they were a century ago. The political silence that surrounded difficult personal questions (unmarried motherhood, contraception, infanticide) for decades is not as noticeable today, although only just as is shown by the political reticence on the history of sexual abuse.

**Equal rights and the right to public visibility, the most fundamental of civic starting points, still need to be asserted or, at least, protected.**

Equal rights and the right to public visibility, the most fundamental of civic starting points, still need to be asserted or, at least, protected. What of the individuals or organisations, secular and religious, who continue to deny women the right to participate? What, for instance, of lesser publicised suffragist aims like eliminating the White Slave Trade, as it used to be called? Surely this old aim has also translated into a new form in an Ireland (and also Europe) that cannot seem to prevent the trafficking of girls and women? How free or protected do those girls and women feel, right now, in a twenty-first century state widely lauded for its sophistication and its economy? The ideal of equality had a fragile and uncertain foundation – its slighting was not regarded as especially controversial, aside from the incisive contribution of women senators. The dismissal of opinion as unrepresentative – a tactic that has endured – offers its own insight into how democratic debate was (and is) interpreted. Finally, given that those writing in revolutionary haste in 1916 could manage to address Irishwomen as well as Irishmen, why does the English language version of the preamble to the Irish constitution, Bunreacht na hEireann, continue to refer to men only? As stated at the outset, information about past ideals and effort is relevant so that women who live in Ireland have access to the full range of civic rights and not just those that suit the pragmatic political, social, economic or religious needs of the moment.

## *Women Elected – The Early Years\**

### *December, 1918 – First Dáil (69 seats)*

- Constance Markievicz is elected and becomes the first woman returned to Westminster Parliament. (St. Patrick's)
- Winifred Carney contested in Belfast though failed to get elected.
- Government of Ireland Act, 1920 to establish parliaments in Belfast and Dublin

### *May, 1921 – Second Dáil (128 seats)*

- Kathleen Clarke (Dublin, Mid), Ada English, (NUI), Mary MacSwiney (Cork City), Constance Markievicz (Dublin South), Kate O'Callaghan (Limerick City and Limerick East), Margaret Pearse (Dublin).
- Articles of Agreement for a Treaty between Great Britain and Ireland (December 1921)

### *June, 1922 – Third Dáil (128 seats)*

- Mary MacSwiney
- Kathleen O'Callaghan

### *August, 1923 – Fourth Dáil (153 seats)*

- Caitlín Brugha (Co. Waterford)
- Margaret Collins-O'Driscoll (Dublin N)
- Dr Kathleen Lynn (Dublin County)
- Mary MacSwiney (Cork City)
- Constance Markievicz (Dublin S)

### *Seanad (60 members) – December, 1922 – abolition of Senate, May, 1936*

- Eileen Costello (1922)
- Ellen Desart (1922)
- Alice Stopford-Green (1922)
- Jennie Wyse-Power (1922)
- Kathleen Clarke (1928)
- Kathleen Brown (1929)

\*For further details of the women and the legislation, see my article "Aspects of Women's Contributions to the Oireachtas Debate in the

Irish Free State, 1922-37", in Maria Luddy and Cliona Murphy (eds), *Women Surviving: Studies in Irish Women's History in the 19th and 20th Centuries* (Dublin, 1989).

## Select Reading Guide – Some Key Texts

The following brief guide is intended as a starting point to introduce readers to key studies, organisations and websites relating to issues covered in the paper.

- Yvonne Galligan et al, *Contesting Politics: Women in Ireland, North and South* (Colorado: Westview Press, 1999)
- Alan Hayes and Diane Urquhart, *The Irish Women's History Reader* (London: Routledge, 2001).
- Maedhbh McNamara and Paschal Mooney, *Women in Parliament: Ireland: 1918-2000* (Dublin: Wolfhound Press, 2000).
- Rosemary Cullen Owens, *A Social History of Women in Ireland, 1870-1970* (Dublin: Gill and Macmillan, 2005).
- Louise Ryan and Margaret Ward, *Irish Women and Nationalism: Soldiers, New Women and Wicked Hags* (Dublin: Irish Academic Press, 2004)
- Diane Urquhart, *Women in Ulster Politics: 1890-1940* (Dublin: Irish Academic Press, 2000)
- Margaret Ward, *Unmanageable Revolutionaries: Women and Irish Nationalism* (Dingle, 1983) and *Hanna Sheehy-Skeffington: A Life* (Attic Press/Cork University Press, 1997)

## Organisations and Websites

- National Women's Council of Ireland/Comhairle Náisiúnta na mBan in Eireann
- Put more women in the picture: a photographic tour through the corridors of power (http://www.nwci.ie)
- Centre for Advancement of Women in Politics, Queen's University Belfast, School of Politics and International Studies (http://www.qub.ac.uk/cawp)
- http://historical-debates.oireachtas.ie

# Senator Martin Mansergh

## Former Adviser to the Taoiseach and Columnist

*Born 1946 and educated at King's School, Canterbury and Christchurch, Oxford(MA, Dphil). Entered the civil service 1974. First Secretary, Department of Foreign Affairs 1974-81. Appointed Special Adviser to the Taoiseach (Charles J. Haughey) in 1982. Joined the Fianna Fáil Party in 1981. Nominated to the Seanad in 2004. Publications include:* The Spirit of the Nation: The Collected Speeches of Charles J. Haughey 1957-86, Parnell and the Leadership of Nationalist Ireland *and* Ireland and the Challenge of European Integration.

## We Are Reaping the Harvest of Our Sovereignty

The question posed by the title of this session, "Have the Ideals of the Men and Women of 1916 Any Relevance in 2006?" is two-edged. The relevance of the ideals of the men and women of 1916 in 2006 involves taking a view on what these ideals were, and whether or not they have been fulfilled. When ideals are fulfilled, they tend to be taken for granted, as the State's independence now is.

Implicit in the State's commemoration of the ninetieth anniversary of 1916 is the notion that the Irish State today in all its prosperity represents a substantial fulfilment of the ideals of 1916.

This is not a new view. In the very different economic and social conditions of 50 years ago, Dorothy Macardle, author of the semi-authorised but still indispensable source book, *The Irish Republic*, written from the anti-Treaty perspective, said in a Thomas Davis lecture on Pearse and Connolly:

> "Perhaps the existence of the sovereign independent Republic of Ireland might seem a sufficient – indeed, a superb reward for all the anxiety and sacrifice, despite its flaws. Defects we have in plenty – and we are not without being told about them … and are we not free? And is not a free-born generation preparing to take the future of the Republic into able and fruitful hands?"

At the other end of the spectrum is the notion conveyed in the title of Brian P. Murphy's *Patrick Pearse and the Lost Republican Ideal* that the ideals of 1916 were abandoned or betrayed, and now survive only in the flickering flame of dissident Republicanism, where, as a Leargas film from ten years ago showed us, someone like the President of Republican Sinn Féin can still talk without irony about "the poison of constitutionalism". There is also a socialist version of this.

**"Defects we have in plenty – and we are not without being told about them … and are we not free? And is not a free-born generation preparing to take the future of the Republic into able and fruitful hands?"**

My view is that, outside of the main issue of separation and full political independence, the Irish revolution was quite conservative in character.

There is a very striking review in 1842 by Thomas Davis of the work of a French historian, Augustin Thierry, who hated military despotism and wanted the greatest possible number of independent guarantees of human freedom. Davis commented:

> "This is the creed of a Conservative Republican – a creed having among its professers many of the greatest men of opposite parties all through Europe. It seeks to guard against the tyranny over the majority or by the majority, and for those great ends it sacrifices some wealth…"

Its enemies were the aristocrat, the free trader (today's neo-liberal), and the demagogue. Davis was essentially contrasting constitutional Republicanism, inclusive of parliamentary right and left, with the violent direct democracy of the French Revolution. Consolidating democracy was not easy anywhere in the 1920s and 1930s. Ireland did well, and did fulfil the promise of the Proclamation, although the implied promise of women's equality beyond the franchise was for several decades taken back and has only been reinstated over the past 30 years.

**Much of the social revolution had taken place under British rule: the dismantling of minority privilege in Church and State, the emocratisation of local government in 1898, and above all the transfer of ownership of the land under the impulsion of the Land League and Michael Davitt ...**

Much of the social revolution had taken place under British rule: the dismantling of minority privilege in Church and State, the democratisation of local government in 1898, and above all the transfer of ownership of the land under the impulsion of the Land League and Michael Davitt, even if the former landlords were given a soft landing, of which he disapproved, with the Wyndham Act in 1903.

Ever since the 1790s, what advanced Nationalists wanted was a separate independent Irish State. Asked why the leaders of the Rising had proclaimed a Republic, Seán MacDiarmada, I quote the new biography by Gerard McAtasney:

> "cited the examples of France and America. The former, he stated, had been a firm friend of Ireland for generations, while millions of Irish people had played a central role in the development of the latter".

On the question of State versus private ownership of the means of production, Pearse was utterly pragmatic. With regard to Church and State, though, Pearse had his quarrel with Maynooth over the Irish language; the 1916 leaders and their successors were arguably more conservative than any previous generation of advanced nationalists.

Even the anti-imperialist strain can be exaggerated. As the reference to "gallant allies in Europe" indicates, many tended to be sympathetic to the German Empire, if very hostile to the British one.

De Valera with his American background was the first to appreciate the value of a country with close links to both Britain and Ireland, as a potentially greater influence on Britain than its traditional continental enemies. There is a telling moment in early 1921, with Lloyd George speculating whether an Irish settlement would make Congress more amenable to making concessions on Britain's war debts to the US.

What is marvellous about the European Union today is that Ireland can have alliances or partnerships with different member countries for different purposes and indeed a very close economic relationship with the United States, all without prejudice to better British-Irish relations which, thanks also to the ease of modern travel and communications, are, at last, free from claustrophobia.

The most resonant phrase in the Proclamation about "cherishing all the children of the nation equally", an antidote to the imperial tactic of "divide and rule", though now given an extended social application, which is legitimate but which has been dwelt on at length elsewhere, is an important statement of intent, on which, as my father wrote 30 years ago, "there was no easy going back".

The 1916 leaders did not want to spark off a sectarian civil war. The Belfast volunteers were instructed by Connolly, who knew the North well, to undertake no activity there, well before the Rising, saying that the issue of Unionism would be addressed later, when other things had fallen into place.

This was even though he was aghast at the idea in the Home Rule debate that under partition a Nationalist minority would be left at the mercy of the Orange party.

There is nothing in the copious writings of the 1916 leaders that suggests they contemplated active coercion of the North as a practical proposition. Indeed, it is interesting that Sinn Féin has tended to highlight more the twenty-fifth anniversary of the death of the Hunger Strikers over the ninetieth anniversary of the Easter Rising, which had very little to say about the North.

Despite later protestations about partition, the priority was independence for the larger part of Ireland, where it would be welcomed. The State that was founded had only to accommodate a small minority, which was, in Archbishop Empey's words, on the losing side of a revolution. Subsequent to that, the record of the State is, I believe, good, but that is a separate debate. With regard to Unionism in Northern Ireland, far from being oblivious of differences, peace requires us to acknowledge differences, and as far as possible to cherish them. With the first official commemoration of the Somme and the upgrading of facilities at the Boyne battlefield, the State has started to make up for some past omissions.

**There is nothing in the copious writings of the 1916 leaders that suggests they contemplated active coercion of the North as a practical proposition.**

Essentially, while priority had been given, up to 1914, to Home Rule with unity when that was clearly not possible, as underlined again by the failure of the Irish Convention in 1917-8, there was nothing further to lose by going for full independence. While taking account of the experience between 1912 and 1922, it has essentially been the task of this generation to find a more satisfactory settlement of North-South relations and relations between these islands and to devise creative solutions.

**While aspects of the 1916 Rising remain controversial, mainly because it has been deployed as a precedent to justify an aggressive not just a defensive IRA campaign in the quite different context of Northern Ireland, the fact is that there is very little abnormal or unusual about a national independence struggle in a twentieth century context ...**

While aspects of the 1916 Rising remain controversial, mainly because it has been deployed as a precedent to justify an aggressive not just a defensive IRA campaign in the quite different context of Northern Ireland, the fact is that there is very little abnormal or unusual about a national independence struggle in a twentieth century context, particularly given that it won two years later a resounding, if retrospective, popular sanction. Very telling was the presence of the British Ambassador on the reviewing stand in front of the GPO this Easter. The independence struggle and the IRA campaign in the North are being disentangled, to be judged separately, not together, notwithstanding the combined objections of the so-called revisionist school and supporters of Sinn Féin and the IRA.

There are huge advantages to being a sovereign state, even in the era of regional supranational organisations like the EU and globalisation. We have made good use of our sovereignty, and are now reaping the harvest.

The cultural justification for independence, in a context where Unionists were denying the existence of any such thing as "the Irish nation", was the strongest suit at the time. The Irish-Ireland ideal and the whole notion of economic and cultural self-sufficiency showed their limitations within a generation. But, as is the case with the economy, different motors provide the power at different points in time.

The year 1916 is a hugely important historical moment, a catalyst, against a background of many other important and earlier contributing efforts, all of which made possible much of what has followed. While the sacrifices deserve to be honoured, 1916 should not be regarded either as an exclusive or all-sufficient inspiration for today. It is the job of our generation to forge history, not just to follow it.

Watering the flowers

Audience at *Reconciling Orange and Green*

Tomás Ó Canainn and Caoimhin Mac Aoidh,
Writers and Musicians

*Chapter 6*

# The Soul of Ireland in Traditional Music

*Traditional Music – A Reflection of Who We Are*
CAOIMHIN MAC AOIDH
**Writer and Musician, Chairman, Donegal Local Development Company**

*The Magic of Traditional Music*
TOMÁS Ó CANAINN
**Writer and Musician**

# Caoimhin Mac Aoidh

**Writer and Musician, Chairman, Donegal Local Development Company**

*Born in Co. Donegal, he is a founder member of Cairdeas na bhFidleiri which promotes the playing and appreciation of Donegal fiddling. He has performed and broadcast extensively in Ireland and abroad and has written many articles on traditional music as well as two books:* The Jigs and the Reels: The Donegal Fiddle Tradition *and* The Scribe: The Life and Works of James O'Neill. *He is CEO of the Donegal Local Development Co. which was set up in 1995 to administer EU regional development programmes in the area.*

## Traditional Music – A Reflection of Who We Are

**The Chieftains, who had been on the road since the 1960s, were a major musical force both at home and internationally. It was increasingly becoming hip to play the uilleann pipes.**

Despite the attainment of national independence in the early years whereby the wave of nationalism defined traditional elements of Irish society as being admirable and of value from an institutional perspective, the economic reality of Irish society saw these traditional elements as badges of poverty, failure and shame. Whatever about comely maidens dancing at the crossroads, jigs and reels did not feed hungry mouths.

When the rock and roll boom of the 1950s and 1960s in America began to become a tired, formulaic extrusion of commercialised blandness, a post-Bill Haley generation sought a musical culture of deeper meaning and statements. They looked backward and found "folk music". Bob Dylan, as inspired by the Clancy Brothers, emerged as a belting, challenging ballad singer and the rest is an exciting history. Directly related to and paralleling this American movement was the discovery, interestingly enough by a dominantly urban-based Irish generation both with and without "Culchie" roots, of Irish traditional music. The Chieftains, who had been on the road since the 1960s, were a major musical force both at home and internationally. It was increasingly becoming hip to play the uilleann pipes. The 1970s inappropriately titled "Revival" of Irish music (it had never died), saw traditional musicians boarding planes and touring the world while tens of thousands of others were boarding planes for the purposes of emigration. Despite these contrasts, there was growing pride in Irish culture and identity at home and abroad. Irish speakers no longer spoke in embarrassed whispers. RTÉ's Long Note radio programme of traditional Irish music established a cult following and was proud to broadcast the artistic elements of traditional society that more institutionalised wings of Irish culture had earlier avoided due to the unpalatable challenge of dealing with "real" people from a rural environment.

## Traditional Music – A Binding Agent

Traditional music has served Irish society well in the recent past going far beyond its primary meaning. I refer to that fact that traditional music has acted as a binding agent across the community divide in Northern Ireland. In the early seventies, I played in sessions which comprised hard line Nationalists and serving members of the RUC. Whatever happened outside the door was another matter. In the session, everyone was a musician and that was that. I should remind you that when loyalist paramilitaries made an announcement proclaiming traditional musicians as being "legitimate targets" as part of the "pan-nationalist front," it was Protestant members of the traditional music community who bravely and rapidly negotiated a withdrawal of that threat. The paramilitaries had bought the stereotype that traditional music was for the Fenians and did not realise that it survived the Troubles as one of the few true cross-community practices which immediately and persistently acknowledge parity of esteem.

> I played in sessions which comprised hard line Nationalists and serving members of the RUC. Whatever happened outside the door was another matter. In the session, everyone was a musician and that was that.

## Societal Changes

The 1980s saw a levelling out in the wave of enthusiasm for traditional Irish culture. It had gained respect and even, quite possibly, respectability! There was even now a traditional Irish music "industry" complete with the associated status such concepts appreciate. The 1990s delivered the greatest and most rapid change in society since man first stepped upon Irish soil. We did not build a Celtic Tiger economy, we built a Celtic Tiger society. I purposely make this distinction since society as a whole adjusted to the economic fortunes which have accrued to us. We have changed as a people and we should not beat ourselves up over that. History has repeatedly demonstrated that societies which experience rapid economic growth change in many facets of their existence. Societal changes in these circumstances are both natural and to be entirely expected.

When we find ourselves having the luxury of freedom of choice, then we are presented with possibilities of incredible opportunities as well as outstanding risks. In short, we are given a stupendous chance to distinguish ourselves or disgrace ourselves. This would seem to be a no-brainer option, yet it is absolutely amazing the number of times throughout history that societies have opted to act as a tidal wave of collective lemmings, hell-bent on jumping over the cliff into an abyss of mess.

Let me clearly mark my stance. We are exactly at that point in our history where this very question is being posed to the Irish people in economic, social and cultural terms. We need to take incredible care as we are in an even more pressurised position than societies of the past who have faced this dilemma in that the pace of change and the demand time for a delivery on the response is no longer a few years, but a screaming deadline in the order of six months to a year maximum. That is the way global change occurs today. Anything slower, is too slow.

I am of the view that this history which I have outlined is generally recognisable to people active in and passionate about the traditional arts. The question of our response remains. It is my view that our responses have both distinguished as well as disgraced ourselves.

## *A Unique Experience*

**Traditional Irish music is at its most brilliant and best in touch with its own soul when that lone musician takes up his or her instrument and plays a tune which he or she has performed possibly thousands of times before, but never in the same way. That performance could occur on centre stage in a sold-out Carnegie Hall or in Jimmy Campbell's kitchen.**

If traditional music is an integral element of the soul of Ireland, we need to understand how it is such before we can make plans and decisions for both the music and the Irish soul. For right or wrong, I agree with the late music scholar and collector, Breandán Breathnach, when he defined the core of the Irish music tradition as founded in solo performance on a limited range of instruments which are, by virtue of their construction, mechanically suitable for producing the specific sounds the music demands. It is not the music performed in bands or large-scale thematic stage shows. These forms of performance are examples of planned, arranged playing whose main objective is to entertain a paying audience as opposed to delivering a melodic line from a purely personal perspective.

Traditional Irish music is at its most brilliant and best in touch with its own soul when that lone musician takes up his or her instrument and plays a tune which he or she has performed possibly thousands of times before, but never in the same way. That performance could occur on centre stage in a sold-out Carnegie Hall or in Jimmy Campbell's kitchen. It is a personal statement in a local accent with melody as the medium of the statement. This accent, or as traditional musicians called it, "style", has a deep and magnificent local identity. Listen for only a few seconds to the fiddle playing of Denis Murphy or Julia Clifford and it is immediately obvious that they had endless hours of musical "conversation", purely through the medium of fiddles, with Pádraig Ó Keeffe of Sliabh Luachra. This is music "spoken" in Kerry-ese.

This aforementioned element of variation in the tune, or the freedom to introduce almost infinite changes to the piece in reaction to the conditions of that specific instant in time, while still allowing it to maintain its integral identity, allows each performance to be a unique experience, not only for the musician but also to anyone respectful enough to listen. When Irish traditional music is soulful, it happens in the manner which I have just described. The variety of expression of this soul is astounding. It can be anything as heartbreaking as John Doherty playing the air "Tiarna Mhaigh Eo" to the wild abandon and celebration in Vincent Campbell's playing of the reel "The Oak Tree".

## The Power and Meaning of Traditional Music

This type of performance of traditional music is in direct contact with our past. It links us in a very real and firm way to those people and events which have gone before us. Today most of us see the Great Famine as something in the past which is slowly fading in the distance. I have sat with and learned from players whose music can be factually documented as having derived from well before that event. In playing such pieces, the performer was making a direct contact with the mind and emotions of a composer whose work was rooted in an almost medieval agrarian society and included some influence and interpretation of that unbroken string of players in the transmission chain to the person performing the tune in my presence.

In societal terms, and even in such abstract philosophical terms as the constituents of any "soul of a people", these are very powerful forces. This continual, "hands-on" crafting of a body of music with its inter-generational connectivity is a very rare phenomenon. In truth, we as a people are immensely indebted to those generations of musicians who have gone before us. By way of comparison, consider those countries who have either industrialised rapidly and on a large scale, undergone state-sponsored "cultural cleansing", or both. They inevitably find themselves without a genuine traditional culture. In the interventionist examples, state authorities invent a new, institutionalised culture, while in the more laissez-faire models, societies wind up with a pervasive ephemeral pop culture which lacks any determined commitment to integrity. I once heard the music generated in the latter cultures described by Vincent Campbell as "disposal music" on the grounds that it is brilliant today and only fit for the bin tomorrow. Vincent is a craftsman in words as well as melodies! If you have doubts concerning the value of meaning and power of traditional Irish music and its ability to transcend cultures, look at its impact on young Germans over the past four decades. When asked why they are so strongly attracted to it they will point out that they have no traditional music of their own while referring to the width of its melodic range of emotions.

> This continual, "hands-on" crafting of a body of music with its inter-generational connectivity is a very rare phenomenon. In truth, we as a people are immensely indebted to those generations of musicians who have gone before us.

If you remain unconvinced of the power and meaning of a form of traditional music in forming the soul of a people, I would encourage you to look at the events surrounding the treatment of traditional music by the centralised Soviet authorities in the former USSR in respect of Polish and Romanian traditional music. These genres were seen as having a particularly strong importance and identity in a national cultural sense which was contrary to the mono-cultural objectives of the soviet. An "approved" curriculum of music was centrally agreed in Moscow which had no national cultural identity. Polish and Romanian university academics were forced to teach only from this curriculum. Those Polish academics who began to dabble in Polish traditional music as well as jazz in the sixties were summarily fired from their posts. It is a scandal that due to the cultural cleansing of Polish music, the genre of the traditional mazurka is now virtually as strong in distant Donegal as it is in Poland where this beautiful rhythm was born.

## The Commercialisation of Traditional Music

The Irish have historically held music in high esteem. The success at international levels of traditional musicians has left the Irish people having a high "spoken" regard for the music. By this I mean that we are quite willing to verbally proclaim our interest and enjoyment in the music, whether that interest has any foundation in their active musical support or choice.

To be honest, as a people we lie to ourselves about traditional music on a massive scale. In my nine-to-five work as a CEO of one of the local area partnership development companies, I can say it is a very rare occasion indeed when a community or town publishes a promotional development brochure that does not state the community has a rich, vibrant traditional music scene. In Donegal, this is a routine occurrence. Yet, as a practicing traditional musician living in the county, I know exactly how hard it is to find a session, even a bad session!

I am not aged by any means, yet I am old enough to remember when walking into a pub with a fiddle case was merely a prompt to an invitation to leave the premises. The massive pub sessions of the seventies and eighties did not occur because publicans were fanatical patrons of the arts. They occurred because there was more money to be made in hosting sessions than in doing something else. During those days, enough of an interested crowd could be gathered to make such events a commercial success. True, there were some legendary hosts who did have a passion for the music but, for the most part, it was a business proposition, exactly the same as line dancing,

> The Irish have historically held music in high esteem. The success at international levels of traditional musicians has left the Irish people having a high "spoken" regard for the music.

karaoke, pub quizzes and a plethora of other fads which have come and gone.

If you require evidence, I could easily point you to one major festival of traditional Irish music which has an elevated national and international market profile which is managed and run by a committee whose members I have never observed in a session of traditional music in my life. In a court of law, I could not truthfully testify whether or not any one of that committee even remotely likes traditional music.

These examples which I have chosen highlight the fact that there is a commercial aspect to traditional music and that is its marketability to foreign visitors. Communities and tourism interests throughout Ireland are well aware of this attraction and see traditional music inclusion as an important objective in their "tourism product range". There is clearly a massive difference between providing traditional music to keep the tourists happy versus ensuring its performance because it is beautiful and holds a deep meaning for you and your community.

## It is Time to be Honest

When I was young and becoming mesmerised by traditional music, the thing which I knew as "traditional Irish music" was that form of handed down music which was played and shaped by the musicians of Ireland. I have come to the realisation in the past decade that this definition no longer holds. Irish traditional music and the community which plays it, and loves it, is no longer a community on the island of Ireland. It is a community with a global presence. It accommodates players as brilliant and deeply rooted in the tradition as the New York fiddler, Brian Conway; Chicago fiddler, Liz Carroll; Randal Bays of the Pacific Northwest; scores of players in Tokyo and even one Antarctic polar explorer. We used to see people from outside of Ireland who had any interest in the music as a wonderful curiosity which confirmed to ourselves that we were a lovely people who owned something nice. Now there are two looming questions, do we own this music at all anymore and do we truly care about it at all?

As I have already stated, we are at a decisions crossroads. Lying to ourselves about how much we value traditional Irish music, while clearly paying it only a mocking lip service, is not a sustainable approach to any element of what is a constituent of the soul of the Irish people. If we really do not care about it, we should have the courage to state that fact and get on with promoting whatever we have a true interest in, whether that be salsa drumming, U2 or Daniel O'Donnell. It is time for an honest show of hands.

There is clearly a massive difference between providing traditional music to keep the tourists happy versus ensuring its performance because it is beautiful and holds a deep meaning for you and your community.

I am not trying to argue that every person in the new multi-cultural Ireland must be an enthusiastic player or follower of traditional music. I aspire to being a rational democrat. I believe in freedom of choice. But if traditional music is to remain an integral part of the soul of Ireland, then it must be at least understood and hold a true place of value amongst the Irish people. The music community must continue to maintain its unbroken connection with our past, but also to continue to change to find relevance and meaning to the society in which we live today. It must continue to act as a powerful mirror which reflects all that we are as a people. Maybe that will be its greatest contribution to the Irish society of the future, by mirroring our soul.

If traditional music is to be genuinely part of the Irish soul then, when that lone flute player begins a tune, it should impact on those listening as a statement of historical, current and future meaning, spoken in a thoughtful and considered local accent in an expression of passion, humour, pathos or celebration. That is a breathtaking challenge to us as a people of culture as well as to us as a community of musicians.

A number of years ago, I acquired a rare tape of the playing of Mickey Doherty made at a house party only a few miles from Glenties. Mickey was requested by another great Donegal fiddler to play the driving three part reel "The Morning Dew". I listened to it with great intent, and, as Mickey would say himself, "I took a conceit on it"! Listening to every nuance of the performance, I suddenly realised that he had played a four part version. I studied the extra part intensely and was struck by the fact that while it was new, there was some curious ring of familiarity about it. Days later while travelling in the car it struck me! The first two bars of Mickey's fourth part were the exact overture to the soul music legend Marvin Gaye's version of "I Heard it Through the Grapevine!" Several weeks later, I played it for an old, but razor sharp, Donegal fiddler remarking on the astounding connection. I expected his response to be as astonished as my own. Instead, he wisely stated: "Sure, that's no surprise at all. It only goes to prove that the Dohertys had soul long before Marvin Gaye ever heard of the word!"

**But if traditional music is to remain an integral part of the soul of Ireland, then it must be at least understood and hold a true place of value amongst the Irish people. The music community must continue to maintain its unbroken connection with our past, but also to continue change to find relevance and meaning to the society in which we live today.**

# Tomás Ó Canainn

Musician, former Dean of Engineering, University
College Cork

*Born in Co. Derry he studied engineering at the University of Liverpool (Ph.D)
and taught there for a number of years. With a keen interest in music since
childhood, he was a founder-member of the Liverpool Ceilí Band. In 1961, he
joined the staff of UCC and became Dean of Engineering. In Cork, he also
founded the traditional music group, Na Filí, which made many recordings
and toured extensively. He studied music at UCC under Aloys Fleichmann and
Seán Ó Riada, gaining a B.Mus. degree, and took over Ó Riada's lectures for a
number of years while still teaching engineering. He has published a number of
books on Irish music, including a biography of Seán Ó Riada, and has published
poetry in both Irish and English.*

## The Magic of Traditional Music

It has taken me some seventy years of involvement with music to
realise that the ancients were right about its meaning. Mind you, I
am not saying that modern behaviourists, psychologists and all the
other learned "-ists" who analyse the effect of music on the formation
of the young are wrong about its beneficial creation of unique paths
within the brain. But that is mere detail.

The ancients saw the bigger and much simpler picture, which it
has taken me all this time to fathom: music is magic and traditional
music is most magic of all. It has a life and soul that continuously
expand across and permeate the generations, never ceasing to make
a home where it finds friendly territory. It is all-pervasive and nearly
all-persuasive! Let me explain how I think that has happened in our
family, down the years…

I never met my grandfather, Francey Murphy, from Carnanban,
near Dungiven in County Derry. He was the local traditional fiddler
and his son Patrick also played. I often heard my uncle Patrick play
and I feel I know Francey well, from all the stories my mother had
about him. What my mother did not tell me was that she and all her
sisters could handle the fiddle but, in those far-off days, only the male
players were recognized as performers. I was 22 before I discovered
my mother's fiddle-playing. It happened this way…

A Northern Protestant, Seán Pasker, used to come to our house
on his bicycle every Sunday evening and I would accompany his
fiddling or singing at the piano. One wet Sunday night he decided
it would be wiser to leave his instrument at our house, rather than

**The ancients
saw the
bigger and
much simpler
picture, which
it has taken me
all this time to
fathom: music
is magic and
traditional
music is most
magic of all.**

letting it get wet on the way home. I was trying out his fiddle next day, when my mother asked, "Could you not do better than that?" I was surprised at her question, as she was normally very encouraging of my frequent efforts to play various instruments.

"Try it yourself", said I, like a cheeky son, "it's not easy". At first, all I heard was the scraping of bow on strings and then the total shock of a reel, "The Flowers of Edinburgh", singing out at me. I bought a fiddle for her and she played it now and then, until my daughter Nuala was outgrowing a three-quarter size instrument. She handed the new fiddle to Nuala and was content to leave it at that.

I myself tried various instruments when I was young and played the accordion for years with the Liverpool Ceilí Band, before taking up the uilleann pipes some forty years ago, on coming to Cork. I played it through the seventies with our group, *Na Filí*. My mother thought no instrument was as good as the fiddle and lost no opportunity of telling me so!

I have tried to see the soul of traditional music in our family through a few poems that I have written. The first concerns my grandfather:

## *Francey*

> Your music has gone, Francey, out of Carnanban
> Though the fields still crop and the trees grow
> And it's little you'd think now there was a time
> When they crowded in to hear your fiddle sing.
>
> But that fine song is long since sung
> And Patrick, your son, who sang it too
> Is taken away and his fiddle's gone
> And the crows caw in Carnanban.
>
> High grow those trees that were young with you
> And have watched these three generations go.
> Christ! Is it right that a tree can stay
> When Francey and his music are blown away.
>
> But no tree will best you Francey Murphy
> For the seed of your song is blown in my mouth
> And you'll lack neither voice nor my fingers' span
> To flower an echo in Carnanban.

My grandfather and his cousin John, who lived in nearby Strone, shared a common song, "The Verdant Braes of Screen", which I sing and have recorded. "Strone John", as he was known locally, would often come down from his home for a session in my grandfather's house and their song would be sung regularly.

When Strone John died, the priest in Dungiven would not allow him to be buried there, even though he had always attended mass in that church. He relented a little when John's neighbours objected and allowed him to be buried in un-blessed ground beside the ditch. It was a sore point among our people for years, though when the graveyard was eventually expanded, poor Strone John came into his own patch of hallowed ground, by default, as it were. I have used a verse from his song, "The Verdant Braes of Screen", to say something about the man:

## Strone John

He crossed the burn in a crooked line
Jumping to each dry stone
An old man abroad on his ceilí
Bringing a song from Strone.

"Oh sit ye down on the grass", he said
"On the dewy grass so green
For the wee birds all have come and gone
Since you my love have been".

The song in his mouth was like the man
Wrack from another tide
With syllables floating on every note
As he feathered his mountainy rhyme
Over the verdant Braes of Screen
Where the wee birds all had flown
And love was filled with the thousand notes
He carried down from Strone.

The singer is gone but his song rings
To spite the man of God
Who refused him a place to lie with his friends
Beneath the well-kept sod.
So he was laid in unhallowed ground
By the priest who had no ear
Like a dog by a ditch at Dungiven Church
For paying his dues elsewhere.

Music has made its way to our three children, Nuala, Úna and Niamh. When Nuala was over in Boston for a period, some years ago, we must have been a bit lonely at home, for I made a poem about how music had found its way to her, from her great grandfather. In the process, I felt again music's magic:

## Nuala's Fiddle

In Boston, Mass. my daughter fingers notes
On a fiddle my grandfather played in Derry.
Her reels dance along overgrown paths
Once cleared by his bow.

Deep in my father's grave
My mother hid music
That her children might not know
She could draw a bow like the rest.

"A pity", she said to my playing
"A pity we didn't buy thon wee fiddle o' the Gormans that time
And you'd not be saddled now wi' them oul' pipes".
But I knew chanter, like bow, would clear its own path.

Years cover up the players, but tunes remain:
Old notes from a bow re-form on pipes
And echo again on fiddle in Boston, Mass.
Chanter or bow is a baton to take for a turn and pass.

But Thomas Moore, in his *Irish Melodies* touched the heart of it all in his song, "On Music", set to the Irish air, "The Banks of Banna". I remember listening to it being sung at the Derry Feis when I was very young:

Music, oh, how faint, how weak,
Language fades before thy spell!
Why should Feeling ever speak,
When thou canst breathe her soul so well

There's nothing more to be said!

Maurice Regan with Caoimhin MacAoidh

Panel for session *The Death Throes of the Irish Language?*

Trevor Sargent, TD and
Jim Higgins, MEP

Robin Bury and Anton Carroll

*Chapter 7*

# The Death Throes of the Irish Language?

*The Irish Language Survives but it Needs Help*
TREVOR SARGENT TD
**Leader of the Green Party**

*The Tide Has Turned*
SENATOR JIM HIGGINS MEP
**Fine Gael**

*The Irish Language, Self-delusion and Hypocrisy*
ROBIN BURY
**Reform Movement**

*The Irish Language is in Distress but Can be Saved*
ANTON CARROLL
**Principal, Greendale Community School**

# Trevor Sargent TD

## Leader, Green Party

*Born in Dublin 1960. Educated at the High School Dublin, the Church of Ireland College, Rathmines and TCD (B.Ed). Formerly national school teacher and principal. First elected to Dáil Éireann in 1992. Member Dublin County Council 1991-3. Opposed to dual mandate of Oireachtas and local council, resigned from Council in 1993. Elected the first leader of the Green Party in 2001. A member of An Taisce, Amnesty International, Irish Wildbird Conservancy, Greenpeace, Irish Organic Society, Earthwatch etc. Cathaoirleach, Craobh Shéamuis Ennis of Conradh na Gaeilge.*

## The Irish Language Survives but it Needs Help

In relation to the Irish language, what I can say is, it may be under pressure but it has survived centuries of efforts to wipe it out. I am here today to appeal for a collective mobilisation not just to preserve but restore "an Ghaeilge" as the principal spoken language in this country. I make that call not just because I love the unique characteristics, usefulness and beauty of Ireland's native language, but because Ireland needs a non-materialist, noble cause around which to unite and build an inclusive caring society which is ecologically sensitive. The wild Irish salmon, like the Irish language is, as the saying goes, "part of what we are".

**I am here today to appeal for a collective mobilisation not just to preserve but restore "an Ghaeilge" as the principal spoken language in this country.**

I know many people who share the view that our placenames often mean more in Irish than the phonetic English versions suggest, e.g. Kill or Cill (the Irish word for a church). The social values shared by many are expressed authentically in Irish e.g. "an meitheal" ( a co-operative way of working ). In a refreshing change from "Paddywhackery", I find visitors like to hear Irish spoken as a normal modern language and see proper bilingual signage. The Irish language is, as well as everything else, an attractive and distinct bonus for tourism.

It is interesting to recall an event 100 years ago on 21 May 1906, when Douglas Hyde, Uachtarán Chonradh na Gaeilge, having just met US President Roosevelt, delivered a lecture to a packed Carnegie Hall in which he said:

> "I am here today to explain to you the life and death struggle upon which we are engaged in Ireland. I see that the papers say that this is the last grand struggle of the Irish race to preserve their language. Oh, ladies and gentlemen! It is

ten times, it is a hundred times, it is a thousand times more far-reaching than that! It is the last possible life and death struggle of the Irish race to preserve not their language but their national identity."

Subsequently, Hyde's cultural crusade was partly eclipsed by the 1916 Rising and the War of Independence. We can contrast the number of Irish language enthusiasts who fought in the GPO during Easter Week 1916 with the difficulty one might have buying a stamp at Árd Oifig an Phoist through Irish these days. If we are in any way serious about encouraging use of Irish surely doing business in the GPO through Irish is a reasonable expectation. Try it and see what happens!

Máirtín Ó Cadhain gave an account of the 1921 Treaty negotiations in London which again gives food for thought in relation to the Irish language. He says:

"On that black night of the sixth of December, 1921, Lloyd George did the trick. A strange dirty little man that. He messed up his own people, he messed up Europe and the world, before he messed us up. I saw him once at the Welsh Eisteddfod. I heard his son and daughter addressing public meetings in Welsh. The language of his household in London, while PM of the British Empire in the days when that Empire was an empire, was Welsh.

When he did not want the Irish delegation in those fateful days of 1921, to understand, he spoke his North Welsh to his secretary. He taunted our delegation with representing a people without a language. And still I think the only sincere thing he said in all those tragic proceedings was when he recommended the Treaty as giving power to Ireland to revive her ancient speech. Because, whatever else it lacked, it certainly gave that power."

After that Treaty was signed and Civil War ensued, could it be that other aspects of life became defining characteristics of being Irish other than "an Ghaeilge"? It seems that each side, pro- or anti-Treaty, regarded the other as less Irish than themselves. That sidelined the language. After that, the State identified closely with the Roman Catholic Church which became a badge of Irishness. That further sidelined the language. To support the GAA was for many the epitome of being Irish. That again sidelined the language apart from the "cúpla focal".

State policy was, and still is, largely to leave the revival of Irish to school children. For the adult population that narrow policy has certainly sidelined the language for many. A successor to Hyde as

It seems that each side, pro- or anti-Treaty, regarded the other as less Irish than themselves. That sidelined the language. After that, the State identified closely with the Roman Catholic Church which became a badge of Irishness. That further sidelined the language.

Uachtarán Chonradh na Gaeilge, Seán Mac Gearailt, spoke in 1955 of how fanciful that policy was without there being an Irish language environment outside the school as well. Duirt se, "Ba gheall le mioruilt é da gcloidis leis an teanga sa timpeallacht ina mbionn orthu an chuid is mó da saol a chaitheamh. Ni hiad na páistí amhain a shlánoidh an Ghaeilge – ach sinn go léir idir óg agus aosta."

In spite of official State policy, which has been tokenistic at best in relation to reviving Irish, the vast majority of the population want Irish to be a written and spoken language and available to them to learn and use. The wonder is that this was so in 1945 and it is still true 61 years later in 2006.

Minutes of a 1945 Conradh na Gaeilge Árd-Fheis report: "Tá daoine ar bís chun an Ghaeilge a fhoghlaim-ach easpa na múinteoirí Gaeilge an rud is mó atá ag cur as dár muintir ar fud na tíre".

To this day, those of us who teach Irish to adults at evening classes still have no easily accessed training course although I understand that NUI in Maynooth is coming to the rescue with a new part time course, buíochas le Dia. I notice the website www.beo.ie has some useful lesson plans for adult Irish classes.

However, by contrast, the proliferation of TEFL courses for teachers and adult pupils highlights how normal it is to be bilingual. It is the speaking of only one language which is odd.

Likewise, it is normal worldwide to speak one's own indigenous language as well as one or more neighbouring or global languages. This truth is reinforced again and again by the "new Irish" coming to work or seek refugee status in Ireland. Last year, 6,209 people were granted refugee status in this state. A number I have met do wish to learn Irish as for them it is the indigenous language of their new home. English is spoken by 309 million people, Spanish is spoken by 322 million and Mandarin by 873 million (2004 figures) so they may also be speaking and learning one or more of these languages too.

For people with two or three languages, learning a fourth or fifth is no big deal. Of course to learn a variety of languages as an infant is no effort whatsoever.

Linguists generally agree that it takes at least 100,000 speakers to sustain a vocabulary which means that 90 per cent of the more than 6,000 languages spoken today could be extinct by 2100AD. The population of Irish speaking areas, "na Gaeltachtaí", is about 50,000. This fact puts it up to all of us – the Government, each parent, each businessperson, every signwriter, every radio and TV station and newspaper – to use our language or lose it.

*Lá*, the daily Irish language paper, sells 5,000 copies every day. Dead languages don't sell newspapers! However, a comprehensive interconnected plan is needed to ensure that at least 100,000 people

**In spite of official State policy, which has been tokenistic at best in relation to reviving Irish, the vast majority of the population want Irish to be a written and spoken language and available to them to learn and use.**

fluently using Irish every day to meet virtually all their linguistic needs can ensure the language not only survives but thrives.

In many ways, the Irish language is better placed than it was 100 years ago to provide an inspiration and a service for the Irish people. We have media, both broadcast and written, available in Irish. TG4 abú! There are plays, books, films, DVDs, CDs etc in the Irish language. There is an education system from pre-school to post-graduate university level "as Gaeilge". There is computer software and websites for Irish and through Irish. If you are looking for a word or phrase, you can e-mail your query to freagra@acmhainn.ie. Check out the website www.acmhainn.ie/freagra.

There is now a whole legal framework to uphold the right of a person to use Irish in law and opportunities to access services through Irish. However, the Irish speaker still needs to have a harder neck very often than the casual English speaker. For example, tours of Government buildings are automatically in English, but for a tour in Irish, you can have one, but only after you ask for this special favour! To read the annual report of An Gárda Síochána, you need an ability to read up-side-down!

In spite of the obstacle courses put in the way of students and speakers of Irish, the 2002 Census indicated that 1.57 million people in the Republic speak the language. In Northern Ireland, 10.4 per cent of the population say they have a knowledge of Irish.

What is missing from Government policy, North and South, however, is that ubiquitous management cliché, "joined up thinking going forward". Sponsoring organisations like Foras na Gaeilge, important as such organisations' work is, will not transform the linguistic landscape of Ireland. A comprehensive language planning process is needed. Is gá próiséas pleanála teanga – the kind of effort that gave us such a successful Special Olympics, that has people queuing in every town and village regularly to give blood because it is the right thing to do. That is the level of enthusiasm I want to bring to the debate on the Irish language.

Finland, Denmark, Israel and many other countries have restored their own languages before us. Finland continues to out perform Ireland in terms of competitiveness economically and Professor J.J. Lee of UCC says about Finland, "far from being associated with the abandonment of her language, her economic performance seems, if anything, to have derived a certain impetus from a highly self-conscious national revival, including considerable emphasis on the language as a bearer of national culture in defiance of imperial power".

The Celtic Tiger has brought material satisfaction to those who could benefit from it at the time. The challenging question now is, can we awaken the vision of an inclusive, self-respecting and distinctive

*... a comprehensive inter-connected plan is needed to ensure that at least 100,000 people fluently using Irish every day to meet virtually all their linguistic needs can ensure the language not only survives but thrives.*

**Our indigenous language, "an Ghaeilge", is still available to fire our imaginations.**

society? Our indigenous language, "an Ghaeilge", is still available to fire our imaginations. A hundred years ago, "an Ghaeilge" worked to inspire amazing changes in Ireland. Let us take up the challenge and restore the potential of our own distinctive language to forge a society of which we can all be proud.

# Jim Higgins MEP

## Member of Seanad Éireann

*Born in Ballyhaunis and educated at St. Jarlath's College, Tuam and UCG (BA, HdipEd). Formerly community school teacher. First elected to Dáil Éireann in 1987. Appointed Fine Gael Chief Whip in 1988. Minister of State at the Department of the Taoiseach, Department of Defence and Government Chief Whip 1995-7. He was a member of Seanad Éireann 1981-2 and 1983-7. He was Chairman of the Fine Gael Party 1994-5. Was a member of Mayo County Council 1979-1995. Elected to Seanad Éireann in 2002 and as a member of the European Parliament in June, 2004.*

## The Tide Has Turned

I attended secondary school at St. Jarlath's College, Tuam. Irish was my least favourite subject. I didn't bring anti-Irish prejudice with me from my primary school days – indeed quite the reverse. I went to a small, rural two-teacher school where both my father and mother were teachers and Irish was sometimes spoken at home but I grew to despise the language at secondary school. First of all, there was the absolute insistence on grammatical precision. One could accept that there had to be a reasonable grasp of the nouns in their five declensions but, for the most part, the verbs were beyond me, particularly when it came to the MFL, the MFC, the AGL, the AGC I was lost. Our teacher was a native Irish speaking priest from Connemara who was a former handball champion and if you didn't master the gymnastics of grammatical correctness one's jaw was likely to be met by an open hand as if he were hitting a half-solid against the backwall of an alley. Is it any wonder I hated Irish and so did the bulk of my classmates? Language is first and foremost a vehicle for oral communications, but it wasn't taught that way. There was little, if any, emphasis on comhra or conversations. And then there was the looming or overhanging cloud of the impending Leaving Certificate where if you failed Irish you failed the whole exam. The language was taught in the very same way as two other languages on the curriculum, Latin and Greek. It was a dead language, killed because of the manner in which it was taught and killed stone dead in the hearts and minds of the students because of compulsion. The day I walked out the gates of St. Jarlath's for the last time I firmly resolved that that was the end of my interest in Celtic studies. So disinterested or disaffected was I with the language that I wouldn't even watch an Irish language programme on TV or listen to

> The language was taught in the very same way as two other languages on the curriculum, Latin and Greek. It was a dead language, killed because of the manner in which it was taught and killed stone dead in the hearts and minds of the students because of compulsion.

the "Nuacht" on radio. Then, in the mid-1980s and Charlie Haughey having coined the phrase, "Health Cuts Hit the Old, the Sick and the Handicapped", and with TDs tied down in a crucial Dáil vote, I was arm-twisted by the Fine Gael Press Office out to RTÉ to defend Barry Desmond's health policies on the Cúrsaí programme. Before going out I had to get the Aire na Gaeltachta's Private Secretary to write out for me words like Cártá Leigheis, Gearraithí Siar and Buiséad. I was pitted against none other than the "bould" Padraic Flynn. I struggled but I got through it and afterwards the presenter Seán Ó Tuairisc said: "Why don't you listen to the radio, improve your vocabulary and you'll get lots of media opportunities?" That I did and not alone did I get plenty of media appearances on TG4 and Radio na Gaeltachta but I have got to genuinely love the language. I am no longer amazed when somebody invariably walks up to me on the street and says: "I saw you on TG4 last night". When Seán Ó Neachtain, Barbara de Brun and myself meet together in Brussels or Strasbourg we generally converse in Irish.

And so to the subject matter: "The Death Throes of the Irish Language". I think that, far from witnessing the death throes of the Irish language, we are currently witnessing a resurgence of the language. After decades of a shrinking Gaeltácht, after years of decline, the rot stopped some years ago, things stabilised. A language renaissance is well and truly underway. I don't know how many of you have visited a Gaelscoil. I have and I visit Gaelscoileanna regularly. What strikes me is the sheer enthusiasm with which the young pupils embrace the language, whether as a subject itself or as a medium through which subjects are taught. The figures speak for themselves. In the school year 2005/2006 there were 132 Gaelscoileanna at primary level with a total enrolment of 24,376 pupils. It is a movement which is growing. Gaelscoileanna are mushrooming all over the country. The most heartening aspect of this is that the greatest concentration of Gaelscoileanna is in the Dublin area. How can one square this blossoming of all-Irish schools with the contention that we are supposed to be witnessing the death throes of the language? The key to the success of the Gaelscoileanna is that the emphasis in the first place is on the oral fluency, giving children the confidence to speak the language – a departure in terms of teaching orthodoxy, getting away from the old style rigid orthodoxy that unless every utterance was grammatically correct, then you were deemed a failure. What must be acknowledged is that when the British set about the anglicisation of Ireland, they used the English language as an effective instrument of anglicisation policy. The aim was to get people to speak the language. It worked. The results are self-evident and that is the reason we are here discussing the topic.

**How can one square this blossoming of all-Irish schools with the contention that we are supposed to be witnessing the death throes of the language?**

I asked a colleague to table a question in the Dáil to the Taoiseach regarding the number of people who indicated that they had an ability to speak Irish or who use Irish on a daily basis. The following is the Taoiseach's reply:

| Year | |
|------|------|
| 1926 | 540,802 |
| 1936 | 666,601 |
| 1946 | 588,725 |
| 1961 | 716,420 |
| 1971 | 789,429 |
| 1981 | 1,018,413 |
| 1986 | 1,042,701 |
| 1991 | 1,095,830 |
| 1996 | 1,430,205 |
| 2002 | 1,570,894 |

While some might question the accuracy or the truthfulness of the respondents' answer to the Census question, and would be tempted to ponder on just how often people really use the language, the reality is that 1,570,894 people in 2002 maintained, and clearly put down on paper, that they used the language, whatever about speaking the language frequently. I believe that it is an indication that while they may not publicly acknowledge it, there is a deeply ingrained affection for the language in the hearts of the majority of Irish people.

What is especially worthy of note is that in the 1971 Census there were 789,429 people who professed to speak Irish whereas in 1981 that figure had jumped to 1,015,413. By 1981, Ireland was nine years a member of the European Union. Instead of losing our national identity, as the anti-EU campaigners had maintained, the direct opposite happened. Membership of the EU triggered a sense of national identity in people's consciousness, a sense of national pride, a sense that while we may be part of an international, political and economic union made up of member states, each with its own identity, culture and language, we too have our own distinctive and unique culture. Traditional music, already beginning to flourish, flourished even more. Irish dance was recognised on the world stage as a spectacular extravaganza and on the language front there was a determination that something precious, a badge of who and what we are, had to be salvaged. It is very much a case of "Tír gan teanga, tír gan anam".

The emergence of Radio na Gaeltachta and TG4 have played a major role in the language's recovery. They have met the challenges

*The emergence of Radio na Gaeltachta and TG4 have played a major role in the language's recovery. They have met the challenges confronting them with vigour and imagination.*

confronting them with vigour and imagination. In both cases they will interview somebody whose Irish may not have the fluency or the flow of the cainteoir dúchais, but who is still able to convey his or her message. The old elitist, puritanical attitude has been abandoned. In TG4's case, they have excellent current affairs programmes, which are sub-titled.

Is it not somewhat ironic that we should be debating the subject of the death throes of our native tongue on the advent of Irish being recognised, after a long struggle, as a working language within the EU?

One of the features of the Irish persona is our difficulty with languages. I was on a French TV programme last May with MEPs from Latvia, Lithuania and Poland. They had perfect French. When we got together for a coffee after the programme they conversed in perfect English. They came from fledgling democracies which for years were locked behind the Iron Curtain in the icy grip of Moscow. The three would have been educated under the old communist regime in their respective countries and yet they had a mastery of three languages. I believe that the Irish person's mental block as regards languages is the legacy that has afflicted us for generations from the way Irish was taught at school – absolute precision and perfection, albeit in written expression, and, of course, compulsion.

I believe that things have changed in the new era of enlightenment. For example, 420 people have applied for the positions of interpreters in the European Parliament and Commission, some of whom will take up their positions on the 1st of January next. The desired standard is Irish and five other languages. I doubt that twenty years ago there would have been such an influx of confident young multi-linguists from this country. The tide has turned. The language has been saved. A unique, beautiful and rhythmical expression of our Irish identity has been reclaimed by the Irish people. Ar aghaidh leis an obair; ar aghaidh leis an teanga.

**I believe that the Irish person's mental block as regards languages is the legacy that has afflicted us for generations from the way Irish was taught at school – absolute precision and perfection, albeit in written expression, and, of course, compulsion.**

# Robin Bury

## Former Chairman, Reform Movement

*Educated at Middleton College, Cork, St. Columba's College, Dublin and TCD. Studied modern history and political science. Spent several years teaching in Africa and Ireland before joining CTT, the Irish Export Board. Worked as export manager with two companies. Formerly President of the Irish Exporters' Association.*

## The Irish Language, Self-Delusion and Hypocrisy

In the Reform Movement we question the compulsory nature of Irish and I will explain why we think Irish and English should be equal national languages and that English should be given precedence in the event of legal conflict.

Let me start by saying it is madness to attack a language and Reform never did that. A language is a thing of beauty and should be cherished. Let us remember that no two languages put the world in the same order. But it is another matter to criticise the way the language has been handled since Independence. My position is that I was taught Irish from 8 to 17 years of age, yet, like most people can only speak a few sentences.

First, a few quotes. The *Irish Independent* reported on 23 June last: "It's official: Standard of spoken Irish has gone into freefall". In the *Irish Times* of 17 January last, Brian Fleming told us: "thousands of students are opting out of learning Irish". A recent ESRI study concludes that Irish is "the least popular subject among school students". As for the Gaeltacht areas, the bedrock for Irish language speakers, here is what Reg Hindley wrote in his book *The Death of the Irish Language*: "A country which cannot adequately support at home the people who speak its dying language will have grave difficulties in sustaining it into the future".

I propose to contrast the status of the Irish language before Independence in 1893, when the Gaelic League started, with the state it is in today. In fact the language had been dying for two and a half centuries before the Gaelic League was founded. It is a myth to state that Irish was spoken widely before 1922. As long ago as 1700, Irish was no longer the first language of Roman Catholic Ireland. By the late eighteenth century, Irish was an interest for scholars and occasional Protestant activists as a medium for conversions.

The writer of the 1871 census wrote: "There can be no error in the belief that within a relatively few years Irish will have taken its

> A language is a thing of beauty and should be cherished. Let us remember that no two languages put the world in the same order. But it is another matter to criticise the way the language has been handled since Independence.

place among the languages that have ceased to exist". In 1905, the Gaelic League paper, *An Claidheamh Soluis,* in despair, asked: "Is the Irish Language Dying?" Desmond FitzGerald, Garret's father, saw the language before the Great War as a dying one. He believed it was losing its richness of expression and idiom.

Here are some of the facts:

- Before Independence, the language had been substantially abandoned by the mass of the population and that of all the main towns.

- Before the League started, only 3.5 per cent of all children under ten spoke Irish.

- In 1911, 16,870 people only spoke Irish. Today no more than 20,000 speak Irish as their native tongue but they all speak English. There are no monolingual Irish speakers left.

- There was a massive decline of 41 per cent of Irish speakers between 1881 and 1924.

- Outside the Gaeltacht areas only 12 per cent spoke Irish by 1926.

- By 1956 there were only 30,000 habitual native speakers.

I believe the motivation to revive Irish, in the name of romantic nationalism, which was very strong in Europe at that time, was very understandable at the time of Independence but it was too late – we are, after all, situated between two huge English-speaking blocks with which we have deep and lasting relationships.

**After a hundred years of using all sorts of ingenious schemes, including compulsion, bribery and discrimination, no more than 20,000 speak Irish as their native tongue and all of these speak English.**

Let us now turn to the state of the Irish language over a century later. After a hundred years of using all sorts of ingenious schemes, including compulsion, bribery and discrimination, no more than 20,000 speak Irish as their native tongue and all of these speak English. The basic and indisputable facts are that the native tongue of the Irish today is English and that we are one of the most monolingual countries in Europe. And Irish has all but disappeared in the Gaeltacht.

Emigration, depopulation, tourism, the advent of the car, mass culture, especially TV and sport, played their part in its decline. Also, there tends to be a paucity of good Irish textbooks, especially in the more technical subjects. Where are the racy magazines and pop culture in Irish language magazines and comics?

As long ago as 50 years, Archbishop McQuaid told De Valera that Irish children would not revive Irish as when they went home their parents spoke English to them. The reply? "The experiment is not yet over." I suggest it is now. McQuaid was right. Since 1956, according to Hindley, "there could not have been more than 30,000 native speakers".

The recently published report by Dr John Harris of Trinity College, Dublin makes the point that McQuaid made: parents do not support learning of the language and their hands off stance to children "greatly increases the chance of the enterprise failing".

The report finds that, compared to 20 years ago, under a third of pupils in 3,000 ordinary primary schools have achieved mastery communication in Irish.

Standards are falling in Gaeltacht schools. General comprehension of speech has dropped from 96.3 per cent in 1985 to 73.3 per cent in 2002.

The best hope seems to be the Gaelscoileanna. There are 127 primary all-Irish schools but we should remember that many years ago there were very many such primary schools and their pupils turned to English as their native tongue when they left school.

The vast majority of people show no inclination to exercise a right to speak Irish which they honour as a symbol. It is unpatriotic to criticise Irish, to tell the truth. People prefer to tell "loyal lies". In the words of Hindley: "It does not matter that the Emperor has no clothes, so long as many wish to believe he has and continue to act accordingly".

Referring to Gaeltacht areas, Gemma O'Doherty of the *Irish Independent* wrote on 11 January 2003 that teenagers have rejected Irish as a language of romance. One said: "But if you went to a disco in Galway and asked in Irish someone to dance, you'd be absolutely shunned. It's just so uncool, man." For sheer compression, as an obituary for a language, that would be very hard to beat.

But the pretence goes on. And the censuses go on playing that game. The last one in 2002 told us that 1,500,000 people speak Irish. Loyal lies are told to uphold morale. The questions asked were: "Can you speak Irish? Yes or no? If 'yes', do you speak Irish weekly, less often, never?" Based on these questions, the census concluded one and a half million people, or 42 per cent of the population, speak Irish. No effort is made to find out how many speak it fluently, how many have a good working knowledge, how many have the cupla focail.

Again, in the words of Reg Hindley: "Irish language census figures have become for the most part worthless as an indicator of Irish survival and use" ... "census language figures are inflated by patriotic and nationalist sentiment and reveal wishful thinking". As Hindley put it: "The fanatics, through ignorance, closed minds, excess of idealism, refuse to accommodate to the reality of an English speaking Ireland."

> The vast majority of people show no inclination to exercise a right to speak Irish which they honour as a symbol. It is unpatriotic to criticise Irish, to tell the truth. People prefer to tell "loyal lies".

"The Irish in Primary Schools" report makes a serious attempt to find out how many parents can speak Irish and concluded that only 7.2 per cent of parents who send their children to ordinary primary schools can understand "most conversations" or have "native speaker ability". I suggest that politicians such as Trevor Sargent and Jim Higgins need to find out what the real situation is in the next census. We, as taxpayers, pay for government spending on the language so we should know how effectively our money is spent.

Irish is compulsory. Hindley believes this is "a fundamental error in social psychology". It is "required" by artificial means. It has become a school language, promoted by propagandists and supported by an urban middle class who send their children to the dying Gaeltacht for a month or so, and sometimes to Irish-speaking schools where they get 10 per cent more points for doing some of their exams in Irish.

It is surrounded by self-delusion and hypocrisy and is practically never used in the Oireachtas. Yet it is our official language, in countless government websites, read by practically no one.

There are now about 150 languages spoken here – yet we still have not had an objective assessment of the problems and failures of language maintenance.

> **It is surrounded by self-delusion and hypocrisy and and is practically never used in the Oireachtas. Yet it is our official language, in countless government websites, read by practically no one.**

## Discrimination

Irish has been used to discriminate, not least of all against Protestants. It also was an anglophobic weapon. Tom Garvin wrote in *National Revolutionaries in Ireland*:

> ... that the Irish language took the high moral ground. English was the language of vulgarity and a vehicle for corruption, a Protestant language"

He went on:

> "the extremists confiscated the language ... they identified the language with a particular ideology. ... Protestants naturally excluded themselves."

I know all about Douglas Hyde, that eccentric atypical Protestant. But even he said that when the lingo-fanatics took charge they forced him out of the Gaelic League: "it was charming until it became powerful". It was to become a weapon for fundamentalist Roman Catholics and was feared by Protestants.

As for Irish and patriotism, Myles Dillon, Senior Professor in the School of Celtic Studies of the Dublin Institute of Advanced Studies and son of the famous John Dillon, asserted in the *University Review*, in 1958 that "to ally Irish to patriotism is at least questionable". He pointed out that Daniel O'Connell despised the language, Connolly and Tom Clarke were not interested in it, nor were Wolfe Tone, Emmett, Grattan, Parnell and Davitt, nor the literary giants Swift, Berkeley, Yeats and Shaw. Sean Lemass could not be persuaded to take up Irish.

Dillon said about Gaeltacht areas: "Native speakers of Irish today think Irish is a misfortune of their birth and an obstacle to their future prosperity in Boston or Birmingham". Dillon also wrote that "it is a pretence that Irish was the native language so it must be made compulsory to preserve it". In fact force-feeding it was "a contributory factor in a wave of disillusionment and apathy that has led thousands of people to quit the country in despair".

And on discrimination and Protestants, here is what he wrote: "The language was a means used to oust Protestants from power from civic and cultural institutions of the state, from the Royal Irish Academy to the National library to the National Gallery to the Royal Botanical Gardens".

## Conclusion

Hindley said, and I agree with him, that there is no room for honest doubt that the Irish language is now dying. English is our language and comes naturally to us and it has brought us huge prosperity.

Reform's position is straightforward. We respect all traditions in this country and on this island – from Orange to Green, to those who want to have the language as their important symbol, something to love and nurture. But we ask, should they impose it on those who do not freely choose it?

Let Myles Dillon have the last word in the interests of pluralism, particularly relevant to today's Ireland. His is "the idea of Ireland that is now growing up, a river fed by many streams, a stone of many colours, like a diamond cut in 6 facets". That was 50 years ago. There are more like 60 facets today.

**We respect all traditions in this country and on this island – from Orange to Green, to those who want to have the language as their important symbol, something to love and nurture. But we ask, should they impose it on those who do not freely choose it?**

# Anton Carroll

## Principal, Greendale Community School

*Born in Gweedore, Co. Donegal. A native Irish speaker, he was educated at St. Patrick's College, Drumcondra, UCC and TCD. He has been Principal of Greendale Community School in Kilbarrack since it was opened some thirty years ago. He was the first National Co-ordinator of the Leaving Certificate Vocational Programme. He has served on the Governing Body of Dublin City University and has also been a member of the Board of the now defunct Health Education Bureau.*

## The Irish Language is in Distress but Can be Saved

It is timely to reflect at this point on the state of well-being of the language as it is, in the view of many, past the point of rescue. It is certainly in serious decline as a vernacular of a people and that is cause for concern. The Irish language is key to so much in our lives that its demise would be an incalculable loss for our heritage and our culture.

I come to this forum with a view informed by observation of the teaching and learning of Irish. I would like to claim that I am objective and that my views are not influenced by any doctrinaire baggage or blinded fanaticism.

### Appraisal of the Current State of the Language

The Irish language is a sophisticated language with a native literature that extends back further than most of the European languages with the exception of Greek. Irish was the language of Fiannaíocht, Ruraíocht, an tSeanchas Mhór, and Céitinns "sceol ó ardmhaigh Fáil". Clearly, it is an inheritance to treasure and preserve. Unfortunately, our efforts at its preservation have been quite ineffective and its decline continues apace.

> The decline of Irish is not really surprising considering the influential circumstance that surrounds its usage. Its linguistic rival is probably the world's most prestigious and desired language.

The decline of Irish is not really surprising considering the influential circumstance that surrounds its usage. Its linguistic rival is probably the world's most prestigious and desired language. Irish does not enjoy the protection of isolation from other languages – it is essentially competing for primacy over English among a relatively small cohort of people who are fluent in both languages.

For the purpose of analogy, I want to suggest to you an image of Irish as a patient with a malaise or illness that is slowly draining the life out of the patient. To treat the sick patient, the first priority is to diagnose the illness. When diagnosis is concluded a course of medication or treatment is prescribed and administered. Progress is monitored and if the treatment is not working the diagnosis will be reviewed and an alternative treatment may be pursued!

But with Irish the approach is different! There is no objective diagnosis as to what has gone wrong. Why, after up to 12 years of daily lessons in Irish, are the majority of the population unable to construct a simple sentence in Irish? Surely there has been a failure of teaching. That, to any objective person, is not an unfair conclusion to draw.

Over the period since Independence, Irish governments have invested huge resources in the promotion of Irish. Up to 30 per cent of school time at primary level has been devoted to the teaching of Irish. Yet, only a small minority use the language competently. That statement may not accord with the views of some, but I challenge any organisation or individual to refute it on the basis of empirical research.

Part of the problem with Irish is that we have not established objectively and reliably what the state of the language is. For example, we indulge in a huge collective delusion that Gaeltachts are Irish-speaking enclaves, when the reality is that not a word of Irish is spoken in many of such designated Gaeltacht areas. Dungloe, a neighbouring town here in Donegal, is, I understand, declared by Donegal County Council as the capital of the Donegal Gaeltacht. This type of fanciful designation does not serve the Irish language; it merely confirms a cynical attachment to a national delusion.

The delusion is that all is well. Ask Foras na Gaeilge. They will cite statistical data from census returns that will portray the country as virtually bilingual. I remember reading some statistical hyperbole that suggested that upwards to 90 per cent of the people of Ashbourne, Co Meath and Thurles, Co. Tipperary could speak Irish. Try doing business tré Ghaeilge in Ashbourne or Thurles!

But the delusion goes on. And challenges to that delusion can be put down. For example, in 2005, the Leaving Certificate results in Irish were so bad that they were suppressed. A new team of correctors was engaged with a dumbed down marking scheme to ensure that the grades achieved would follow the normal bell-curve that typifies mark distribution in any test administered to a large cohort of people.

So rather than submit to an objective diagnosis and the possibility of different treatment, we keep administering the same old medicine even though it is not proving efficacious.

Without doubt, the Irish language is in distress. Yet we are

**Why, after up to 12 years of daily lessons in Irish, are the majority of the population unable to construct a simple sentence in Irish? Surely there has been a failure of teaching.**

treating it like some primitive tribe might treat its dying chief; we go into denial about its decline. We call places like Achill, "Gaeltachtaí"; we put up road signs exclusively in Irish and we pretend the natives speak Irish! We insist that Clare Co. Council spends €30,000 on translating its County Development Plan even though there is absolutely no public demand for the Irish version. Why do we treat Irish as we do?

## Towards a More Realistic Strategy

He [Enda Kenny] questioned the doctrine of compulsion and he succeeded in forcing an evaluation of the norms of teaching and promotion that we've adhered to for many decades with diminishing returns and demoralising results.

Enda Kenny did us a service when he invited us to look critically at what current strategies are achieving. He questioned the doctrine of compulsion and he succeeded in forcing an evaluation of the norms of teaching and promotion that we've adhered to for many decades with diminishing returns and demoralising results.

For some years, my organisation, Association of Community and Comprehensive Schools (ACCS), has been concerned about the standard of Irish in our schools. We have been aware, anecdotally, of falling standards at intake from primary schools and we have been aware of a growing antagonism towards the language. The points race has forced students into choices and priorities in respect of subjects. For most students, Irish is not regarded as likely to yield a rich harvest of points. Its imposed inclusion in their list of subjects is resented by many as they see it as a threat to their chances of garnering high quantities of points.

We have been considering this matter for some years and Mr. Kenny's comments have given fresh impetus and renewed focus to our concerns. Perhaps our diagnosis of the ailment will not meet with general consensus but here it is:

1. The standard of Irish of many primary teachers is inadequate for the teaching of Irish. If the teaching of Irish is to be prioritised, there must be specialist teachers of Irish assigned to individual primary schools.

2. The emphasis in teaching Irish must be placed primarily on communicative linguistic competence.

3. The Leaving Certificate Irish programme should be divided into two separately examinable subjects: Irish language and, separately, Irish literature and cultural studies.

4. Irish language should be a required subject for entry into public service employment. The level of competence should be set in reference to a National Standardised set of tests. These tests should be modelled on concepts like the ECDL and modules could

be taken at any time throughout schooling or afterwards. A set of levels, such as are used in piano competence grading, could be employed to certify different levels of competence in Irish. There should be nationally approved self-tutoring aids such as CD's and booklets to facilitate the acquisition of competence. Such resources would equip anyone including non-nationals to acquire the entry threshold level appropriate to whatever public service job they aspired to. Perhaps we could set levels of competence appropriate to Taoisigh and Ministers if we had such a national set of criteria!

5. Generous scholarships should be made available to encourage students to locate in the Gaeltacht for upwards to a year of secondary schooling.

6. Government should resource Gaeltacht and all-Irish schools with good quality text books and I.T. facilities to ensure high quality teaching through Irish of the full range of second level subjects. On a recent study trip to Wales we have seen a model for financing and monitoring such an initiative.

7. Government should set up a national strategic plan for the conservation of the Irish language.

That strategic plan should set out:

• What is the desired vision?

• What incremental steps are to be taken towards the attainment of that vision?

• Who is to complete each task?

• When is it to be done?

• What interim objectives are to be met along the way?

• What resources are needed?

• What monitoring mechanisms are to be used to measure and report progress?

To set out a realistic plan, the Government must engage dispassionate, objective expertise, preferably with an international profile. Such an expert panel charged with formulating a National Strategic Plan for Irish should include not just linguists of the highest standing but also sociologists, economists and marketing experts.

We have endured for too long the afflictions imposed by well-meaning enthusiasts. We do not doubt the goodwill of the many

We have endured for too long the afflictions imposed by well-meaning enthusiasts. We do not doubt the goodwill of the many enthusiasts but, as in all aspects of life, performance is judged by outcomes.

enthusiasts but, as in all aspects of life, performance is judged by outcomes. The outcomes for the Irish language condemn past initiatives largely to failure. Therefore, a new approach is required. There may be elements and aspects of the current repertoire of initiatives that can be retained and expanded. One such element, in my view, is the Gaelscoileanna. They have been a remarkable success but there is at least one weakness that even the strongest proponents of Gaelscoileanna acknowledge, that is, that the linguistic purity and richness of Irish is considerably diluted in the Gaelscoileanna for lack of contact with and immersion in a truly Irish-speaking experience.

This gives rise to a fear among some that the Gaelscoileanna may act as an agent of mutation, turning the spoken Irish language into a patois with a new construct and vocabulary that are largely borrowed from English.

**If Gaelscoileanna are to be enriched and enabled in their mission, they must be given the resources to link with truly Gaeltacht communities where their students can occasionally have total immersion experience of the Irish language.**

If Gaelscoileanna are to be enriched and enabled in their mission, they must be given the resources to link with truly Gaeltacht communities where their students can occasionally have total immersion experience of the Irish language.

On the recent study trip to Wales, which I mentioned earlier, we found a thriving Welsh language schools sector. However, even their advocates and proponents conceded that their prevailing vernacular did not have the "blas" or the linguistic richness of native Welsh speaking areas. This problem, in my view, is but a relatively minor flaw in an essentially excellent project. What I am arguing though is that a Gaelscoil cannot replicate total immersion in an Irish-speaking community. To be really effective the Gaelscoil must have the resources to link meaningfully with a host Gaeltacht.

There is one other area of major concern to us about the erosion of Gaeltachtaí – that is inward migration. Because of industrialisation in the Gaeltachtaí and the growth of affluence and tourism there have been considerable levels of inward migration of English speakers to the Gaeltachtaí, many of them of school-going age.

Because they are usually monoglots and the Gaeltacht children are bilingual, the medium of communication becomes English. This might start out as a courtesy to the stranger but it quickly becomes institutionalised as the norm. This experience has been conspicuously noticeable in Gaoth Dobhair. As you are aware, there has been very considerable industrialisation there in the past 30 years. A major downside of this has been the decline of the Irish language. Although Irish is still the vernacular of the over-40s, it is not the vernacular of their children in the schoolyard or in social discourse.

This presents a huge dilemma to Údarás na Gaeltachta – on one hand, charged with preserving the Irish language and, on the other, with developing sustainable communities where there is employment.

Perhaps we can take a lesson from Gwynedd in North-West Wales. Or perhaps we're too late!

Anyhow, for what it's worth, Gwynedd, a Welsh-speaking district, faced with the same problem of natives reverting to English in deference to newly arrived English-speaking migrants, resorted to imposing a total immersion experience for all newly arrived non-Welsh speaking school pupils. They set up special schools for inducting these new pupils into the Welsh-speaking schools and communities. Only when an adequate fluency in Welsh is attained are pupils allowed integrate into the Welsh-speaking schools.

In ranging over the problems of minority languages the recurring difficulties are similar. The positive influences are not only similar but virtually identical.

## Conclusion

No one, nowadays, seriously entertains De Valera's vision of revival of the Irish language. But we can preserve it and expand its usage. To do this, we must improve the competence of people to speak the language and we must improve the public's disposition towards the language. However, we must firstly acknowledge failed strategies and replace them with expertly planned initiatives that are grounded in realistic appraisal of what is possible and what is attainable in encouraging increments.

*... we must firstly acknowledge failed strategies and replace them with expertly planned initiatives that are grounded in realistic appraisal of what is possible and what is attainable in encouraging increments.*

The question posed for this evening's deliberations is: "Are we facing the imminent death of Irish?" I'm afraid the answer is yes, but qualified!

Look at the Gaelifying of place names by Local Authorities. I get despondent. I know of a place now that is called Long Cogaidh. I saw in Malahide a street named Sráid Sean. I saw recently a Gaelscoil named Gaelscoil Dara. Unquestionably, we're losing the richness of the language. I believe the loss of quality Irish by abandonment in the Gaeltachts is not being compensated for by uptake in the Galltachts, and whatever uptake there is is hardly worth crowing about. Listen to TG4. Very often, what is presented as Irish is, what the Connemara man said was, "Ní Gaeilge nó Béarla é ach big fata mór".

If present decline of Irish continues unabated for another generation, its demise will be complete within two generations. As a patient, it is, unquestionably, seriously ill. I do not have confidence in its medical team and I don't believe current treatment will prove efficacious. The prognosis is not good but the language, in my view, is not yet in the death throes. A restoration to moderately active life-style is still possible.

Dr Diarmuid Martin, Archbishop of Dublin and
Right Rev Ken Good, Bishop of Derry and Raphoe

Prof Michael Paul Gallagher SJ
Dean of Theology,
Gregorian University, Rome

Prof Michael Paul Gallagher, Right Rev Ken Good and Most Rev Dr Diarmuid Martin

*Chapter 8*

# Secularisation and the Loss of Religious Identity

*Hope of a Different, More Mature, More Lively Church*
MOST REV DR DIARMUID MARTIN
**Archbishop of Dublin**

*The Content of Faith, Beliefs and Values Will Not Change*
RIGHT REV KEN GOOD
**Bishop of Derry and Raphoe**

*The Shrinking of Spiritual Horizons*
PROF MICHAEL PAUL GALLAGHER SJ
**Gregorian University, Rome**

# Most Rev Dr Diarmuid Martin

## Archbishop of Dublin and Primate of Ireland

*Born in Dublin 1945 and educated at Oblate School, Inchicore and De La Salle School, Ballyfermot. He studied philosophy at UCD and theology at Holy Cross College, Clonliffe. Ordained in 1969. Studied moral theology at the Pontifical University of St. Thomas Aquinas. Served as curate in the parish of St. Brigid in Cabinteely. Entered the service of the Holy See in 1976. In 1986 he was appointed Under-secretary of the Pontifical Council for Justice and Peace. In 1998, he was appointed Titular Bishop of Glendalough and in 2001 was elevated to the rank of Archbishop and became Permanent Observer of the Holy See at several international agencies including the UN. He Succeeded Cardinal Connell as Archbishop of Dublin in 2004.*

## Hope of a Different, More Mature, More Lively Church

A few days ago I hosted a gathering to launch a new book on the contribution of Irish missionaries to Nigeria written by Irene Lynch, the wife of a former Irish Ambassador to Nigeria. It is a simple book in which missionaries of various ages, from various religious congregations and from various parts of Ireland tell their stories.

Two things struck me about the stories and the photos that form part of the book. The first is that they are images and stories of happy people, free from many of the doubts and questionings and dissatisfactions that are so often the stuff of reflection on the Church in Ireland today. Let me stress that what these men and women talk about is very far from any authoritarian strain of a Church made up of people who believe they know everything and had gotten everything right. What I came away with was the impression of people who knew that they had played their part with enthusiasm and who were convinced of the intrinsic worth of their effort.

The second thing that struck me is that almost all of the contributors linked whatever success they had had in Nigeria with an original inspiration, an intuition that they had had in Ireland. The story of their contribution to a better world was the story of their vocation.

It is important for us all to remember that the "Catholic Ireland" of the past was not just marked by power-seeking, abuse of children, scandals and censorship, but it was also a history of the lives and dedication of many extraordinary people of whom we should be proud and to whom many of us are personally indebted.

The Catholic school, for example, was not the place of

> It is important for us all to remember that the "Catholic Ireland" of the past was not just marked by power-seeking, abuse of children, scandals and censorship, but it was also a history of the lives and dedication of many extraordinary people ...

indoctrination and repression, of conformism and of moral rigidity it was often presented as. The Catholic school was a place where people were enhanced in their creativity. It was a place where so many of the less fortunate were given an opportunity to get on and from where they did get on. Likewise, in the debates about education today, far too little attention is given to the extraordinary work that is being done in Catholic schools in welcoming children of many nationalities into one school community. When I look at the situation in the diocese of Dublin, it is most often the Catholic school in an area which is the most representative in terms of nationalities and religious denominations, while still maintaining its Catholic ethos. Indeed, there is a sense in which it is the Catholic ethos, also in the wide sense of the word catholic, which gives rise to openness and welcome. The contribution of these schools and their teachers has been exceptional and almost totally unrecognised.

We have every reason to be optimistic about that Church in Ireland and its institutions. There is a great deal of renewal going on. I visit extraordinarily lively parishes every Sunday, parishes with great purpose, energy and solidarity. Saying this does not mean that numbers have not gone down. Saying this does not mean that we have any less the obligation to learn and explore the lessons of our past mistakes and errors, at times grave. Whereas I would love to be able to dedicate myself to the most satisfactory dimension of my ministry, sharing with people the freeing power which comes from following the teaching of Jesus Christ, I have to spend huge amounts of time trying to identify in greater detail the extent of the failings of the Church and the ways an institution had lost track with what is essential in the Christian faith.

Christian faith is not just a faith about doctrines or about rules and regulations or about ethical standards against which we have to measure our own or, as was very much an Irish tradition, other persons' moral behaviour.

The message of the Church is the message of God who loves us before any merit on our part. It is a God who reveals; who speaks to us, engages with us and allows us to understand something of the inner life of God, which is a life of communication and of love. It is a faith which is about truth, but truth which is to be discovered in the life of a person, Jesus Christ, who revealed himself through total self-giving. It is about a God who is generous and whose followers should witness in their lives to the fact that being truly human has much more to do with giving than about having.

The concept of a God, who is characterised by love and mercy, by compassion and forgiveness, is at times hard to fully comprehend in today's culture, which is at the same time extraordinarily tolerant

**Christian faith is not just a faith about doctrines or about rules and regulations or about ethical standards against which we have to measure our own or, as was very much an Irish tradition, other persons' moral behaviour.**

and extraordinarily intolerant. For some, a culture of forgiveness can only lead to a culture of impunity, where the concept of mercy and forgiveness is used to evade bringing persons before the full force of justice and judgement. For others, it leads them to a vision of God who forgives and tolerates any behaviour and who is satisfied with whatever results we bring to his challenge. This is the difficult paradox of a God who is demanding and is yet merciful, a God who speaks about justice, and yet enters into a dialogue with an ever-unfaithful people.

Christianity is not a religion of cheap repentance, but is a religion of a God whose mercy heals and restores the converted into being the people that God wants them to be and never doubts the ability of any person to be so, even within the framework of continued brokenness. It is a Church which is not a holy elite, but a community of repentant sinners confident that they can be led along a path which overcomes weakness and doubt.

... can a world be tolerant if it does not have some absolutes around which to construct its basic orientation? These are questions which Irish society must ask and find workable answers to if it is to be a truly inclusive society.

Is there place for a religion of absolutes in a world of tolerance? Indeed, is our world of tolerance capable of being tolerant of those who hold views that appear absolute? On the other hand, can a world be tolerant if it does not have some absolutes around which to construct its basic orientation? These are questions which Irish society must ask and find workable answers to if it is to be a truly inclusive society.

I do not wish today to get into the details of discussions about where the public morality in a future Ireland will find its roots. Let me simply say that these discussions are too important to be left to "others". Everyone and every institution must be able to, and should, play its part and bring its contribution to the debate. Such questions require open, mature and broad discussion in society. They require a discussion which goes beyond superficial media sound-bytes and beyond spin. They should not be left alone to judges, functionaries or committees.

We have discussions going on these days about what I heard someone recently describe as "the contentious issue of the right to life". I would have expected that the right to life was *un-contentious matter* in any democracy. This is not simply a playing on words. If the right to life is such a primordial principle, the real basis of democracy and the rule of law, then the debate on how that right is legally interpreted should be wide and mature.

I for one was surprised to learn that the Irish constitution might consider a foetus not protected in Irish law if there was an indication that its life after birth might be short. I am surprised that a judge will have to make a decision on the constitutional significance of the human embryo in an almost total legislative vacuum, and in the absence of a broader public debate. I do not deny that in the real world decisions on such matters have to be reached. My point is that such decisions require much more open debate.

Where is the Church in these areas? The Church draws its teaching from the message of Jesus Christ, but that teaching is read and mediated within the realities of life and of science and may lead one to read these realities in a way which is different to others, but nonetheless to a reading which is valid within a democratic process where no philosophy has a monopoly. As a Catholic Bishop, I have every right to stress views, even if they are not shared by all. I have every right to present my Church's position with vigour, even if this is said by others to be divisive. If there is no clear unity of vision every position could be called divisive. The Church will not impose, but it has every right to propose its position and to be countercultural. Affirming a right to life from the moment of conception until the moment of natural death is appealing to an ideal, a vision which is not unscientific, but an affirmation of the uniqueness of every human individual, which is not ours to play around with. In a world in which the possibilities to play with life have grown, the call to absolute respect for human life is more valid than ever.

When I spoke earlier of the message of Jesus Christ being a message of care, I am naturally drawn to recall the parable of the good Samaritan. Here was this outsider who shows us what is involved in caring for a brother and sister: noticing and recognising, encountering face to face, carrying, caring and even returning to see that the wounded is really fully restored to life. This is a vision not just of the good person, but of the caring society, which is a society not of delegation to others but of participation by all in the reality of care. The Good Samaritan wrote no letter to the editor. He simply became the carer.

When we talk about that parable of the Good Samaritan all our attention is usually focussed on the figure of the Samaritan. But who is the one who fell among the thieves? The Gospels tell us only that he was "a man", a human person. It is not important to know anything else. It is the simple fact of "humanity", of being a human being, which gives rise to the duty of care. When a society begins to make its own decisions about categories of humanity deserving less care than others, then fundamental discrimination takes root.

"Secularisation and the Loss of Religious Identity" is the title of our session. Is this a true description of what is happening in Ireland? Is there secularisation? Yes! Is there loss of religious identity? Yes! Is this the entire picture? No! As I said earlier, there is extraordinary vitality in the Irish catholic community. There are parishes which

> As a Catholic Bishop, I have every right to stress views, even if they are not shared by all. I have every right to present my Church's position with vigour, even if this is said by others to be divisive.

have never been so active and participatory in their history. There are, on the periphery of Dublin, examples of Church-inspired care and working together which are showing how to turn the suburban "social deserts" left by the planners and developers of the decades gone by into forward looking, hope-filled and flourishing communities. It is easy – perhaps even cynical – somehow to say that such examples are the fruit of the few who stand up to the institution. I for one can only express admiration for the manner in which so many are not prepared to sit on the ditch commenting, but take on responsibility and solidarity that they receive from the Gospel message and make it their own. That is the sort of Church I am proud to belong to.

My feeling is that what I am talking about is not just a Roman Catholic phenomenon. Talking to other church leaders in Dublin, I have the impression that they also encounter the same tensions and difficulties, but also the same new hope of a different, more mature, more lively Church, where the Bishop is enthused by the power of real Christian commitment of lay persons in a way that we never experienced in the past. I for one believe that this common experience offers us also new frontiers for cooperation between churches, in both the North and the South and, indeed, between religious groups North and South. But we still do not know one another enough to be able to do this.

Finally, lest my enthusiasm sweeps me away, I would not be honest without asking myself and you about young people. I do not meet that many of them in churches. But when I meet young people I find that it is easy to come to a meeting of minds. Young people are asking questions which my generation asked much later in life, if ever. Young people encounter the reality such as the suicide of their own contemporaries and ask the deeper questions about life. Young people are ambitious for a better and more just world, not by just talking about it but by showing that they want to be part of the construction of that world through their own work and creativity. Again, we do not provide enough occasions for such engagement with young people.

There are so many reasons to have negative feelings about the Church in Ireland and about religious identity in Ireland. But reading that book about the missionaries and seeing happy faces which represent fulfilled lives reminds me that long faces rarely win many hearts. The Church in Ireland needs purification, as the Church composed of humans always needs purification. But purification is not just purification of institutions, but conversation of hearts and renewal of enthusiasm around what is essential in the Christian life. I find plenty of enthusiasm about being involved in such a Church. Even the convinced secularist might like to have another look.

**The Church in Ireland needs purification, as the Church composed of humans always needs purification. But purification is not just purification of institutions, but conversation of hearts and renewal of enthusiasm around what is essential in the Christian life.**

# The Right Rev Ken Good

## Bishop of Derry and Raphoe

*Born in Co. Cork, he was educated at Cork Grammar School and Middleton College and studied languages at TCD, theology at Nottingham University and education at UCC. He was ordained Deacon in 1997 and Priest in 1998. He served as curate in Willowfield Parish in Belfast and from 1979 to 1984 was chaplain and Head of RE in Ashton Comprehensive School, Cork. He was rector in Dunganstown, Co. Wicklow, Glendalough and in Shankill Parish, Lurgan, one of the biggest parishes in the Church of Ireland. He took a three-month sabbatical in 2001 during which he visited churches in the USA, Singapore, Australia and New Zealand. He was elected Bishop of Derry and Raphoe in March 2002.*

## The Content of Faith, Beliefs and Values Will Not Change

Whether in the Celtic Tiger economy of the Republic, or the steady but less spectacular growth of the UK, and even in a city like Derry where statistics reveal that childhood poverty is considerably more serious than elsewhere, greater wealth now provides more choices and more options for self-reliance in the pursuit of self-fulfilment.

The Church of England Bishop of Maidstone, Dr Graham Cray, puts it aptly when he suggests that Descartes' slogan for today's consumerist society could well be, *Tesco ergo sum!* An apt motto at least for the majority, but for the substantial minority of those who feel least able to keep in the rush for the shops, the feelings of alienation and dissatisfaction become more acute.

Having choices like we never had before has an obvious impact on religious belief, practice and identity of modern Ireland.

*1) A multi-cultural Ireland*, is evident in many parts of the country, not least in Letterkenny, not far from here. Irish people who, until relatively recently, knew where they stood in a homogeneous and predictable society, now find themselves in a new diversity if not a multiplicity of religious beliefs. This, obviously, has an impact on the shape of religious identity and religious awareness.

*2) A more questioning or sceptical Ireland* where traditional Christian churches (along with all traditional institutions) and, therefore Christian beliefs, are coming under closer scrutiny than ever before. Status, tradition and position do not make anyone or anything immune from having to justify their position in the face of

> Irish people who, until relatively recently, knew where they stood in a homogeneous and predictable society, now find themselves in a new diversity if not a multiplicity of religious beliefs.

probing questioning and sceptical analysis.

But there is a strangely interesting relationship, still, between this growing scepticism on the one hand and quite strong spiritual or religious conviction on the other. Just this month in the *Derry Journal* (11 July 2006), the findings of a survey of social and religious attitudes in Donegal are reported (as conducted by the Derry Journal Group).

While undoubtedly there are changes in levels of religious belief and practice, I am happy to remind you that right now you are in the county of Donegal where, according to the *Derry Journal*, 88 per cent of people say they believe in God, where 85 per cent of people are regular churchgoers and where 81 per cent intend to bring their children up in the Christian faith. I also note from the survey one finding that gives food for thought for politicians. Despite the increasing religious scepticism and secularisation, 63 per cent of people say they still trust clergy, whereas only 36 cent say they trust politicians! I resist making any comment.

*3) A post-modern Ireland.* In every post-modern society, as we know, there is a diminishing acceptance of a shared meta narrative or a bigger picture reality, into which everything fits and makes sense. The big (Christian) story, in the light of which our common history in Ireland has been understood over the centuries, is being replaced in the minds of some by numerous smaller and more individual stories or narratives.

While there is still undoubtedly the high level of spiritual interest reflected in the Co. Donegal survey, even if in some parts of the country it is expressed in less committed church allegiance, there is much more of a "pick-and-mix" spirituality in which people choose the bits of various faith perspectives which suit them and leave to one side those parts which they find less meaningful or agreeable.

*4) An individualistic Ireland.* Many organisations in Ireland which traditionally have relied upon regular participation and commitment to group activity are experiencing a drop in numbers, such as trade unions, team sports and more structured youth organisations. In contrast, activities which require involvement without regular corporate attendance have experienced growth in interest — societies for the protection of the environment, personal fitness, hill walking and golf clubs. This trend undoubtedly can have an impact on aspects of church life in general, and on attendance at corporate worship in particular.

*5) A politically correct Ireland* where there is a growing determination to not offend anyone and to avoid creating any impression that one view or faith or conviction might be better than another. Although we may not quite have arrived at the

... according to the *Derry Journal*, **88 per cent of people say they believe in God, where 85 per cent of people are regular churchgoers and where 81 per cent intend to bring their children up in the Christian faith.**

situation reached elsewhere where a *Happy Christmas* greeting has compulsorily been replaced by a *Happy Holiday* one, and *Christmas* itself has been watered down to *Winterfest*, in case offence might possibly be caused, that day is probably not very far away here, too.

While fairness, justice and sensitivity are obviously important social values, I trust I am not alone in this gathering in expressing concern that when political correctness is overdone, it can all too easily result in a neutralising culture in which the lowest common denominator becomes the only permitted option and where pluralism can become an insipid neutralising of healthy conviction in diversity.

## *The Diagnosis?*

So the modern Ireland in which I live and which I observe is one which, like a teenager, appears to be throwing off some of the long-established family values, boundaries and belief systems which it now feels to be overly restrictive, and is opting instead for a more do-it-yourself system of individually selected life-choices, many of which can seem to be chosen on the grounds of short-term individual gratification and expediency rather than for any longer-term social or corporate benefit.

At the very same time, it would also seem to me that the Ireland in which I now live hasn't yet found a new set of life-enhancing values, moral boundaries or guiding principles that really work, which can replace what has been, at least in part, rejected as outdated. The liberation which was eagerly anticipated by breaking free from restrictive shackles has not brought the hoped for freedom, nor the personal sense of fulfilment which it promised. If anything, all this has come at the price of a deeper alienation and relational damage, and left us somewhat valueless and rudderless.

The overall title of this year's MacGill Summer School is *The Soul of Ireland*. We are aware that it was Jesus of Nazareth who spoke with some clarity about the pitfall of "gaining the whole world" and, in so doing, of "losing one's soul". He followed up this statement with a question: "What can we give that will buy back our own soul once we have lost it?" (Matthew 16:26)

It was a rhetorical question, without a clear answer. But it was surely a word of warning which contained the caution that the business of soul-losing is something to be avoided at all costs because, once lost, it is very difficult to find it again.

In what ways might soul-losing manifest itself in any society? Might it not be where there is a widespread fragmentation and breakdown of relationships, where there is a diminished sense of

> The liberation which was eagerly anticipated by breaking free from restrictive shackles has not brought the hoped for freedom, nor the personal sense of fulfilment which it promised.

community and an exaggerated preoccupation with self-fulfilment and individualism? Where low level depression, anxiety and alienation are on the increase; where alcohol and substance abuse and dependence take a stronger and stronger grip on us; where the increase in death by suicide becomes alarming; where aspects of youth culture and behaviour give cause for concern? The evidence would suggest that symptoms such as these, each of which is becoming apparent in today's affluent Ireland, is an indicator that all is not well with our inner being, that there is something not right with our soul.

## The Remedy?

So what then are we to do? Are we to look back and try to go back to an idyllic golden age when religious practice and religious identity in Ireland were the panacea for all ills?

I was interested to read in this year's Summer School Programme Patrick MacGill's poem, "Going Home", where he speaks nostalgically of "going back to Glenties and the wave washed Donegal, to the hills I tramped so long ago".

There is a wistful sense of longing to escape from the harsh realities of his new environment by going back to this beautiful part of the world where, he now imagines at a distance, all must surely be idyllically and wonderfully well.

> I've seen the smile of innocence become the frown of crime.
> I've seen the wrong rise high and strong, I've seen the fair betrayed.

**What we acknowledge now is that there were aspects of our religious past in Ireland that were less than the entirely golden, idyllic or halcyon days that some might have claimed.**

Was Glenties ever the idyllic antidote to all the world's ills? I suspect not. Nor were Ireland's religious times of yore. What we acknowledge now is that there were aspects of our religious past in Ireland that were less than the entirely golden, idyllic or halcyon days that some might have claimed.

Colum Kenny, in his thought-provoking assessment of the shaping of modern Ireland, *Moments that Changed Us,* reminds us of a time when Christian denominations treated each other with contempt, when their members were forbidden from attending one another's church ceremonies, when the *Ne Temere* decree discouraged inter-church marriage, and when government ministers felt unable to grieve for their Church of Ireland President, Douglas Hyde, at his funeral in St Patrick's Cathedral. (Kenny describes that episode as the "nadir of feebleness" in inter-church relationships.) The way in which we worked out our sectarian struggles, especially in the North, but in the Republic too, are something of which none of us can feel very proud.

No, the answer is not to attempt to turn the clock back to a former time, the answer is to move forward as a society allowing our values, our principles, our aspirations and our priorities to be shaped in such a way that our soul becomes more healthy, our spirit more enlivened, our heart more generous, our sense of community more prominent and our levels of faith more developed.

My personal conviction is that the main challenge to the Christian church today, in this country, is not from any external threat, be it secularism, materialism, consumerism or postmodernism. The main challenge is the internal one of ensuring that the integrity, the reality, and the relevance of the church's life and worship, its teaching and communication, must strike a meaningful chord in a society that still has an appetite for spiritual reality. Where people see in our churches that our walk matches our talk, where they see, lived out in the daily pressures of life, real hope, truth, conviction, commitment, forgiveness, wholeness, community, generosity, concern for the poor, lives and situations transformed, where they see God at work then their interest will follow.

It is also my conviction that this does not mean that the church should try to do whatever it can to accommodate the cultural preferences of the day, or to be blown in whatever direction the secular breezes of the times appear to be wafting. No, the apparent irony is that churches which try to adjust or dumb down their message in an attempt to make it more acceptable to our times, or more politically correct in a way that doesn't challenge anybody, are on a path that leads nowhere useful. Instead, an approach that is willing, when necessary, to be more robustly and unapologetically counter-cultural in addressing the issues of the day will be taken more seriously and will attract more attention and interest. The way in which our beliefs and values are expressed, communicated or packaged may need to change, but the essential content of the faith, the root beliefs and core values, the doctrinal and ethical foundations will not.

The society in which the church operates today requires of us a genuine humility where we have to earn the right to be listened to rather than demanding or expecting it. Compassionate servanthood that is Christlike will attract attention, whereas any attempts at exercising power or control over people will not. Former notions of enthronement, of prelates and of palaces are better replaced with those of leading by inspiration, by effective spiritual nurture and by realistic pastoral support.

The soul of Ireland has for centuries been nourished by its Christian heritage and I have no doubt that this rich well has much more nourishment still to offer us for this and future generations.

*... the apparent irony is that churches which try to adjust or dumb down their message in an attempt to make it more acceptable to our times, or more politically correct in a way that doesn't challenge anybody, are on a path that leads nowhere useful.*

# Michael Paul Gallagher SJ

Professor and Dean of Theology, Gregorian University, Rome

*Born in Co. Sligo, he graduated from UCD with an M.A. in 1962 and from Oxford with an M.Litt. in 1968. He entered religious life in 1972. He did further research in literature and theology at Oxford, John Hopkins and Queen's University, Belfast. From 1972 to 1990 he lectured in English and American literature at UCD. From 1990 to 1995 he worked in the Vatican in the Pontifical Council for Dialogue with Non-Believers and the Pontifical Council for Culture. Since 1995 he has been Professor of Fundamental Theology at the Gregorian University in Rome where he was appointed Dean of the Faculty of Theology in 2005. He has contributed extensively to Irish and international journals and has published some ten books.*

## The Shrinking of Spiritual Horizons

Inevitably a short contribution is going to select a particular focus on our theme and leave many important aspects untouched. For instance, there is a hen and egg problem about secularisation: one theory sees the decline of personal belief as the cause of the secularisation of public life; another sees the loss of public credibility by the churches as the source of personal unbelief. Also, we find clashing theories summarised in slogans: are we in a situation of "believing without belonging" (Grace Davie) or of "belonging without believing" (the tendency of Helen Hervieu Leger)? I want to change the agenda somewhat away from the externals of sociology and towards a more anthropological reading of secularisation as a crisis of shared spiritual imagination.

It seems suitable in view of the figure we celebrate in Patrick MacGill to begin with some literary scaffolding. I offer four short references, two from outside Ireland and two from Irish writers. The first comes from Albert Camus who once suggested that tragedy gets written when people are changing their gods. Last year in Sebastian Barry's novel, *A Long Long Way*, a certain Mr Lawlor complains that "the curse of the world is people thinking thoughts that ... have been given to them. ... Their own thoughts are tossed out and cuckoo thoughts put in instead". The third is from Seamus Heaney's book of a few months ago, *District and Circle*, where a poem entitled "Out of this World" explores the birth of religious unbelief and has the simple but striking line: "The loss occurred off stage". In this light, I want to propose that rapid secularisation entails some anthropological

> ... are we in a situation of "believing without belonging" (Grace Davie) or of "belonging without believing" (the tendency of Helen Hervieu Leger)?

dangers, recognisable as dangers, I would hope, by both believers and non-believers alike. When people are changing their gods is a painful and vulnerable moment, potentially creative of tragedy, but also potentially shrinking consciousness to cuckoo thoughts. My argument will be that the real loss occurs off-stage, in other words, away from the big headlines about church troubles or the sociological statistics about religious change. Where exactly does secularisation have its deepest impact? Here, I call my fourth literary witness, the poet T. S. Eliot, who said some 60 years ago that the religious crisis of modernity was not "merely the inability to believe certain things about God which our forefathers believed, but the inability to feel towards God and man as they did". In other words, secularisation can have its greatest impact not on the level of our ideas but on our spiritual imagination. It involves not simply a reduced public role for religion but (literally) a radical change in the symbolic sensibility of a people.

That is the first shift of perspective that I want to suggest for our reflections – to place the drama of secularisation not in the realm of explicit worldviews but in the more delicate zone of our intuitive or imaginative interpretations of life. In much the same line, I also want to propose a second adjustment of focus, from a social to a more specifically cultural understanding of secularisation.

Thirty years ago, many theologians and even official statements of the Catholic Church largely welcomed what they then viewed as secularisation. It was described as a coming of age, a process whereby the rightful autonomy of secular disciplines and goals were differentiated from religious control. This new acceptance of human autonomy was seen as a healthy challenge to develop more mature languages of faith, born from personal freedom responding to God's word. If secularisation in the sixties or the seventies was seen as mainly social rather than cultural, in more recent decades thinkers such as Charles Taylor have criticised what they see as the superficiality of a merely social understanding of secularisation. Society, in this sense, refers to the more measurable aspects of our living together (urbanisation, work patterns, external religious practice and so on), whereas culture points to more subtle and hidden dimensions of meaning, value and (once again) imagination. If society is visible, culture is more like an iceberg, nine-tenths invisible. It includes not only externally measurable behaviour but all the non-explicit attitudes and assumptions we live by. To return to the Heaney image, culture is more off-stage than society, pointing to a more tacit level *underlying* (Lonergan) our social life and, therefore, cultural secularisation affects our self-images, our collective imagination of the real.

... secularisation can have its greatest impact not on the level of our ideas but on our spiritual imagination. It involves not simply a reduced public role for religion but (literally) a radical change in the symbolic sensibility of a people.

It is in this more subtle field of culture as sensibility that the German theologian, Johann Baptist Metz, has diagnosed a "new secularisation". It is more a matter of images than of ideas, expressed more in life-styles than in arguments or philosophies. In earlier decades Metz was enthusiastic about secularisation as a product of a Christian sense of responsibility for creation and for history. But he now adds some important qualifications. Looking at our lived and anchorless post-modernity, Metz is alarmed by a secularisation that is self-destructive of our humanity. Thinking of the impact on our spiritual imagination of hours and hours spent passively assimilating the banality of most television programmes, Metz locates the "new secularisation" in what he calls a "massive loss of sensitivity" to the full range of our humanity and in particular to the pain of history around us, the two-thirds world of poverty and violence. Older sociological debates were about quantitative secularisation. Now the focus has moved to what we can call qualitative secularisation.

If this is so, a deeper reflection on secularisation is called for, where, as I mentioned, believers and non-believers alike could hopefully develop a different quality of conversation. Do we know what we are doing to ourselves when we change our sense of what is real, when we move from older symbolic worlds of transcendence to narrow and largely pragmatic horizons of fragmented externals? The religious crisis of secularisation, clearly evident in Ireland in the last two decades, can provoke an anthropological crisis. It causes a painful dearth of shared meaning on the level of our self-images, and the existential pain seems more acute because of the speed of the move from pre-modernity to post-modernity without the normal upheavals and transitions of modernity.

If our spiritual imagination is the battleground of our lived self-meaning, we need to reflect on this deeper secularisation of the sensibility beyond the more obvious sociological crisis of religious structures in a more open society. It involves not just a measurable crisis of belonging and believing but a crisis of our images of ultimate identity. When a spiritual horizon is lost so rapidly, it is humanly disturbing for many people. What Newman called the "religious imagination" remains wounded and undernourished. Instead of a faith tradition, that served both as stimulus of compassion and as ultimate serenity concerning life's meaning (in spite of all its warts and sometimes shocking infidelities), what takes over can be a set of unworthy and frustrating images of the good life. McWilliams' book, *The Pope's Children,* would seem to diagnose an illness and alienation beneath the froth of the new economic boom. When anchors are lost, people seem to keep moving in order to avoid their confusion about identity. But in the words of Will Kymlicka, the Canadian political

When a spiritual horizon is lost so rapidly, it is humanly disturbing for many people. What Newman called the "religious imagination" remains wounded and under-nourished.

philosopher and not himself religious, it is only through having a "secure cultural structure that people can become aware … of the options available to them, and intelligently examine their value". Cultures, in short, provide environments for choice and identity, and what happens within cultures, in Kymlicka's view, shapes the frontiers of what is imaginable. Let me add to this a comment by another Canadian, the distinguished philosopher Charles Taylor, who speaks of religious faith as "being called to a change of identity" and ultimately as trusting that a different "stream of love" is "a possibility of us humans".

In this light I have been proposing that secularisation is not only a question of the social decline of religion but a larger drama of the shrinking of spiritual horizons. I have been suggesting that a different quality of debate is needed, starting from an anthropological concern about what is happening to our collective self-images. For more than 15 years now, I have been living in Italy where there is often a remarkable level of respectful reflection together by both believers and non-believers on such fundamental issues. Ireland, by comparison, seems frequently adolescent in its tone of discussing religious issues in the public arena. Surface points are scored while deeper issues seem neglected. What I have said here has been a plea to realise the delicacy of what happens within people's imagination of life and death in a time of cultural secularisation. To conclude, as we began, with our quartet of literary witnesses for the prosecution: in a period of rapid secularisation of sensibility let us beware of passivity and cuckoo thoughts, which can damage our imagination in hidden ways, off-stage so to speak. When people are changing their sense of God, their sense of humanity is also in transition, and in ways that can be not only trivialising but tragic and, especially so, if we do not reach worthy wavelengths to discern together these cultural transformations.

**Ireland, by comparison, seems frequently adolescent in its tone of discussing religious issues in the public arena. Surface points are scored while deeper issues seem neglected.**

Sean Kelly, Mary Coughlan TD, Prof Mike Cronin
and Micheál Ó Muircheartaigh

*Chapter 9*

# Gaelic Games and Cultural Identity

*The GAA – Reflecting All That is Good in Irish Culture*
SEAN KELLY
**Former President, GAA**

*Glamour, Masculinity, Nationhood and Amateurism*
PROF MIKE CRONIN
**Academic Director of Boston College and author of** *Sport and Nationalism in Ireland*

*The GAA and the National Cultural Identity*
MICHEÁL Ó MUIRCHEARTAIGH
**Writer and Broadcaster**

# Sean Kelly

## CEO, Irish Institute of Sport, former President, GAA

*Born in Kilcummin, Co. Kerry in 1952 and educated at Tralee CBS, St. Brendan's, Killarney, St. Patrick's College of Education, Dublin and UCD (B. Ed). Formerly a schoolteacher, he was sworn in as the 35th President of the GAA in April 2003 – the first Kerryman to hold the position. During his tenure as President, which ended in 2006, he oversaw the continuing development of Croke Park, the improvement in players' conditions and the introduction of rule changes and particularly Rule 42. He is credited with the successful conclusion of arrangements for the temporary use of Croke Park by the IRFU and the FAI and is seen as one of the most dynamic GAA leaders of modern times. In July, 2006 he was appointed CEO of the Irish Sports Institute.*

## The GAA – Reflecting All That is Good in Irish Culture

The GAA hasn't really changed its focus since it was founded. If you look at the aims of the association today, they are the exact same now as they were 122 years ago. It was founded basically to revive Irish games and pastimes and those are still the aims of the association. The latest edition of the rule book states that the association shall actively support all our major games and promote them, support the Irish language, support camogie and ladies football and support Irish industry. In other words, the GAA encompasses all aspects of culture in this country and the most successful clubs in particular look at themselves in a broad rather than a narrow way.

In the past, perhaps, clubs looked at themselves as a football club, or a hurling club, or a camogie club, or a ladies football club whereas nowadays they look at it in a much broader context. We are a cultural club within the parish taking in all aspects of Irish culture and trying to cater for them, and that is certainly the way we are trying to position our clubs into the future.

Now, 122 years on, where are we? Without a doubt, the health of the association has never been stronger and its activities never more popular. Its games have never had bigger attendances, there have never been more players playing and there have never been more games being played. Nor have we ever had so many facilities. The situation can be summarised thus: 80,000 members, 2,000 clubs, 300,000 players and, in the case of ladies' football, started a little over 30 years ago, it is going from strength to strength. Camogie is also doing quite well and both games, I think, are enjoying renewed

> **In other words, the GAA encompasses all aspects of culture in this country and the most successful clubs in particular look at themselves in a broad rather than a narrow way.**

popularity which is excellent. Just last Sunday, 82,000 people watched the Leinster final. The same will continue on to the quarter-finals, semi-finals and finals which will have the biggest attendance at any sporting events, not just in Europe but probably in the world. TV audiences last year watched 380 hours of live television, 86 games were covered at 17 different venues – all GAA venues – and 75 per cent of the population tuned in at some stage or other. Added to that, you have, as Micheal O Muircheartaigh has said, the extensive exposure in the newspapers and on radio and people like the great O'Muircheartaigh himself, with his melodious voice, carrying the games all the way around the world through the Internet and so on.

Economically, we have done very well with gate receipts probably at €25 million this year and commercial income between €10 and €12 million, maybe €15 million over the year. Certainly the GAA is, without any shadow of doubt, in really good health. You have to ask yourself why? Well the reason is quite obvious enough in the sense that, as Archbishop Croke said, at a time when English games and the English language were taking over, our games are racy of this soil. In other words, they were what we were meant to play and reflected what we were about. As far as the GAA is concerned, that is still the case. At local level, these are the games we like to play. They are good games, they are popular games, they are skilful games, they are passionate games. I suppose passion is very important. They generate loyalty and certainly they reflect all that is good in Irish culture. The voluntary effort is very significant because voluntary effort is what put the GAA there, the feature that has made it what it is in every club throughout the country and indeed abroad and we have about 450 clubs abroad. It is the voluntary effort, the pride that makes people say: this is our club, this is our parish, we want the best for our children, we are going to do it ourselves regardless of what we get from anyone else and we are going to do it well. When they have a club they want to win, win for the county, win for the country, win for themselves and they want to be able to boast about it. That is the pride you want in clubs, that is what makes them what they are.

The other thing is the voluntary effort and the amateur status it has given to the association which is, I think, vital. Everybody is equal and there are no real prima donnas in the GAA. The greatest players, the Gooches of this world, the Anthony Molloys, the Adrian Sweeneys, the D.J. Careys all go to work the following day. So, they are all equal, whether it's a player at inter-county level or at club level, and of course the inter-county players play at club level as well which is a fundamental element, I think, of what makes the games popular. The same is true of the administration. Whether they are at national level, county level, local or club level, they are all equal

> It is the voluntary effort, the pride that makes people say: this is our club, this is our parish, we want the best for our children, we are going to do it ourselves regardless of what we get from anyone else and we are going to do it well.

and there is nobody really saying that one person is more important than the other. This comes from the amateur status, it comes from the voluntary effort and that has made the association what it is today. Another thing which is important, I think, is that we have had no scandals and that is because the GAA has been transparent. It is one of the few bodies I know where, at the county AGM, the provincial council convention, the national congress, the full accounts are thrown open on the table and are given out. Every journalist can get a copy of them and they can write about them. Very few private businesses will do that. They may give you the profit and loss accounts but the actual details would not be given. I think that one of the reasons why the GAA is so respected is because it has nothing to hide. Everything is by and large above board. Occasionally, the odd person will do something untoward but, in general, there are good systems in place whereby things are accounted for. I think this is very important, because it creates confidence. People know that, when they are going through the gates, the money is being put to good use down along the line.

> I think that one of the reasons why the GAA is so respected is because it has nothing to hide. Everything is by and large above board.

The other thing we avoided is splits. We might have plenty of rows now and again but we haven't had splits. Brendan Behan once said that the first thing on the agenda of any organisation in Ireland when it is founded is what are we going to split about? The GAA went through a difficult time in the beginning and came through turbulent times, particularly at the time of the War of Independence and the Civil War, but it never split. In actual fact, it became a healthy bond rather than a dividing issue for people in this country. Of course, it all comes back to the honour and glory of the little village. That is what it is all about. Kickham said, and it is true of every single club in the country, that it is all about the honour and glory of the little village and then, of course, about the honour and pride of your country. An ESRI report was published by the Sports Council last year which looked at the whole issue of volunteerism in this country. They were amazed to find that by far and away the organisation with most support was the GAA. In fact, 42 per cent of all the people in this country who volunteer for anything do so for the GAA. In other words, almost 50 per cent of them are in the GAA and the other 50 per cent are divided up, between maybe 200 or 300 or perhaps many more other organisations in this country. So, it just shows you the drawing power of the organisation and the sense of commitment and it all comes back to what I said – the honour and glory of the village, the transparency, the honesty, I suppose, and of course the equality that comes from amateurism.

Michael Cronin mentioned in his paper that the GAA was willing to change. That is true but for the GAA change comes dropping slow, and that is not a bad thing. In other words, bans which were introduced probably to protect the association in the initial period, possibly outlived their usefulness by years.

The ban on foreign games, Rule 7, should probably have gone years and years before it went in 1971. The same is true of the ban on British forces, Rule 21, that took years before it was abandoned. In the South, it was gone probably 50 years ago but because the North was in a different situation, the Southern counties, and my own county in particular, said we are never going to support the abolition of it until we know the Northern counties are in favour of it as well. That was sensible. Rule 42, which was amended last year, was again a ground breaking decision for the association but, in time, I think it will be seen as a very wise decision and certainly I have found over the last 12 months that the goodwill factor towards the association has increased enormously since we decided to make Croke Park available for the Internationals on a temporary basis starting on 11 February next year. All of those developments have been important.

Now look at the games themselves and again how they were slow to change. The championship, for instance, for 100 years was a knock-out – one game and you were out. Then people began to question it and gradually we eventually changed, but we didn't change it over night. We brought in the "back door" just for the losing provincial finalists and then it got extended and it probably might be extended a bit further. Again, that is a sensible way to approach things rather than diving in, making mistakes and then trying to retrieve the situation afterwards.

Croke Park itself is probably the iconic cathedral of modern Ireland. It perhaps reflects all that is good about the Celtic Tiger in the sense that it is a symbol of what Ireland can achieve in the modern era. Again, looking at the support for Croke Park, we thought we would never be able to sell the boxes at €250,000 each but when we renewed the rents last year we had a waiting list of 20. The same is true of the premium seats: €10,000 for ten years, €6,500 for five years and we have a waiting list of about 500 or 600 people trying to get in. This, to a certain extent, probably reflects the wealth in the country but it is also due to the attractiveness of Croke Park as a venue. People want to be there. It is the place to be and it is probably the expression of Irish culture in the best possible way for an awful lot of people. Undoubtedly, with the global village that we have at the moment and so many outside influences which are good in themselves, Irish people at the same time want to be different as well. I think there is a return to supporting all things Irish and I suppose the GAA is probably the best example of that for a lot of people. That is why in some respects we are enjoying renewed popularity. Croke Park is generating big money and the gates and the players are putting in

*... I have found over the last 12 months that the goodwill factor towards the association has increased enormously since we decided to make Croke Park available for the Internationals ...*

bigger efforts. So where does all of this leave us as we go forward?

There are probably some storm clouds gathering. I think that a couple of the biggest challenges facing the association are at grass roots level, and the biggest challenge facing the association at grass roots level is the change in demographics in Ireland. Will clubs be able to cope, will they be able to keep that community identity with so many people moving in? I know that in my own little parish in Kilcummin, there were three houses in the village for 80 years but in the last four years, I suppose, 350 new houses have gone up there. That is a huge change and that is happening right throughout an awful lot of clubs and parishes. How is the GAA going to adapt to that? How are those people coming in going to feel part of the association? How is the organisation going to reach out and cater for them? It will mean for an awful lot of clubs, and it is happening already, expanding, getting new facilities, buying extra ground to cater for the players. We have a growing population with people playing a lot more, a lot more teams, which is a great thing. But with the price of land going up we see a lot of clubs for which the cost of land is going out of their reach. That is going to be a big problem for us as our population continues to grow – putting the infrastructure in place and, secondly, creating the leadership, because in every club in the past there had to be leadership that knitted it together and who gave their whole lives to the association. That will be needed more than ever into the future – people who are willing to give of their time for the club and bring other people in. As well as that, of course, you have the new immigrants coming in. They will have their own culture but they should be encouraged to experience our culture, and where better to do this than in the GAA. Again, it will be up to GAA clubs to open their arms and encourage people to come in, regardless of their background, regardless of religion. That is very obvious, particularly in the case of Northern Ireland. All those things are going to be important in the future as the GAA continues to grow. In other words, we will have to play the Irish card and play it well and, therefore, we'll have to be all embracing.

**We are professional in approach without a doubt but I think that if we were to go professional as an organisation, it would be the death knell of the association.**

The other thing which is going to be a big headache, I suppose, is how we are going to deal with the growing call for professionalism. We are professional in approach without a doubt but I think that if we were to go professional as an organisation, it would be the death knell of the Association. Against that, you cannot continue to say to players that they must train harder, reach higher standards, make more of a commitment and particularly more of a commitment in terms of pressure and expectation than was there in the past. Recently, I was talking to a former Kerry footballer who is a great friend of mine, Sean Walsh, who played full back in mid-field for

Kerry for a number of years. I said to him, "All of this talk about players training harder now than before isn't really true because I saw you training in the 70s and you trained as hard as anyone". His answer was, "yes, we did train as hard but the pressures weren't half as much as they are now". The microscope on players on television, in the media in general, in the pubs as well as the expectations are real pressure. If you read, for instance, Christy O'Connor's recently published book, *Last Man Standing*, you will see that the pressure which goal keepers are under, for example, is absolutely abominable, with the abuse they get. So, players will have to be taken care of and the big challenge for the GAA is to do it without actually breaching the professionalism and not dividing the club and the county. That is the real connection for the GAA. It is not professionalism as such. It is actually breaking the connection between club and county, because if you go professional at inter-county level then it is inevitable that the clubs will have to follow suit. Then it is inevitable that a transfer system is going to come into being and it is inevitable that loyalty goes out the door. In professionalism it's money that takes over, it's business that is going to be the bottom line and we have to guard against that. At the same time, I think, there is plenty of room to manoeuvre, ways to cater for players, to sit down with them and discuss things with them because, from my experience with them, players are very reasonable. They don't want to be professional as such, but they want to be treated properly. Obviously, they see the cake getting bigger and particularly now, when Croke Park is no longer a millstone around our necks like it was going to be when I took over as President. At that time, we were looking at a debt of €100 million. Now, it is a very manageable debt of about €25 million and there is no point in pretending otherwise. So, we have to come up with a system whereby the players at inter-county level, who are being pressurised, who are producing the performances, who are the reason for the big gates, are going to feel that they are rewarded in some way and respected without breaching the amateur status. That's the challenge for us, and I think that it can be done because, once you give players due recognition, they will be happy and I think that, as I said, there are plenty of ways in which to do this.

So, in essence the challenge for us will be to maintain our cultural identity, because at the end of the day we are what I would call *the* cultural body in Ireland. We have preserved, better than possibly anybody else, the basic aspects of our culture. It all comes down to grass roots level and that's what makes the GAA and that's what will sustain it.

> ... we have to come up with a system whereby the players at inter-county level, who are being pressurised, who are producing the performances, who are the reason for the big gates, are going to feel that they are rewarded in some way and respected without breaching the amateur status.

# Prof Mike Cronin

Academic Director for Irish Programmes at Boston College

*Author of* Sport and Nationalism in Ireland: Gaelic Games, Soccer and National Identity since 1884 *(1999),* Wearing the Green: A History of St. Patrick's Day *(with Daryl Adair (2002), and, as editor with John Bale,* Sport and Postcolonialism *(2003). He has written extensively on the history and relevance of sport in Ireland and is currently working on a history of major state spectacles staged in Ireland since Independence.*

## Glamour, Masculinity, Nationhood and Amateurism

The "GAA man" was intimately connected with the ideologies of masculinity that propelled both empires and revolutionary national movements.

The GAA has prided itself, ever since its foundation in 1884, on the value of its games as ones that produce strong and skilful men who are imbued, by virtue of playing the game, with the associated positive values of team spirit, fair conduct and acceptance of the rules. However, this mode of masculinity as a viable ideal has been in crisis recently. This is in part due to an increasing disregard for the rules that regulated and channeled on-pitch aggression as reported in the press in recent years. These reports told of on-field violence and occasional events off-field, namely the previously hidden problems of alcohol and sexual abuse in team sports.[1] These events were evidence of the displacement of the mode of masculinity that underwrites the GAA's constitution in recent articulations of national success. The GAA was founded at a time of nascent nationalism and the breakdown of empire across Europe. The "GAA man" was intimately connected with the ideologies of masculinity that propelled both empires and revolutionary national movements. Both needed men to volunteer for frontline activity and they invested heavily in an ideology of masculinity in which a "man" was one who was prepared to sacrifice himself for, be disciplined for, and submit to the greater good, for the glory of something else.[2]

### The GAA and Contemporary Irish Society

The GAA was founded, in 1884, at a time of massive social and political change in Ireland.[3] Its existence, although part of a wider European and American organisation of sport along modern lines, owed much to the spirit of the cultural revival.[4] However, while other organisations of the revival, such as the Gaelic League, failed to flourish and remain at the centre of Irish life in the long term, the GAA has remained a staple feature of community life across the island since the late nineteenth century. Due to its connections with the cultural revival, the close connection of many of its members with the forces of advanced nationalism and its ban on foreign games, the GAA can be seen as an unchanging, irredentist force speaking for and representing a particular brand of Irish nationalism.[5] While these associations do much to explain the early success of the GAA, the Association itself has always been a consummately able marketing machine, and thanks to its efforts, the GAA club became, and remains, an essential part of Irish community life. The appeal of the spectacle of highly skilled players competing ensured its popularity but, more importantly, its organisation around the parish system powerfully ensured that it would become part of the daily fabric at the heart of small communities. Gaelic games became a national passion: a performance of what it is to be from "your" parish or county, and thus, by extension, what it means to be Irish.

This sense of national cohesion was reinforced by the GAA's willingness to use and be used by a range of media. When the fledgling national radio station, 2RN, was seeking to appeal to listeners it started broadcasting major hurling and football games.[6] The same was true in the 1960s of RTE's television coverage: GAA games were the first sports it covered. By using the new forms of mass media (a process that was reinforced by high levels of coverage in the print media), the GAA reinforced its place at the heart of Irish life.[7] Through radio and television, and the legendary commentary of Micheál Ó Hehir and Micheál Ó Muireachtaigh, the GAA traveled directly from the field of play at Croke Park, Semple Stadium or Casement Park, into homes and pubs across the land. It transformed the localised space of Ireland's native games, which were essentially rural pursuits, into the modern spectacle of mass media sport that bound together the all-important imagined national community.[8] Because of this mediation from the local to the national, the GAA ensured continued support, based on parochial local rivalries and attachment to counties of origin for those who had migrated to cities. Except for the Catholic Church, and perhaps Fianna Fáil, no single Irish organisation had a relationship with its community of followers and supporters that inspired such loyalty. The imagined "organisicm" that bound country and city, parish and nation, is reinforced by the renewing of ties with the games every spring, when supporters and players alike looked forward with hope to glory in September.

The patterns of community life as well as the institutions with which the GAA were associated underwent considerable change in the later decades of the twentieth century and the early years of the twenty-first, when many of the institutions and morally central bodies on which the Irish nation-state was founded entered periods of sustained crisis.[9] How has the GAA not only survived, but prospered, when many of its core values and practices were associated with bodies and groups that had fallen far out of flavour, and when what it seemed to represent was increasingly considered retrogressive and irrelevant in the new (post-modern) Ireland? The exposure of institutional and sexual abuse significantly reduced the power and moral authority of the Catholic Church in Ireland and the central dominance of Fianna Fáil in the nation's political life has been undermined by the methods of modern politics and media coverage (as well as the intrusions of successive tribunals). Whilst other stalwarts of Irish national life have been partially undone by the media, the GAA has prospered from its associations with the same. A comparison of older footage of the GAA with more recent footage shows how it has managed to embody whatever it is the nation needs. Old footage of GAA matches in the 1960s and 1970s often features the old guard of De Valera or McQuaid in the stand, a stadium that is old-fashioned with pitch-side and programme advertisements for agricultural products and machinery. Equally, modern coverage of an all-Ireland final, at the refurbished Croke Park, shows brash, self-confident and, above all, successful GAA supporters enjoying pre-match drinks and food in corporate boxes, pitch-side advertising that speaks of a global economy and a general sense of affluence demonstrating the spirit of Celtic Tiger Ireland. The cyclical patterning of the season, with its organicist metaphors and language and tied so cleverly to the rites of spring and harvest, reveals a capacity for re-branding that has enabled the association to repackage itself for a nation of ideology-scarified post-nationalists.

**The GAA was faced with the challenge of retaining the support, hearts and minds of its young players, who were being tempted by the attractions of highly paid and very visible soccer stars, and by the dream of playing in the green shirt of Ireland rather than in the colours of the home county.**

The GAA administration was galvanized into action by, amongst other things, the success of the Irish soccer team in the early 1990s. It had to be able to compete with the spectre of a glamorous, massively exposed and successful sport. The GAA was faced with the challenge of retaining the support, hearts and minds of its young players, who were being tempted by the attractions of highly paid and very visible soccer stars, and by the dream of playing in the green shirt of Ireland rather than in the colours of the home county. Poor quality stadiums, lacklustre marketing and technologically staid media coverage with poor presentation qualities also beset it, like many other sports in Europe at the time. While soccer was being transformed by the money, modern technologies, multiple camera angles and high quality production values of satellite television companies, the GAA was stuck with the dated production values of RTÉ (fixed camera angles, little pre- and post-match analysis and no real sense of occasion and excitement). As well as this, the Association's own constitution was proving to be a problem as rules 21 and 42 were increasingly viewed by a European and integrationist Ireland as unnecessarily exclusionary and as an embodiment of a backward-looking nationalism that depended on an oppositional and insular articulation of Irishness. The former banned all security forces in the North from taking parts in the games, while the latter kept GAA facilities closed to foreign games.

The GAA secured money from central government to modernise Croke Park, making it one of the best sports stadiums anywhere in Europe. RTE's coverage of the games was improved to the level of that associated with soccer, and extra television exposure of the League and women's games by TG4 introduced an element of competition to the market that was much needed and kept standards improving. After a carefully managed process, Rules 21 and 42 were removed from the rulebook.[10] While hotly debated within the GAA, the changes to the rules were widely applauded by commentators, politicians and other sporting organisations.[11] The GAA's proactive approach ensured that the games didn't lose their base and it actually led to a renewed and ever growing enthusiasm for hurling and Gaelic football which made them more popular than any other sport in the country. In 2004, the GAA dominated attendance figures at sporting events taking 57 per cent of the total sports audience. Of the 400,000 people in Ireland who took a voluntary role in sport that year, 40 per cent of them took part in Gaelic games.[12]

As a result of modernisation, the GAA continued to prosper as something that functioned as a safe repository for a traditional, yet largely uncontroversial, Irishness. This in turn was what made the GAA so attractive to sponsors. Thus, despite the changes to the rulebook that threatened the integrity of the playing field, and thus the national space, by moving into the simulated space of televisual land it has kept alive the spirit of national identity that has been so important to its success since the late nineteenth century. Retaining the amateur system allowed them to recast the ideal GAA man as the opposite of the foreign-identified metrosexual. It allowed the integration of an Irish identity with domestic products, as opposed to a society and a marketplace that often felt saturated by global forces and foreign goods.[13] By re-presenting and refashioning the games of the GAA, the sponsors were able to offer a depiction of a tradition of the games that spoke, in a post-modern fashion, to a culture that was refashioning its history as well as itself. As with national products and identity processes in other economies, the link between the GAA – as a repository of national character – and its corporate sponsors, "displays a type of national sentiment".

By using famous athletes or celebrities, advertisers believe that they will be able to influence consumer behaviour. This is due to the belief "that celebrities can enhance the audience perceptions of the product in terms of image and performance".[14] The function of sports-related advertisement is when "athlete endorsers are expected to accomplish a number of objectives, including: capture the attention of the product, give the message credibility, increase product attractiveness, increase liking and recall of the ad, and increase the likelihood of purchase".[15] In the GAA, however, all the "superstars" are actually amateurs, and actual players have rarely appeared centre stage in the campaigns of the Bank of Ireland, Guinness or Vodafone. So, unlike "foreign sports" which privilege their "superstars", the GAA (which undoubtedly has its superstars) gives primacy to the game rather than the individual, by the dominant practice of omitting named or instantly recognised players or places in advertisements associated with it. This use of the nameless and placeless and its eschewing of the national and the international stage ironically means that it becomes a signifier of a nationalism that is as available to the diaspora as well as those living on the island, and can be exported along with Guinness as a marker of Irish identity to other countries. By emphasising the team and not the individual, consumer and player alike are asked to sublimate their selves in the cause of the "greater good, the greater glory", and thus the game, despite using the operations of international corporate sponsorship and media, becomes more emphatically a repository of an Irishness predicated on a communitarian anti-globalisation, built like the nation's foundational definition of Irishness on what it's not, on an essential anti-foreignness.

All of the advertisements discussed here build on the viewer's common social knowledge, and invite them into a preconstructed world – which is built around Gaelic games – that is Irish, communitarian and positive. Once it is accepted that these are the values of the games, the same value judgment can be made of the products themselves.

Bank of Ireland began its sponsorship of Gaelic football in 1994 with a four-year campaign entitled "Answer the Call", which focused on the bravery of supporters in following their team. While moderately successful, feedback on the campaign made it clear that the partnership between the GAA and the Bank was not fully recognised by the public. In 1998, a decision was made to switch the direction of the campaign under the guidance of advertising agency McCann Erickson. The aim of the campaign was to suggest that the GAA, and by extension the Bank of Ireland, were central to Irish life. McCann Erickson's research into the mindset of the GAA supporter

*... the game, despite using the operations of international corporate sponsorship and media, becomes more emphatically a repository of an Irishness predicated on a communitarian anti-globalisation, built like the nation's foundational definition of Irishness, on what it's not, on an essential anti-foreignness.*

revealed that love of the game and the county drove the supporter, and not necessarily a belief that their county was actually good enough to lift the Sam Maguire trophy. The report concluded:

> The insight was that the games meant that they [the supporters] had a chance to express their local identity. It was less about the winning and more about the taking part. By focusing on each fan's love and passion for their county of birth, we [McCann Erickson] included every GAA fan in the county regardless of how good their team was.[16]

The result was a campaign, launched in 1997, titled "Ask". The campaign won industry awards in Ireland and the United States, as well as the prestigious Silver Shark at the Kinsale International Advertising Festival. The campaign was brilliantly simple. It reminded GAA supporters of their allegiance to county, and showed that support for the team was woven into the fabric of daily living and was not confined to Sunday afternoons on the side of a pitch. The central point of "Ask" was that it recognised that fans could make no demands on their team. The key issue was what they could do for their county to show their love and support for their home place. This is in marked contrast to the "Answer the Call" campaign, which had demanded a fealty from the consumer along the lines of old-style volunteerism. "Ask" inverted this relationship, recasting love for a cause, dedication to the greater glory as a passionate choice, and not a duty. The consumer was constructed via the images of the supporter as giving their loyalty through choice, in a world full of choices, rather than inheriting the unmediated political values of the "old Ireland" of the preceding generation.

The campaign was brilliantly simple. It reminded GAA supporters of their allegiance to county, and showed that support for the team was woven into the fabric of daily living and was not confined to Sunday afternoons on the side of a pitch.

The various campaigns promoting the renamed Guinness Hurling Championship have been highly successful. In 1994, aggregate attendance figures for the hurling championship were 289,281. This figure had risen to 543,335 by 1999 and over 600,000 by 2005. The number of active players grew by 50 per cent in the first five years of the campaign, and the number of live games shown by RTE increased dramatically. In 1993, only three championship matches were broadcast live, but by 2005 that figure had risen to 14.[17] The sponsorship campaign was worth €5 million to the GAA in the first five years, and Guinness invested a further €10 million in supporting the game at the grass roots level, including €3,000 hurling scholarships for players attending the University of Limerick, University College Cork and University College Dublin. The most successful and identifiable advertisement promoting the Guinness connection with hurling, although not specifically connected with promoting the championship, was titled "Free In". Although the campaign was the subject of a complaint to the Advertising Standards

Authority for Ireland because a viewer felt that it equated sporting success with the consumption of alcohol, the advertisement was a huge success.[18] Like the Bank of Ireland campaign, the Guinness advertisement relied on the relationship between sport and the local. The game as depicted was not played in one of the main stadiums, but could have been any local match anywhere in the country. Likewise, the player's imaginary celebration is not national acclaim played out in front of mass media attention, but a homecoming to the congratulations of locals in a parish bar, a grounded return to origin. At the heart of "Free In" was a recognition of the local, authentic and ancestral values of Irishness, that is, a set of values which were to be revered as somehow being at the heart of what it is to be Irish.

The Vodafone campaign, like those of the Bank of Ireland and Guinness, linked the passion of the players with that of the supporters. Most importantly, in the context of the amateur status of the GAA, the campaign reinforced the fact that the stars of the game were not spending the cold, wet and windy months of preparation before the championship matches cosseted and pampered like the million pound stars of soccer, but were simply playing, in difficult circumstances, for the love of the game and home, the hope of success. The final line of the Vodafone advertisement implied that players had no choice to do what they did (because the force of the GAA is stronger even than DNA). Equally, the Bank of Ireland advertisement demonstrated that the Irish, whether player or county fan, are born into the GAA and have no choices of who to follow. The multinational emphasis on ancestral Irishness ("DNA") is in stark contrast to the "Irish" sponsors, who instead employed international signifiers of playful choice ("Ask") and open boundaries ("Free In") in a global market of sports. What they all had in common was the rejection of "outsider" masculinity and an appeal to a national identity that is above all male, white and physically able. It may not be for the glamour, but it's still for the glory.

*... the Guinness advertisement relied on the relationship between sport and the local. The game as depicted was not played in one of the main stadia, but could have been any local match anywhere in the country.*

## Endnotes

[1] For example, see conviction of Offaly footballer for onfield violence, *The Kingdom*, 10 November 2005; the high profile trial that led to the acquittal of Kerry footballer Declan Quill on sexual assault charges on the evening of an All-Ireland semi-final, *Examiner*, 11 August 2002; and the GAA's own investigation into the problems of the drink culture within the game, Gaelic Athletic Association, *A Report by the GAA Task Force into Alcohol and Substance Abuse*, GAA, Dublin: 2004.

[2] The embrace of masculinity through sport has been a common feature of diverse ideological and political movements. See J.A. Mangan (ed.), *Shaping the Superman: Fascist Body as Political Icon - Aryan Fascism*, Frank Cass, London, 1999; Clifford Putney, *Muscular Christianity: Manhood*

*and Sports in Protestant America, 1880-1920*, Harvard University Press, Harvard, 2003; and Pierre Arnaud and Jim Riordan (eds.), *Sport and International Politics: The Impact of Fascism and Communism on Sport*, Spon, London, 1998.

[3] For a history of the GAA see Mike Cronin, *Sport and Nationalism in Ireland: Gaelic Games, Soccer and National Identity Since 1884*, Dublin, Four Courts, 1999, and Marcus de Burca, *The GAA: A History*, Dublin: Gill and Macmillan, 2000.

[4] For a general understanding of the birth of modern sport and the associated processes see Neil Tranter, *Sport, Economy and Society in Britain, 1750-1914*, Cambridge, Cambridge University Press, 1998, and for the link between sport and the period of the cultural revival see Tom Hunt, *The Development of Sport in County Westmeath, 1850-1905*, unpublished PhD thesis, De Montfort University, 2004.

[5] For a critical engagement with the nationalist history of the GAA see Mike Cronin, "An Historical Identity: Historians and the Making of Irish Nationalist Identity in the Gaelic Athletic Association" in *Football Studies*, 1, 2, 1998: 89-102.

[6] See Raymond Boyle, "From our Gaelic Fields: Radio, Sport and Nation in Post-Partition Ireland" in *Media, Culture and Society*, 14, 1992: 623-36.

[7] For the early relationship between the GAA and the print media see Paul Rouse, "Sport and Ireland in 1881" in Alan Bairner (ed.), *Sport and the Irish: Histories, Identities, Issues*, Dublin, University College Dublin Press, 2003.

[8] For the idea of the imagined community, see Benedict Anderson, *Imagined Communities: Reflections on the Origin and Spread of Nationalism*, London, Verso, 1991, and for a sporting application, see Joseph Maguire, Grant Jarvie, Louise Mansfield and Joe Bradley, *Sports Worlds: A Sociological Perspective*, Human Kinetics, Champaign, Illinois, 2002.

[9] For a review of these issues see Luke Gibbons, Peadar Kirby and Michael Cronin, *Reinventing Ireland: Culture, Society and the Global Economy*, London, Pluto Press, 2002.

[10] For the history of the Rule 21 debate see David Hassan, "The Gaelic Athletic Association, Rule 21 and Police Reform in Northern Ireland" in *Journal of Sport and Social Issues*, 29, 1, 2005: 60-78.

[11] For example, see extensive coverage on the decision to open Croke Park to soccer and rugby, *Irish Times*, 18 January 2006.

[12] "Time is ripe for GAA to make serious money", *Sunday Times*, 6 November 2005.

[13] This is an adaption of arguments made in the context of Chinese nationalism. Dai Jinhua, "Behind Global Spectacle and National Image Making" in *Positions*, 9, 1, 2001: 165.

[14] Chris Kambitsis, Yvonne Harahousou, Nicholas Theodorakis and Giannis Chatzibeis, "Sports advertising in print media: The case of the

2000 Olympic Games" in *Corporate Communications: An International Journal,* 7, 3, 2002: 156.

[15] James H Martin, "Is the athlete's sport important when picking an athlete to endorse a nonsport product", in *Journal of Consumer Marketing,* 13, 6, 1996: 28.

[16] Institute of Advertising Practitioners in Ireland, *ADFX,* 3, 2000: 73-9.

[17] Figures taken from "Sponsorship: A successful partnership between the GAA and Guinness", www.business2000.ie/cases/cases/cases413.htm.

[18] There is now a serious debate within the GAA over whether it can continue its relationship with Guinness given the Association's commitment to promoting youth sport. For a coverage of the debate see Richard Gillis, "Last Orders" in *Sports Business,* August 2004: 12-14.

# Micheál Ó Muircheartaigh

## Writer and Broadcaster

*Born in 1930 in An Daingean, Co. Kerry. A native Irish speaker, formerly a teacher. Began commentating on games in his late teens. Came to prominence after the All-Ireland Senior Football Football Championship Final in New York in 1947. For a number of years commentated on Minor GAA matches in the Irish language and in the early 80s became a full-time commentator with RTÉ, eventually succeeding the legendary Micheal O Hehir. In 2004, he published his autobiography,* From Dún Sion to Croke Park *and in 2006* From Borroloola to Mangerton.

## The GAA and the National Cultural Identity

Whatever organisation was to develop from the now famous meeting that took place in Hayes's Hotel in Thurles on 1 November 1884 was destined to be committed to the preservation of sports that were deemed to be part of the Irish identity.

We gather that much from the letter sent out on 27 October of the same year. It was signed by Michael Cusack and Maurice Davin and invited people to a meeting "to take steps for the formation of a Gaelic Athletic Association for the preservation and cultivation of the national pastimes and for proposed amusements for the Irish people during their leisure hours".

The attendance at the meeting was sparse in the extreme, seven in all, but the GAA was founded and the first step taken in the greatest social revolution Ireland has ever known.

In essence it was a call to the people of Ireland to stop and ponder on what was in danger of being lost of the Irish way of life, a way that had kept the hope alive that Ireland would one day, in the words of the Knocknagoshel Parnellite Banner, "take her place among the nations of the earth".

I do not intend to trace the development of the GAA into the sporting megalith it is today but rather to pick some of its actions over the years that demonstrated its willingness to be part of the cultural identity of the country. Less than three years after the foundation in Thurles, the notion of holding All-Ireland championships in hurling and football was given the go ahead by an association that had no physical assets by way of grounds and little knowledge of the logistics of organising such an undertaking.

But it had one invaluable asset – the goodwill and respect of the people generally on account of its acting to try and save some of the good of the past. The new term "All-Ireland championships" in

> ... it was a call to the people of Ireland to stop and ponder on what was in danger of being lost of the Irish way of life, a way that had kept the hope alive that Ireland would one day, in the words of the Knocknagoshel Parnellite Banner, "take her place among the nations of the earth".

hurling and football had a wholesome ring to it that made ordinary people feel good about themselves. Hitherto hurling and football were never included in sports programmes and thus the inauguration of All-Ireland championships for basically Irish sports was a major advance and a platform for the identity the GAA wished to promulgate.

Lord De Frenche placed his estate at Elm Park, in Dublin's Merrion district, at their disposal for the playing of the opening matches and saw fit to attend. Not alone was he impressed by the quality of the games he witnessed, he went further and invited Limerick's captain, Malachi O'Brien, to dinner with himself and Lady De Frenche, thus making the Commercials player the recipient of the first ever "Man of the Match" award. Of course there were hitches. Some teams that entered failed to show but, eventually by the early months of 1888, the first All-Ireland champions had been crowned, Tipperary in hurling and Limerick in football.

**Some teams that entered failed to show but eventually by the early months of 1888, the first All-Ireland champions had been crowned, Tipperary in hurling and Limerick in football.**

Bíonn gach tosnú lag adeirtear. Only five teams took part in the hurling and eight in football and there was no representation from Ulster. But the vehicle for a cultural identity for Irish people was now there and a glance back at recent events highlights how it has been nurtured in the meantime. The attendance of 82,000 at the Leinster football championship final in Croke Park this year constituted the largest crowd watching any sporting fixture the world over that day, and both McHale Park in Castlebar and Páirc Uí Chaoimh in Cork added another 60,000.

The remainder of 1888 was more extraordinary still. Kilkenny had won the Leinster double of hurling and football on the road towards the second All-Ireland, Cork and Clare were through to the Munster hurling final and Tipperary were Munster champions in football, when a decision was taken to abandon all and instead go on a promotional tour of hurling and athletics to the USA.

Athletics were part of the GAA brief at the time and hurling was a distinctively traditional Irish pastime boasting a long lineage so it was thought that the proposed tour would show the sporting world that Ireland did have a cultural heritage of its own, and America really was Ireland's world in the closing years of the nineteenth century. The tour was called the American Invasion, a new type of invasion – a Cultural Invasion.

There are historians "go leor" present here in Glenties this week and they would be able to confirm that many invasions go wrong and it was the same with our one of 1888. But we cannot but admire the idealism of those who conjured the notion even if it was only giving credence to the old proverb "Mura bhfuil agat ach Pocán Gabhair bí i Lár an Aonaigh leis"– even if you have only a puck goat for sale be in the middle of the fair.

They were certainly in the middle of the fair in the proceedings before departure to the USA and could teach the modern association a fair bit about promotion of their wares. A group of a little over fifty was chosen, divided almost equally between athletes and hurlers, and they met in Dublin for kitting out about six days before departure. The organisers were conscious of the need to promote the national identity and the first step was a march down Dame Street in Dublin and on to O'Connell Street, headed by bands, before journeying to Donnybrook where exhibitions of hurling and athletics were given in the early afternoon. This was a high profile and very visible demonstration of an infant identity that was novel to the Dublin of 1888. The same exercise was repeated in Dún Laoghaire, then known as Kingstown, in the late afternoon but I see significance in the fact that the promotional tour was extended far outside of Dublin. There were no cars in those days so it was a train journey to Dundalk on the following day for more exhibitions, to Tullamore next, then Kilkenny.

As the founding place of the Association four years earlier, Thurles held an honoured place on the itinerary and a decision to undertake the Kilkenny/Thurles section by means of horses and sidecars added to the promotional value and aspect.

Cork was the last stop before boarding a liner at Queenstown and the invasion was then truly underway. They were met by a massive welcoming crowd on the shores of America but in many ways that was the highlight. An American presidential election campaign was in progress, there was a split in local athletics and the tour ended in financial losses. The GAA still had no financial assets but Michael Davitt, founder of the Land League and one of the Patrons of the GAA, cleared the debts by way of a loan. He never asked for repayment and it was fitting that the GAA contributed greatly to the creation of a museum in his honour years later in his native place of Stráid, Co. Mhaigh Eo.

Though the American venture failed to have the desired impact, nevertheless it succeeded in highlighting at home at least that the new organisation wished to be perceived as one that was placing the preservation and cultivation of the sporting aspects of Irish culture at the forefront and that they were anxious to spread the gospel, at least as far as sport was concerned.

The founding of Conradh na Gaeilge or the Gaelic League in 1893 was the next event that had significance for the GAA. Its objective was to take steps to preserve the Irish language and increase its usage among the public. From the start, this was looked upon by the GAA as a kindred organisation and a great number of people became active in both movements. The language was seen as another wing of the cultural identity and many GAA meetings of Central Council

**The founding of Conradh na Gaeilge or the Gaelic League in 1893 was the next event that had significance for the GAA. Its objective was to take steps to preserve the Irish language and increase its usage among the public.**

and provincial councils and other executive bodies were conducted through the medium of Irish.

It was the same with the emergence of the Sinn Féin movement in the early years of the 1900s, and the principle of nurturing an indigenous Irish industry was one that appealed specially to GAA and Conradh na Gaeilge members alike. Again, there was the phenomenon of widespread common membership in keeping with the GAA's tenet of supporting Irish identity in as many fields as possible, almost like a crusade.

I got an excellent indication of this from a former Dublin Gaelic player, Frank Burke, who has the distinction of being one of the fifteen who have won All-Ireland titles in both hurling and football. All in all, he played in five All-Ireland football finals and four in hurling between 1917 and 1924, winning three in football and two in hurling.

But for me, the most interesting feature of the Kildare-born man's life was his devotion to the furtherance of Irish cultural identity. He enjoyed a long life well into his 90s and I had the privilege of meeting him on several occasions but can never recall him speaking other than through the medium of the Irish language.

The family moved to Rathfarnham in Dublin while he was young and he was sent as a boarder to the Diocesan College of Knockbeg, Co. Carlow in the early 1900s. He was very keen on sports, hurling in particular, and brought his hurley with him when enrolling in Knockbeg. He never forgot the shock it was to him to be informed solemnly that cricket was the game of the school and that there was to be no accommodation for hurling.

There was no such thing as student power in those days and he survived by keeping the rules in vogue at the College but did manage to get a few pucks with his camán on odd occasions.

Then, by pure chance, when walking in Rathfarnham during the summer holidays that followed his first year in Knockbeg, he happened to read a notice in a shop window advertising Padraig Pearse's new school, Scoil Éanna, nearby. It appealed to him, principally because it stated at the end: "Hurling is the game of this school". He went forthwith to his mother and informed her that he did not intend to return to Knockbeg but was going to the hurling school instead.

He did so, went from there to University College Dublin and returned as a teacher to a school that was immersed in Irish cultural identity, language, games, music and dance. It led him in time to be side by side with Pearse and plenty more from Scoil Éanna in the GPO in 1916, and later to be the player marking Michael Hogan of Grangemockler when the Tipperary player was shot dead in Croke

Again, there was the phenomenon of widespread common membership in keeping with the GAA's tenet of supporting Irish identity in as many fields as possible, almost like a crusade.

Park on Bloody Sunday 1921 during a football match between the counties.

It is not for me to elaborate on those troubled times but I merely give Frank Burke as an example of many more like him in the GAA who saw real relevance for Ireland's future in re-establishing the cultural traditions that had survived but were in danger of being lost.

I thought of Frank when attending the final of the All-Ireland Colleges Football Championship of 2005 when Knockbeg claimed the title for the first time.

I now move on to the founding of Ireland's first Radio station, 2RN, in January 1926. Being run by the Department of Posts and Telegraphs it is understandable that it would have an Irish ethos and the choice of Douglas Hyde as the first person to speak from the station gave substance to the desire that it be seen as sort of custodian of the country's heritage. The man who became President of Ireland thirteen years later spoke "as Gaeilge".

It was taken a step further in the month of August the same year when an t-Uasal Ó hEigeartaigh, representing the infant 2RN, arrived in Croke Park in an excited state about a novel idea he wished the GAA to consider. His idea looks ridiculously simple now but it was revolutionary in the ambience of 1926. He suggested that 2RN had equipment that would make it possible to relay news of the All-Ireland hurling semi-final between Kilkenny and Galway, scheduled for Croke Park on the following Sunday, by means of a special transmission.

I say it was revolutionary because the art of sports broadcasting was unknown in the sporting world at the time, though it transpired later that ninety seconds of a sports meeting had been relayed in America some time earlier and that some part of a yacht race in Kingstown harbour had received some coverage through Marconi in the early years of the century.

At any rate it is interesting that it was to the GAA that 2RN went to inaugurate this new service for listeners in 1926, and it is certain that the reason was that it was seen as an organisation that was always anxious to promote the national cultural identity, as was the new national radio service.

The GAA acceded to Ó hEigeartaigh's request on that day in 1926 and it is fitting that the massive industry which sports broadcasting is today first saw the light of day to the accompaniment of the sound of the clash of the ash and the flashing camáns of Kilkenny and Galway on 29 August 1926.

It was big business the world over by the time RTE television came on the air in 1962. There was a culture developing in many

*... it is interesting that it was to the GAA that 2RN went to inaugurate this new service for listeners in 1926 and it is certain that the reason was that it was seen as an organisation that was always anxious to promote the national cultural identity, as was the new national radio service.*

counties at the time that live transmissions of sport on television would have a detrimental effect on attendances. Of course, RTE was anxious to include sport in its programming but the GAA was alone in permitting live transmissions from the start. Greater exposure for the national games was the primary consideration but it had wider implications for the cultural movement because the GAA insisted that fifty per cent of commentary would be through the medium of the Irish language. That is still the case with the semi-finals and finals of the All-Ireland championships when the commentary on the minor games is "tré mheán na Gaeilge". RTÉ now pay GAA for the broadcasting rights but in the early years only a nominal fee of ten pounds annually was required.

**RTE now pay GAA for the broadcasting rights but in the early years only a nominal fee of ten pounds annually was required.**

While the promotion of the games is the GAA's core business there has always been strong support there for the Irish language and other elements of Irish identity. There is an officer in Croke Park dealing with the Irish language and the GAA supplies well over a thousand scholarships a year for young people to courses in the different Gaeltachtaí. This is administered through clubs, county boards and the provincial councils and is perceived as a very effective means of promoting the language. There is a thriving annual football competition also between Gaeltacht teams, Comórtas Peile Na Gaeltachta, that has now been staged for over thirty years in conjunction with blanket coverage "as Gaeilge" from Radio na Gaeltachta and TG4. There is also a strong link between the GAA and the many sessions Comhaltas Ceoltóirí Éireann organise throughout the country.

I will finish with something brought to my notice in faraway Sydney and for me it highlighted the importance the young people of today attach to cultural identity.

A priest from one of the churches in that city got an idea one day to place a notice in one of the local Irish papers or journals inviting the young Irish on a year's break in that country to consider coming to mass on a given Sunday wearing their county colours. He was not prepared for the response. They came in massive numbers – the green and gold of Kerry, Donegal, Meath and Leitrim, the blood and bandage of Cork, the orange of Armagh and all combinations that go to make up the flavours of club, county and country.

Apparently, it was simply amazing and they lingered afterwards, talking, swapping stories, exchanging jerseys, young men and women with an unswerving love of their heritage and proud of a chance to display it – a wonderful generation and I would add that the GAA has played its part in bringing that about since the time of that fortunate meeting in Hayes's Hotel in Thurles 122 years ago.

Audience on a hot day

Martin Mansergh in discussion with Sinn Féin

Fr. Dermot McCarthy, Emily Logan and John Lonergan

John Waters, Robert Ballagh and Mary Cloake

*Chapter 10*

# The Irish Imagination

*Irishness in Art is Difficult to Define*
ROBERT BALLAGH
**Artist and Designer**

*The Role of the Arts in Defining Our Cultural Identity*
MARY CLOAKE
**Director of the Arts Council**

*Autobiography – The Ethical Difficulties*
JOHN WATERS
**Writer and Broadcaster**

# Robert Ballagh

## Artist and Designer

*Born 1943 in Dublin. Studied architecture at Bolton St. Technical College. Worked as an engineering draughtsman, a postman and a musician (guitarist with the Chessmen) before taking up painting in 1967. Represented Ireland at the Paris Biennale in 1969. His paintings are held in collections in Ireland and abroad including the National Gallery of Ireland, the Ulster Museum, the Hugh Lane Municipal Gallery and the Albrecht Durer House, Nuremberg. As a designer, has been involved in major projects including designing stamps for An Post, and the final series of Irish banknotes before the introduction of the euro. His stage design includes sets for productions of Beckett's work at the Gate Theatre and for the show* Riverdance.

## Irishness in Art is Difficult to Define

Iwould like to discuss the topic "The Irish Imagination" from the perspective of the visual arts. In 1971 an important exhibition of Irish art with the title "The Irish Imagination" was held in Dublin. It was curated by the artist Brian O'Doherty and he made an interesting statement in one of the essays in the catalogue. "Irish artists occupy the gate lodge to the literary Big House, listening to the heavy traffic up and down the driveway." This pithy remark seemed to confirm the oft-expressed view that, compared to our rich literary tradition, the visual arts in Ireland have remained almost invisible. Of course the reality is much more complex.

I suppose the last time that visual representation was not only dominant but also accepted as expressing a truly Irish characteristic was during the golden age of Gaelic culture. Here I speak of the production of illuminated manuscripts, high crosses and round towers. However, this so-called golden age was brought to an end by the arrival of the Vikings and the succeeding centuries produced a complicated history with divided allegiances. Fundamentally, an independent Ireland was always seen as a threat to England's defence. This meant that Ireland never enjoyed a period of peace or even the dubious benefit of a conquering monarch who could unify the people and create the conditions for cultural development. After the Battle of the Boyne in 1690 a new social structure emerged. The old Catholic aristocracy was replaced by a Protestant one and a new middle class emerged composed of settlers from outside. Many of these settlers assimilated Irish customs and traditions. The title "Anglo Irish" was used to distinguish these people who, while not

> "Irish artists occupy the gate lodge to the literary Big House, listening to the heavy traffic up and down the driveway." This pithy remark seemed to confirm the oft expressed view that, compared to our rich literary tradition, the visual arts in Ireland have remained almost invisible.

Irish in origin, became Irish in many ways. These circumstances led to the emergence of two artistic traditions in Ireland – the Anglo Irish and the native tradition. For many years, from the perspective of the native Irish, "classical music, opera, ballet, and the visual arts tended to be seen as more exclusive than, for example, traditional forms of music and dance". Therefore, the history of the visual arts in Ireland, up to recent times, has been a history of Anglo Irish painting. Also, it's worth noting that this particular history is difficult to construct. Anne Crookshank, the art historian, noted:

> ... time has been harder on Ireland's works of art than those of most European countries – little could survive the wars, rebellions and peace settlements of the seventeenth century which all resulted in destruction and changed the ownership of land and wealth in Ireland. The social changes which began with the Act of Union in 1801 and which were accelerated by the numerous Land Acts of the nineteenth century led to the gradual dispersal of the Anglo Irish gentry who had been the patrons of the arts.

This meant that artists of ambition naturally followed, so that any flowering of Irish talent in the nineteenth century occurred outside Ireland and there is ample evidence of such talent. John Foley was undoubtedly the finest Irish sculptor of the nineteenth century and he achieved great fame in his day, living in London and working on commissions in England, India and Ireland. In London he sculpted both Prince Albert and the Asia group for the Albert Memorial. In Dublin his Burke and Goldsmith stand outside Trinity College and his O'Connell marks the beginning of O'Connell Street.

Daniel Maclise came from Cork but went to England to make a living. He became a hugely successful painter of large canvasses on great themes. He painted the great murals for the House of Lords in London with such subjects as the "Death of Nelson". John Lavery was born in Belfast and became a painter of international renown both for his landscapes and his portraits.

William Orpen was the most brilliant draughtsman of his day and became one of the most fashionable portrait painters in London. He was appointed official war artist and at the end of the First World War was commissioned to paint the signing of the Treaty of Versailles. This partial listing of Irish artists gives some indication of their contemporary importance. Some may say that, because most of these artists lived and worked outside Ireland, they therefore should not be considered Irish. However, we have never disqualified our Anglo Irish authors on that score. Nevertheless, we should note that there was nothing characteristically Irish in the work of these artists; most were working in the English mainstream and created work that was similar

**... the history of the visual arts in Ireland, up to recent times, has been a history of Anglo Irish painting.**

in style and content to that produced by their English contemporaries. The Easter Rising in Dublin in 1916 led to a War of Independence which resulted in self-government for the 26 counties and a separate government under the British crown for the remaining six counties. The new government in the southern "Irish Free State", eagerly searching for an "Irish" school of painting, thought it had found one in the work of such painters as Paul Henry and Sean Keating. Brian Fallon, the art critic, correctly recognised that "the cultural commissars of the new Irish state knew very little about painting but they could recognise a haycock or a west of Ireland cottage when they saw one". Fallon humorously noted that such "Free State Art" was rather like those old cast iron letter boxes left behind by the British but subsequently over-painted by the new regime with green paint applied all over the crest and initials of Victoria Regina or Edwardus Rex.

This self-deception in the arts echoed the political reality in the country where the potential for change in a new independent state was being sacrificed to a resurgent conservatism. Terence Brown, in his book *Ireland: A Social and Cultural History*, questions why "a revolution fought on behalf of exhilarating ideals, ideals which had been crystallised in the heroic crucible of the Easter Rising, should have led to the establishment of an Irish state notable for a stultifying lack of social, cultural and economic ambition". The year 1923 saw the introduction of the Censorship of Films Act and in 1929 the Censorship of Publications Act was passed. When Fianna Fáil entered the Dáil many thought, indeed some feared, that they would introduce a dash of radicalism to Irish political and cultural life. This was not to be – the 1930s, if anything, deepened the conservatism of Irish life. An attitude of xenophobic suspicion often greeted any manifestation of anything that reflected cosmopolitan standards. Not only a tariff wall was erected around Ireland to protect the economy from outside competition, but a cultural wall as well to protect the people from foreign cultural contamination. This cautious mode of existence continued into the period of the Second World War, or the Emergency as it was called here, which forced Ireland into some of its dullest isolation. According to Brian O'Doherty, "the spiritual powers of tradition and the secular power of the Church were equally oppressive and food and intelligence were both rationed. Yet, for painting, the war proved fortunate in the most unexpected way." He remarked that "isolation allowed ideas to be examined and developed within the context of local needs", but acknowledged, "that to call it a national quality could be an exaggeration".

Artists like Patrick Collins and Nano Reid responded to those ideas in an atmospheric mode of painting, a style characterised by "an uneasy restless fix on the unimportant and a reluctance to disclose

**An attitude of xenophobic suspicion often greeted any manifestation of anything that reflected cosmopolitan standards. Not only a tariff wall was erected around Ireland to protect the economy from outside competition, but a cultural wall as well to protect the people from foreign cultural contamination.**

anything about what is painted let alone make a positive statement about it". Patrick Collins remarked: "when I see a few bottles on a table I feel that there is more than a few bottles. It is this something more that I try to paint". This "evasiveness summarises a whole defensive and infinitely discursive mode of existence in Ireland in the 40s and 50s", which was challenged in the mid-1960s by the return from New York by Micheal Farrell whose work was aggressive and intellectually hard. The economic changes introduced by Séan Lemass in 1959 created a small new audience prepared to accept the kind of work being done by Farrell and those that followed his lead. Under the premiership of Lemass protectionism was abandoned and the country was opened up to foreign investment. Slowly the economy began to develop and by the mid-1960s there was a buoyant feeling of optimism within the business community. I feel that it was no accident that the new bright, mainly abstract, painting and sculpture were chosen to mark this new-found confidence. Anne Crookshank wrote that "the first impact of the Bank of Ireland collection as a whole is one of vitality". However, things were to change; the 1980s brought economic stagnation and many artists responded to this situation with a vigorous expressionist style of painting. The New York artist Martha Rosler wrote: "the adoption of expressionism seems to represent the failed confidence of managerial and financial elites ... a sense that certainties are retreating".

Eventually, however, the gloom of the 80s gave way to the boom of the 90s, as Ireland became more integrated into the global economy and the multinational corporations became more dominant in our affairs. One consequence of this has been economic and cultural homogeneity. The stores on our high streets are the same as everywhere else and the fare in our museums and galleries provide us with the visual equivalent of the menu at McDonald's. If international artists are unavailable then Irish artists seem ready, willing and able to provide local variations of styles and approaches to art practice that obtain elsewhere. Such local translations of international modes represent what Brian O'Doherty calls "doppelganger provincialism", and he admits that "such ventriloquism of the latest trends extracts a pity that tends to bring out the worst in one".

At this stage, having trawled through almost one and a half millennia of visual expression in Ireland, with the exception of the work of the monks in their mossy cells, I have singularly failed to settle on anything that can be seen to have been inspired by something uniquely Irish in character, and yet I have to admit that many Irish artists produce work that is quintessentially different to work produced by artists from other countries/societies. That is a conundrum with no easy answer. For example, to resort to

**Slowly the economy began to develop and by the mid-1960s there was a buoyant feeling of optimism within the business community. I feel that it was no accident that the new bright, mainly abstract, painting and sculpture were chosen to mark this new-found confidence.**

the employment of Celtic ornament in an attempt to create a valid contemporary statement seems entirely bogus to me. Unlike traditional music, for example, there is no unbroken visual tradition to buy into. With music, each generation refreshes and invigorates the tradition! Also the adoption of so-called Irish subject matter, the thatched cottage, for example, will not necessarily result in a picture with a strong Irish characteristic. Obviously a thatched cottage painted by a German artist will look different to one painted by a Japanese artist and to one painted by an Irish artist.

It was in 1975 that the nature of this difference became apparent to me and this revelation occurred quite by accident. At that time, I was commissioned to paint two large pictures for a restaurant and bar in Clonmel, Co. Tipperary, with the proviso that they be of local interest. After long research to find a subject that would be relevant I finally settled on the famous eighteenth century author Laurence Sterne, who, in fact, had been born in Clonmel in 1713. Sterne's family lived with, or more likely off, their Irish relatives in Carrickfergus, Mullingar, Dublin and Annamoe until, finally, Laurence left for schooling in Halifax and then to Cambridge. I read his famous book, *The Life and Opinions of Tristram Shandy, Gentleman*, for the first time in 1975 and was immediately struck by what I felt to be a common sensibility even though we were separated in time by two centuries. Kieran Hickey, the film director, said, with tongue in cheek, that "if Sterne had not existed it would eventually have been necessary for Robert Ballagh to invent him". I first felt that we simply shared a common artistic purpose but slowly it occurred to me that the book was steeped in what I can only call an Irish sensibility. The conversational style of the writing, the sense of irony, humour and the "frisky digressions" all go to create a book that, however un-Irish it may appear on the surface and however much Sterne may be categorised as an English writer, has at its core, incontestably, a real "Irishness". In my opinion, Laurence Sterne quite naturally absorbed these various qualities during his formative years in Ireland.

I now sensed that "Irishness" is not something that can be superficially imposed on a work of art, for example through the employment of Celtic ornament, but rather that it is something that goes much deeper and is in essence difficult to define. It could be summarised possibly as an attitude to life, or more accurately a way of dealing with life, consisting of, perhaps, a preponderance to irony, satire or metaphor, a sense of humour, an enjoyment of parody and, above all, a healthy scepticism. These qualities are not uniquely Irish, but nonetheless the Irish do have them in abundance. And there are sound historical reasons as to why this should be the case. The Irish have been a subjected people, sometimes willing, sometimes

I now sensed that "Irishness" is not something that can be superficially imposed on a work of art, for example through the employment of Celtic ornament, but rather that it is something that goes much deeper and is in essence difficult to define.

not, for many centuries. This has meant that, in the past, whenever subversive ideas were to be communicated it became necessary to employ some sort of disguise. For example, the poets frequently used metaphor in order to communicate their true feelings when a direct statement would undoubtedly have been considered treasonable. Over the years, this technique of saying one thing while meaning another has become second nature to the Irish. So we can conclude that because of their troubled history the Irish were forced by circumstances to adopt qualities that have had the effect of enriching the national character.

**Over the years, this technique of saying one thing while meaning another has become second nature to the Irish.**

So, to sum up, perhaps we shouldn't be striving so hard to identify a specific "Irish Imagination" in Irish art, but should be happy instead to recognise that most honest Irish artists exhibit a subtle Irish sensibility which is no more than a conscious or unconscious acceptance of our history, culture and traditions.

# Mary Cloake

## Director, The Arts Council

*Born in Co. Wexford, educated at DCU (M.A.) and TCD (B.A. Mod) she joined the Arts Council in 1993 as Regional Development Officer and was appointed Development Director in 1997. She has held the post of Director since 2004. Formerly, she worked as Arts Officer for Dundalk Urban District Council. She is a member of RTÉ's Audience Council and in 2006 was a member of the Bloomsday 100 Committee. In February 2005 she was appointed to the board of Culture Ireland – the new agency to promote Irish arts overseas.*

## The Role of the Arts in Defining Our Cultural Identity

My starting point is an assertion: that the Irish imagination is distinctive in the world, and makes a contribution to the world; that the state of the arts in Ireland is thriving beyond all expectations and disproportionately to the status, attention and resources we give them; that the role of the arts is, has been and will continue to be absolutely central in "shaping the soul of Ireland". This centrality is not limited to simply expressing the multiple cultural identities we have had in the past and have now, but also in creating our future society, our economy, our body politic, in pushing the boundaries of our technology and in creating our capacity to innovate in shaping our environment.

The Irish imagination has been the subject of much commentary. From the many qualities attributed to it, three distinguishing characteristics emerge.

First, the Irish imagination lives easily with, and even thrives on, paradox. Richard Kearney has said that we can hold two thoughts simultaneously, that we can take two opposing points of view, seemingly irreconcilable, and rest them together without apparent conflict. Second, that the Irish imagination is inclined often to take an alternative or outside view, to look for and hold a perspective outside convention. Third, the Irish imagination is adept at surfing the waves of globalising influences – as a nation we absorb mainstream world culture but at the same time process it, render it our own and still maintain our specificity.

These distinguishing characteristics arguably arise from our unique place in the world – we are a small country but live in close proximity to a large neighbour; we have carved a cultural space for ourselves between Europe and America, where we draw influences from West

> ... the Irish imagination is adept at surfing the waves of globalising influences – as a nation we absorb mainstream world culture but at the same time process it, render it our own and still maintain our specificity.

and East. Our diaspora has thrived in every major country in the world and our emigrants' remittances have been not just financial, but social, cultural and political as well. We use a major world language and yet we have our own which, despite fears to the contrary, is all around us, in our idiom and in our world view. Our language remains a formative influence on our imagination – we are aware from our first linguistic moments that there is more than one way of thinking about the world. This imbues the way we communicate, it allows us to weigh up options, alternatives and possibilities and arguably, has given us the ability to generate the quick and creative responses necessary to thrive in the contemporary international arena. Our historical identity has given us the best of both worlds, the small and specific, the overarching and global. The lateral thinking which has resulted from this mix has been the key to our success, the engine of economic growth and the driver of our disproportionate influence on the world stage.

> **Our historical identity has given us the best of both worlds, the small and specific, the overarching and global.**

What, then, is the role of the arts? How do they relate to this imagination?

Art has many roles in society, some of which appear to be contradictory. The art of storytelling in their various forms – literature and film, for example – give us insights into the lives, emotions, values and perspectives of "the Other"; of people from far away places, people of different ages, gender and political persuasions. Stories open up worlds for us outside our lived experience.

Complementing this is the ability of the arts to articulate our own experience. "Good" art – art that "works" – is often characterised by moments of recognition, a work that describes a present or past reality which has been either too complex, too awful or too intuitive to acknowledge. Seamus Heaney in his description of how poetry "works" suggests that the auditory experience of the sounds of poetry connect with our intuition, provoking a response which makes us want to say to the poet "thank you for putting words on this – its something I always knew, deep down, but could never express and perhaps could not even acknowledge".

By articulating, in a carefully observed way, our current reality, the arts describe who we are and through this enable us to recognise, understand and celebrate what we discover as latent experience. We know this when a work of art, in whatever form, "rings true". By expressing our complex and hybrid imagination, the arts give us confidence, confidence to be different, confidence to speak from outside the mainstream of global cultural influences and confidence to lead. Robert Ballagh has acknowledged the political value of the artist in simply recording their time, their society and their experience. Through this record, we can see and acknowledge ourselves and others can see the values of the time really clearly.

But art at its very best – and arguably in its most important role – is about the recognition of what could be, about imagining a future that's different. The greatest of art, therefore, sends us beyond our own experience to imagine a world that is different from the one we know and suggests ways of being that we could aspire to. This is the art that is inspirational, and it is also the art that changes societies.

It has been said that reasonable people accept things the way they are, they accept the world as it is. Only unreasonable people do not accept things the way they are and only unreasonable people take a negative view and ask "is this all there is?" And it is to the artist we look to bring this "unreasonableness". The world depends on, the future depends on, the artist who imagines another way of being. This is a crucially valuable counterpoint to an everyday life in which most of us "go with the flow". Far from being a negative, or complaining contribution, the genuine or valuable form of critique is to imagining something different.

> **The world depends on, the future depends on, the artist who imagines another way of being. This is a crucially valuable counterpoint to an everyday life in which most of us "go with the flow".**

The role of the artist, then, can be to imagine another way of being. When this work of imagination touches a chord – when it is a good work of art – we respond to it. The most obvious example of this is given in works based on the idea of Utopia. By positing a perfect world of the future there is an implicit criticism of the world of the present. And the obverse of this, the concept of Dystopia, brings negative or latent elements of current society to their relentless logical conclusion. We see finely worked examples of this in George Orwell's *1984* or Aldous Huxley's *The Doors of Perception*.

The extreme example of Dystopia is only one end of a continuum within which new political and social possibilities are suggested by the artist. "Imagining the future" does not have to depict cataclysmic change, as Utopia or Dystopia, but can work in more incremental ways, through small steps in which the artist says of society or ways of living "this is not the way".

Any desirable new reality has to exist in the imagination before it exists in reality. Once it exists in the imagination, then the desire to change can follow. And this is one of the important jobs of our artists – to provide us with a vision of possible new realities, great or small, to assist us in the creation of the future. This can happen in subtle and intuitive ways. The birth of the nation, the concept of "Ireland", has imaginative origins dating back to earliest times. Each century made its contribution. In the nineteenth century, the poetry of Mangan and the melodies of Moore reflected a new consciousness of country as landscape and as a historical entity. These were part of the "route maps" which brought us to the Ireland we know today.

Imagining the future is not confined to story-telling or to nation-building, but applies right across the spectrum of the arts in different ways. A good piece of architecture, or a well-thought-through piece of public art, for example, can make us look at our environment differently and see the imaginative possibilities of our public space. The "breaking ground" project in Ballymun – a major public art initiative – has literally broken ground in both senses of the word, in the new buildings to replace the tower blocks in this 60s suburb, and in creating new ways of thinking about Ballymun.

Similarly, in their respective fields the artist James Coleman and the poet Maeve McGuckian opened up new ways of thinking. These artists have been referred to as "ahead of their time", but the futures they imagine have now become part of our present, our reality. We have absorbed their critique, however implicit, just as we have absorbed the critique of O'Casey's anti-militaristic *Plough and the Stars*, and Joyce's critique of a narrow nationalism in *Ulysses*.

The inevitable byproduct of this "imagining the future" is a critique of the present, a critique on which the health of democracy depends. The ability to accommodate a diversity of voices – pluralism – is a central pillar of democracy. Societies have always looked to artists to provide this critique. In the past, to be oppositional, artists often had to leave, they had to be outside the country to think outside the system. Sometimes this is still the case, but less so than in the past. We have at least some of our artists here, reflecting on our daily life and work.

If we are at a cultural and social turning point, if we are facing the challenge of creating a sense of identity in our country which is changing shape before our eyes, if we have to now invent a new reality in an increasingly culturally diverse Ireland, if we have to restate or re-examine our values, if our ability to live with ambiguity is being put to the test, then it is to the artists we must look, as every society has looked to in the past, to imagine the kinds of ways things can be.

This, then, is why we must appreciate this work that artists do for us, and ensure that they have enough time, attention, status and resources to fulfil their crucial role within society – investing, questioning and renewing the soul of Ireland for each generation.

But do we appreciate this work that artists do for us? Are we giving them enough time, attention, status and resources? Some improvements have been made in the conditions for artists, the establishment of Aosdana, in the 1980s, was a gesture in this respect, and supports from the State through the Arts Council have improved in recent years. Some artists have achieved financial and critical success, but for the majority of artists, life is not an easy one financially. A study published by the Arts Council in 2005 showed that the average annual income of a theatre practitioner is €10,620.

> ... if we have to now invent a new reality in an increasingly cultural diverse Ireland, if we have to restate or re-examine our values, if our ability to live with ambiguity is being put to the test, then it is to the artists we must look ...

Three-quarters of these have third level qualifications. Nearly half cannot take a holiday of any kind (as compared with a quarter of the rest of the population) and half are never likely to own their own homes.

And the poor state of the artist's lot does not relate exclusively to the financial. Do we take their contributions seriously? Are our print and broadcast media, themselves hugely influential shapers of our values and identities, making time and space for the alternative views of the artist? I contend that it is not healthy for the media alone to be the definer of the cultural identity of the nation, given the commercial pressures under which many of them operate.

At a time when there has been an unprecedented rise in wealth in Ireland, when we are – it has been claimed – the second wealthiest country in the world, ahead of the UK, the USA, Italy, France, Germany and Canada, we need to revisit the status of our artists.

And we need to be sure that our education system provides for people to understand and enjoy the languages of the arts, to be able to make the arts themselves, and for the few of us who become artists, we need to make sure that these gifted individuals can master the traditions and craft of the arts, and to add something of your own.

**We need to ensure the arts at local level are supported to enable diverse regional cultural identities to emerge and to respect and value.**

We need to ensure the arts at local level are supported to enable diverse regional cultural identities to emerge and to respect and value these identities,which in turn are shifting and growing, each in its individual way.

The arts play a critical role in "shaping the soul of Ireland". They help us to imagine a better future. We need to make sure that they can continue to do this.

# John Waters

## Writer and Broadcaster

*Born in Castlerea, Co. Roscommon, his career as a journalist began in the 80s with the magazine,* Hotpress. *He came to national prominence with the publication in 1991 of his quasi-autobiographical work,* Jiving at the Crossroads. *He has also written* An Intelligent Person's Guide to Modern Ireland *(2000) and* The Politburo Has Decided You Are Unwell *(2004). He has also written a number of plays for stage and television. His next book,* Lapsed Agnostic, *will be published by Continuum in 2007. He is currently a columnist with the* Irish Times *and is a frequent contributor to radio and television.*

## Autobiography – The Ethical Difficulties

My basic thesis today is that the Irish imagination has recently shifted, or is in the process of shifting, from a fascination with fiction to a fascination with fact – from magic to realism, if you like. I would like to explore the reasons for this and also to look at some of the possible pitfalls.

Working recently as editor of a new fundraising book project for the Irish Hospice Foundation, I verified something I'd been only half aware of. The book is called *LifeStory*, and is basically a template to allow people to write their own or their family's life stories, with a little guidance from the book and its editor.

In the course of preparing the book, we hunted down innumerable biographies in search of the first lines, which we used as a motif throughout *LifeStory*. We were looking also for about 20 or so suitable passages from Irish memoirs to introduce the various sections of the book. In doing this, it struck me that the most influential and widely read books of the past decade or so have not been novels but memoirs: Frank McCourt, Hugo Hamilton, John McGahern, Nuala O Faolain, Nell McCafferty etc. It also struck me that many of these books seem to mark a new direction in Irish writing in that they have taken on many of the qualities of the novel, and in that sense might be seen as seeking, and possibly succeeding, to supplant the hitherto central place of the novel in the Irish imagination.

> ... it struck me that the most influential and widely read books of the past decade or so have not been novels but memoirs ...

There are a number of difficulties with this form, which I will deal with more comprehensively later. One of the more immediately obvious is that this might appear to be a shift away from imagination itself – the replacement of creativity with mere recollection. However, for reasons that I'll go into, this does not look like being a real danger: it actually creates a problem of a different kind.

I am more interested in the social context, and would hazard the following brief exposition of what I believe is happening: In the past, particularly in the early years of independence, we attempted to create a literature that both sought to imagine an uncertain future and depict an ambiguous reality. This, though in some respects successful from a literary viewpoint, failed us in the context of the collective imagination. This most likely occurred because of the inability of post-colonial societies to agree on the nature of reality.

There is always this mix of the pre-existing and respected, the pre-existing and disrespected, of the imposed and adopted and the imposed and rejected. And of course each of these categories is different for virtually every individual citizen. Fiction, then, or at least Irish fiction, or at least Irish fiction set in Ireland, became a disconcertingly slippery activity for a writer. Because there was no agreed reality, a piece of fiction risked instant political categorisation in the context of the disputed meanings of history and culture. Patrick Kavanagh struggled with this conundrum for much of his life – the idea of the "Irish" poem, the "Irish" book, the "Irish" thing.

He concluded that there was no such entity, that there was "no virtue in a place". I believe he slightly mis-stated the issue. It was not the idea of place that was problematic, but the confusion of meanings infecting each place, and the iconography of that place and its different meanings for those from within and without, and the consequent infection of narratives with external, largely political, meanings. The very landscape was infected in this way. A thatched cottage might sit on a landscape and seem to itself and its occupants no more or less than reality, but to the observer it might be a flash of the ideal Ireland, a relic of a kitschified countryside, or an ironic statement of post-modern knowingness, a wink at a passing Yank. And yet, the cottage was quite simply there, very often inhabited by real Irish people, not crones or comely maidens, or, at least, not by old or young women answering to those descriptions. The problem for the writer, then, was how to write it into a book without opting for one or other definition and so categorising the book as either nostalgia or reaction. And, as in the broader cultural context, this fractured reality led to the creation of what might be called a reactive literature in recent years, a literature without thatched cottages, but as a deliberate, indeed a political, omission.

We did, as I say, create a successful literature, but we created it, let us remember, as a provincial outpost of London, which perceived us in a certain way and praised us when we delivered on its preconceptions. I think we have to be cautious when we talk about Irish literature in the twentieth century. How many of our great writers are not so much Irish writers as writers writing about

*... we attempted to create a literature that both sought to imagine an uncertain future and depict an ambiguous reality. This, though in some respects successful from a literary viewpoint, failed us in the context of the collective imagination.*

Ireland from an English perspective? Many of our more successful novelists of recent times, in fact, have set most of their work outside Ireland. This is not normal. Roth writes of America, Klima of Prague, McEwan of London, Brookner of Paris and London and the connection between the two. The Irish writer writes of Spain and Argentina and, to the extent that we remark upon it, it is to wonder at his adaptability.

It seems to me, therefore, that what is happening at the moment is not so much a shift away from fiction as an experiment with Irish reality but more as a means of getting a new fictional perspective on that reality. It's a bit like learning to swim, failing at the front crawl, moving on the breast stroke as a way of getting around that failure, with a hope of returning to the crawl later. What you find is that your version of the crawl has improved greatly while you've been avoiding it.

The thing about autobiography is that it is relatively incontrovertible. My story is my story and I am the best one to tell it. I have authority over it in a way that, strangely, few Irish writers have been able to assert authority over a fictional reality. This, I know, is a controversial view since the popular wisdom would have it that Irish writing is among the best in the English language. (Perhaps that's the problem.) Joyce did it by creating a new Dublin, over which he instantly claimed ownership. I think Pat McCabe did it with *The Butcher Boy* by discovering a voice that was so irrefutably authentic that the story he told – grotesque and horrific though it was – became plausible.

Less sure-footed or less ambitious writers simply borrow the existing reality, perhaps often not realising how contaminated it is by history and politics.

There are no real parallels in the modern world with Irish society – post-colonial, European, white like our colonisers, speaking the same language as our colonisers albeit "on top of" a rich and vibrant culture which still exhibits spectacular life of its own. What discussion there is about the nature of our post-colonial condition is by definition circumscribed by its own nature, and therefore happens, when or if it happens, in highly controlled contexts and with a high capacity for misunderstanding.

In his classic work, *The Wretched of the Earth*, Frantz Fanon argues that there are three distinct cultural phases in the journey of a formerly colonised people towards freedom. The first is what he called unqualified assimilation, in other words an attempt in the damaged culture to demonstrate its worth by comparison with the coloniser's. In this phase you get writers who write within the parameters established by the dominant colonial culture. You get imitation and impersonation, mimicry and pretentiousness. The second phase is an attempt to remember, a return to the past in search of solid ground under the marsh created by colonisation. "Old legends," he writes, "will be reinterpreted in the light of a borrowed ascetism and of a conception of the world which was discovered under other skies". I believe you might plausibly present this as a description of the most recent phase of Irish literature, in which writers have been trying to shake off the colonial embrace while remaining trapped within it. And this is what I believe is the meaning of the present shift to biography. It is a transitional phase, a period of experimentation with the stuff of reality, a way of testing that reality and perhaps of cleansing it of its impurities, a way of freeing Irish writing from the ambiguous legacy of its Anglican roots, a process of decontamination. And the third phase in Fanon's prediction? In this, he said, "a great many men and women who, up until then would never have thought of producing a literary work, feel the need to speak to their nation, to compose the sentence which expresses the heart of the people and to become the mouthpiece of a new reality in action".

I don't wish to labour this theory or its application to Ireland, but simply to point to it as a way of seeing what is happening. The "new reality" Fanon spoke of is a complex entity that combines elements of colonisation and elements of freedom, and these can often be beyond the grasp of a public order and a public conversation that remains trapped in the post-colonial prescriptions. But our own reality is indisputably ours. When I write of my life, I have a right to an acceptance of, and respect for, my description of reality that does not necessarily accrue to me when I write fiction using the common landscape. Then I use something that is held in common, even if disputedly, ambiguously, variously. And that is what we are looking at in the recent works of Hamilton, O Faolain, McCourt et al.

**Many of the new breed of books noticeably have the stature and style of novels, but they seek to deal in the stuff of fact. And this is where some difficulties may arise ...**

Many of the new breed of books noticeably have the stature and style of novels, but they seek to deal in the stuff of fact. And this is where some difficulties may arise, and I'd like to touch briefly on these also. There are a number of ethical difficulties with writing autobiography. I have some experience of this, since I myself wrote a kind of memoir 15 years ago, *Jiving at the Crossroads*. I know the challenges and limits of writing about real people, even dead ones. The first, and perhaps least contentious, is the use of novelistic techniques to recreate the sensibility of fiction. There are obvious difficulties. How could a six-year-old child record the precise dialogue that occurred between his father and a shopkeeper? But, beyond that, we need to get to the meaning of truth, the difference between truth and fact, the inevitable subjectivity of apprehension and memory, and the need to agree on a broader and perhaps deeper meaning to the exercise.

A related and more serious matter, then, is the inability of many of those characterised in such memoirs to "answer back" – by virtue usually of being deceased.

There is also the issue of the sensitivities of those still alive, which must be respected in a way that sometimes circumscribes the truth telling. I came across both of these problems in writing about my parents in *Jiving at the Crossroads*. I wanted to write primarily about my father and my relationship with him, but I did not want to say anything in the book that would disrespect his memory. This made inevitable a certain degree of minor whitewashing, which some people find problematic in literary terms. And there is here, I believe, a clash between morals and literature, which morals should win but nowadays does so with less and less frequency. I believe there are many ethical issues arising from the modern fad for making literal literature out of the raw reality of real human lives, especially of those – generally males – who become so blackened in the reporting as to leave the world only a negative impression, of which the victim, by virtue of being deceased, is unable to offer a rebuttal. Similarly, I did not write much in my own book about my mother, simply because she was and is alive and I did not want to embarrass her. This led to accusations by some critics, notably Nuala O Faolain, that I had written my mother, and by extension Irish women, out of the story.

Now nobody could accuse Nuala of writing her parents out of her story, but is this necessarily a good thing? Is it good for us and our culture that so much of our truth is becoming literalised, that the lives and frailties of real people are being exposed to huge audiences in a way that allows them or their memory no redresss? Is it healthy that Hugo Hamilton, in his beautifully written book *The Speckled People*, accuses his dead father of anti-Semitism?

Then there is the case of John McGahern, venerated as perhaps the finest Irish writer of the past fifty years. In fact, this very conundrum is one he himself addressed at one time. "Real life," McGahern once observed, "is too thin to be art." I forget where he said it, but I remember that he was talking about the limitations of autobiography. Yet his final book, written at the very end of his life, was his own autobiography, *Memoir*, which is no "thinner" than any of the novels or stories he wrote over the previous 40-odd years, and indeed revisited their themes and characters in no uncertain manner. Among the many interesting insights to be gleaned from *Memoir* is the confirmation it provides of what had previously been a woolly impression concerning the extent of McGahern's re-working in his stories of the detail of his own life.

It could plausibly be argued that *Memoir* was McGahern's single literary mistake. That is certainly my view of it. I believe that, by chronicling the literal reality from which he had forged so much of his fiction, it exposes the undercarriage of his imagination to a scrutiny which may ultimately risk damage to his reputation. And this underlines the difficulty with the present phase of Irish writing as a means of getting to the larger truths about who we are and where we are going. Before the publication of *Memoir*, McGahern's other books had a total life of their own, set free from literal connections by the nature of the fictional contract. After *Memoir*, they become something else – not fact, but no longer quite fiction either.

And then there is the treatment in *Memoir* of the author's father, Frank, which brought back to me my own difficulties of 15 years ago. Although dominated by McGahern's memories of his parents – the mother who died when he was a child and the father with whom he carried on a disturbed relationship into adulthood – the book has a feeling of being artistically incomplete, and this arises largely because of the lack of resolution in the relationship between John McGahern and his father.

Several times McGahern writes that he never understood his father. Actually, it's clear that he disliked, perhaps even hated, him and that this dislike or hatred has not in any degree been dissipated by the time the book ends. But at no point does the author seem to reflect on this in a detached manner. There is no moment of grace between father and son which might be deemed the cathartic moment of the book. Whether McGahern should have written *Memoir* is beside the point: what interests me more is what all this tells us about how a culture manages to preserve a convenient self-image of itself long after this has become outdated or even irrelevant. I say this as someone who, having read his books repeatedly and derived a wealth of nourishment from them, regards McGahern as a giant of fiction-writing. But I also believe that one claim made frequently since his death – that he was a faithful and comprehensive chronicler of Irish life – is spurious. And this leads me to doubt whether, without a vibrant climate of discussion, the present autobiographical phase of Irish writing can really take us to the truth.

To be fair, McGahern would have been the first to repudiate the idea that he had a role as a social historian. The truth he wrote was his own truth and was forged, as *Memoir* reveals in remarkable detail, in the white heat of his own experience. Another writer, encountering the same experience, would have written an entirely different set of stories, or at least offered different slants on their meaning.

The reviews of *Memoir* have been universally glowing and, in many respects, deservedly. But I have been struck by the ignoring in both these reviews, and the commentary following McGahern's death, of the extent to which this remarkable writer harmonised

> ... McGahern would have been the first to repudiate the idea that he had a role as a social historian. The truth he wrote was his own truth and was forged, as *Memoir* reveals in remarkable detail, in the white heat of his own experience.

with the discordances of a deeply damaged culture. There has, for example, been much guff about McGahern's depiction of the "patriarchal reality of Irish society". By this analysis, the character Moran in *Amongst Women* (more than loosely based on McGahern's father) is the tyrant king who rules over all within his gaze. Before I read *Memoir*, I would have said that this was a crude ideological reading of a character who was victim of a culture in which he had, in reality, very little power. Now I have to admit that this crudity may have been part of the author's intention. I don't want to labour the sociology, but this was a society which had been traumatised twice – by famine and civil war – and in which the Church had assumed the role of moral government, recruiting the mother in the home as its agent of control and, with her assistance, reducing the father to tolerated provider devoid of moral authority. Caught between the hyper-visible power of the Church and the invisible power of an undeclared matriarchy, Moran's rage was really the rage of the impotent. And then this culture that has raised Mother to the status of Madonna and banished Father to the fields or the fair, laughably interprets a rage born of marginalisation as the roar of the oppressor. What may be a factual account of the life of a family may here be a highly subjectivised and indeed ideological interpretation of social reality.

What may be a factual account of the life of a family may here be a highly subjectivised and indeed ideological interpretation of social reality.

Just as it is clear from *Memoir* that McGahern had little interest in the roots or nature of his father's demons, so also is it obvious that he accepted at face value many of the flimsiest myths of his society. It is unsurprising that this goes unremarked by the procession of contemporary writers and ideological appropriators who monopolised the public grieving in the wake of his death. I myself declined several invitations to talk on radio about him, not because I disrespected him or in any sense would have been seeking to denigrate his achievement, but because I might have, in the interests of truth, wished to talk about ways in which he too was imprisoned within the broader culture. I think that perhaps this is a more appropriate venue for a respectful assessment of a truly great writer.

Dr Alasdair McDonnell MP, MLA
Deputy Leader, SDLP

Gregory Campbell MP, MLA
Democratic Unionist Party

Martin McGuinness MP, MLA
Chief Negotiator, Sinn Féin

Tom Elliott MLA
Ulster Unionist Party

*Chapter 11*

# Reconciling Orange and Green

*Have We Lived Together But Haven't Integrated?*
TOM ELLIOTT **MLA**
**Ulster Unionist Party**

*The Terrible Emotional and Sectarian Legacy Lives On*
DR ALASDAIR MCDONNELL **MP, MLA**
**Deputy Leader, SDLP**

*Eradicating Sectarianism Will be a Huge Step*
GREGORY CAMPBELL **MP, MLA**
**Democratic Unionist Party**

*Building Trust and Confidence*
MARTIN MCGUINNESS **MP, MLA**
**Chief Negotiator, Sinn Féin**

# Cllr Tom Elliott MLA

## Ulster Unionist Party Spokesperson on Agriculture and Rural Affairs

*Born and educated in Co. Fermanagh. Elected to Fermanagh District Council in 2001 and to the Stormont Assembly in 2003. Hon. Sec. of Fermanagh Unionist Association since 1998. Formerly a part-time soldier of the Ulster Defence Regiment and the Royal Irish Regiment. Election Agent for UUP candidate James Cooper in Westminster elections of 2001. Member of several committees of Fermanagh District Council insluding the Sports Advisory Committee, the Hospital Steering Group and the Agricultural Task Force. A dairy and beef farmer, he is actively involved in the activities of his local church and is currently County Grand Master of Fermanagh L.O.L.*

## Have We Lived Together But Haven't Integrated?

> It is our collective shame that in the year 2006, in a developed world country, we still have to make speeches on how to reconcile orange and green.

Have we lived together but haven't integrated? It is our collective shame that in the year 2006, in a developed world country, we still have to make speeches on how to reconcile orange and green. Many have wrestled with this question and related issues for hundreds of years and, time and time again, politicians and society have snatched defeat from the jaws of victory.

This week, here at the MacGill School, is itself part of the reconciliation process; individuals from a variety of backgrounds sharing their opinions in a frank and open manner. For too long, the reluctance to air such issues has hampered progress.

When one considers the ongoing "war on terror" and the differences between Christians and Muslims, or the Middle East where many are still caught up in a bitter, violent war, it makes the differences between orange and green, Unionist and Nationalist, Protestant and Roman Catholic seem but a trifle.

It is somewhat of a cliché but the inescapable fact is that we have much more in common than many would care to admit. We all want to live and work in a peaceful, prosperous society, one in which we are free to observe our religious and cultural beliefs, and pass such a society on to our children. In rural, farming areas, Protestant and Roman Catholic neighbours have traditionally banded together to help win hay or assist in a difficult calving case. Decades ago, such acts were often a matter of life and death.

Very often we, as a people from different community or religious backgrounds, have worked together, visited each other and helped each other. However, I believe we have never truly integrated. I can often remember my younger days when working on the farm and some local Roman Catholics helping out. During the working days and around the dinner table there were very seldom discussions about what we differed about, no discussions about the GAA or Orange Order or about the differences in our church traditions. Maybe that is where our ancestors were wrong. We need to be more open with each other about our own traditions, which could hopefully lead to a better understanding of one another's beliefs and traditions and help build respect for each other.

Such traditions of mutual help and support continue. Sadly, the actions of a few from both sides during the troubles meant that distrust and suspicion flourished. Many such relationships in border areas and city estates were gravely damaged.

However, such experiences show that if there is a common goal, something to benefit everyone, then reconciliation can take place. At a time of political uncertainty and polarised representation, there are common goals that require cross-party, cross-community, and yes, cross-border cooperation.

Poorly funded infrastructure, rationalisation of essential services, a struggling private sector, loss of EU funding to eastern European countries, cross-border racketeering to name but a few, all require a united sense of purpose.

A clear, unambiguous direction from those in power is required if these issues are to stand any chance of being tackled effectively.

It is useful to look more in-depth as to how we as a people from different traditions have moved forward in recent years.

- No longer has the Southern Irish government a territorial claim over Northern Ireland following the removal of Articles 2 and 3 from its constitution.

- We do not currently have the campaign of murder of many innocent Protestants and Roman Catholics that we endured in the 70s, 80s and early 90s.

- We have many Unionists who previously poured scorn on the very idea of visiting the Irish Republic or meeting Irish government officials now engaged in proactive discussions with the Irish government, including the Irish Premier.

- We have Irish Republicans, many of them were possibly IRA members, accepting partition who have played, and wanting to do so again, an active role in a Northern Ireland Assembly, within the constitutional position of Northern Ireland being an integral part of the United Kingdom.

> During the working days and around the dinner table there were very seldom discussions about what we differed about, no discussions about the GAA or Orange Order or about the differences in our church traditions.

- Gone are the days of the calls of "No return to Stormont" on one side and "Smash Sinn Féin" on the other.

But we must not attempt to force opposing traditions together. Any attempt at reconciliation or coming together must be cushioned along and given time and space to develop.

There must be further acceptance that there is never going to be widespread recognition of and participation by traditional organisations from opposing communities, e.g. the GAA is traditionally an Irish Nationalist organisation whose participants come mainly from the Nationalist/Roman Catholic community. On the other side, the Orange Order is an organisation whose membership is mainly from the Unionist/Protestant community. There must be a respect for these traditions from the opposing communities and an acceptance that it is unlikely that we are ever going to have any meaningful participation from the opposing community.

This year, the ninetieth anniversary of the Battle of the Somme was commemorated across the globe. And, much closer to home, we saw the Irish government finally commemorating its own great losses in that battle, a battle which has been a major part of the Ulster psyche since that fateful day in July 1916.

Such an event was unthinkable a few short years ago. It took decades of work by many to bring about such an event. Sadly, it is too late for many from the Republic who fought in many of the campaigns of the First World War.

I was lucky to be present at the service on 1st July last in Dublin and spoke to an elderly Dubliner who had served in the British Army and his father had been a survivor of the Somme. His main regret was that his father never had the opportunity to celebrate this event in his own country. However, it may be cold comfort for many but its better late than never.

From my own perspective, as an Orangeman, I am delighted that this year's twelfth celebrations passed off so peacefully. This is how my forefathers and the founders of the Order perceived the commemoration taking place. The founding principles of the Order, if adhered to, can only but benefit all in the province, be they Protestant, Roman Catholic, Muslim, or Jew.

Sadly portrayed by many as an organisation with the sole purpose of attacking the Roman Catholic Church, it is, if anything, designed to be defensive of the teachings of the entire Christian ethos and principles. It is unfortunate that Irish Republicans have sought for many years to deprive this organisation of its freedom and civil rights.

**There must be a respect for these traditions from the opposing communities and an acceptance that it is unlikely that we are ever going to have any meaningful participation from the opposing community.**

The erosion of such unique traditions is sadly a common feature of the "global village". The "golden arches", I-pods and the like have meant an amalgamation of traditions right around the world. We watch with wonder as China opens up to western culture in a way that would have been unthinkable a few decades ago.

There are now, of course, a large number of people from other nationalities living and working throughout Ireland, with many communities having great difficulty dealing with the many diverse issues that they bring. Dublin has now one of the largest multi-cultural city populations in Europe.

This issue gives everyone from both Northern and Southern Ireland a new focus and challenge outside our traditional orange and green difficulties and differences. Our traditions must be preserved for future generations, be they orange, green or something else.

Of course, it would be remiss of me not to look at the future of the Northern Ireland institutions. Will we have the restoration of the Assembly? I have highlighted earlier how issues have progressed in both Northern and Southern Ireland during recent years. There is a clear coming together of the two main parties in Northern Ireland.

- It is no longer unattainable for representatives of these two parties to share a TV studio or even a debating platform like this one together.

- Quite often we recognise that Republicans are not discouraging their people from directly involving themselves with the Police Service of Northern Ireland.

- The two main parties do not have any difficulty in equally sharing the chairmanship of the Assembly Preparation for Government committee.

With this mutual willingness of the two main parties I, therefore, believe that during the next eight or nine months it is highly possible that we will have the restoration of the Northern Ireland Assembly and a power-sharing Executive.

But this comes with a warning. How committed will Republicans be to the stabilisation of the entity of Northern Ireland? When this was followed through in the past, Republicans always sabotaged the process. Even when a deal was close in December 2004, the Northern Bank robbery was being planned. Many strongly believe that this was carried out to "shaft" the Unionists who may have entered into the Comprehensive Agreement of that time. If Republicans have been prepared to do it several times in the past, will they not do the same again?

> This issue gives everyone from both Northern and Southern Ireland a new focus and challenge outside our traditional orange and green difficulties and differences. Our traditions must be preserved for future generations, be they orange, green or something else.

I cannot ever see a time when I will trust Sinn Féin because of their history and links with the IRA that have murdered many of my friends and those from my community. There appeared to be a recent campaign in which Republicans were attempting to justify their murderous campaign since 1969, but nothing they can ever put forward will justify their brutal past of killing their fellow countrymen.

However, as we move forward, while it is obvious that we will not always have agreement, all communities must exercise tolerance and respect for each other.

The fact is that reconciliation between "orange" and "green", by its very definition, is probably never likely to take place, but reconciliation between neighbours, reconciliation between work colleagues or schoolmates can, is, and will continue to occur and, hopefully, progress. It has to!

**The fact is that reconciliation between "orange" and "green", by its very definition, is probably never likely to take place ...**

# Dr Alasdair McDonnell MP, MLA

## Deputy Leader, SDLP

*Born in Cushendall, Co. Antrim. Studied medicine at UCD which recently awarded him an Honorary Fellowship of the School of Medicine and Medical Sciences. Has practised as a GP in South Belfast since 1979. Elected to Belfast City Council in 1977. Deputy-Mayor of Belfast 1995-6. Elected to the Northern Ireland Assembly in 1998. Elected to Westminster in 2005. Became Deputy Leader of the SDLP in 2004. Member of the N.I. Select Affairs Committee at Westminster.*

## The Terrible Emotional and Sectarian Legacy Lives On

That often repeated rationale for our national flag – the reconciliation of the green and orange traditions on our island – has, unfortunately, become something of a cliché in Northern Nationalist politics.

The treatment of the flag by a minority of Nationalists over the last 40 years means that its promise as a symbol of hope and reconciliation has been damaged but not, I hope, damaged beyond repair. For while its symbolism may have been tarnished, and its rationale may have become clichéd, its aspiration is as relevant and powerful today as ever it was.

As the representative of a constituency where we have people loyal to the boldest green and others loyal to the brightest orange, I know at first hand the importance of encouraging greater understanding between those two – I know at first hand and have long been motivated by the enormous social potential that could be unleashed if they could finally be reconciled.

The basic political philosophy that this motion is based on:

- That only through mutual respect and understanding can the people of this island live at peace together, which has long been a cornerstone of the SDLP's thinking.

- It is one of the greatest tragedies in Ireland's history that it took others so long, and so many lives, to come to the same conclusion.

The awful violence inflicted upon the community as a whole by the militant fundamentalists on either side of the religious and constitutional political divide has had a terrible legacy. While some

*The treatment of the flag by a minority of Nationalists over the last 40 years means that its promise as a symbol of hope and reconciliation has been damaged but not, I hope, damaged beyond repair.*

economic development across the North and a property boom continues to transform the physical element of that legacy, the great pain and mistrust – the terrible emotional and sectarian legacy – lives on.

But we are where we are, and those of us who have always stood by the aim of reconciling our people, of *uniting* Catholic, Protestant and Dissenter in the fashion of Wolfe Tone, have a greater responsibility than ever to use our influence and move that agenda forward.

Now more than ever we must work to encourage and make progress on those things that already bring our people together and shine a light on those things that are used to keep us apart.

In some respects, the green and orange are closer together than ever. Working families from both traditions share the same hopes and fears for their children. The struggle to pay the mortgage, afford childcare, find enough quality time with a young family and bring up kids with self-respect and opportunity is the same difficult struggle in all corners of my constituency and in all corners of Northern Ireland.

Concerns about spiralling household rates and water bills, the environment, the state of our hospitals and the safety of our seniors are the same, whether you live in Crossmaglen or Carrickfergus. In the most vulnerable and marginalised corners of the North, where paramilitary thugs of every hue encourage and feed off the worries and the fears of people struggling to improve their lives, where small businesses are regularly shaken down mafia-style and where the victims of crime are asked to "sort it out" through recourse to local godfathers, the desire for opportunity is the same, the desire for accountable justice is the same, the need for hope is the same.

> ... in many other respects the green and orange are further apart now than at any time in many decades. *The Economist*, for example, reported recently that more than 97 per cent of public housing in Northern Ireland is segregated.

But alas, in many other respects the green and orange are further apart now than at any time in many decades. *The Economist*, for example, reported recently that more than 97 per cent of public housing in Northern Ireland is segregated. At the time of the first ceasefire there were nine peacelines in Belfast. At the last count there were nearly 40 and the number is likely to grow further

There has been much analysis about why this is the case. Working, as I do, in a constituency with some of the most marginalised single identity communities in the North, it's a question I've thought a lot about. There are, I believe, three major themes that underlie this increasing division, three themes that remain as the roadblocks to reconciliation between orange and green. They are:

• The needs of *victims*

• The lack of *shared space*

• And (with apologies to Pat Spillane) the *puke politics* that are the order of the day in Northern Ireland in 2006.

The issue of victims and the concept of victimhood is an enormously sensitive and difficult subject, but it is also of central importance if there is to be any real reconciliation on this island. In basic, stark terms, insufficient attention was paid to the needs of those innocent people and families who were broken by violence.

They were asked to accept prisoner releases without any real empathy and have been virtually ignored by the Government ever since. They watched as some victims' cases were elevated (often for very good reason) while the majority were ignored; they watch this year as monuments to the hunger strikers are erected in every Nationalist town, village and housing estate, while the Provisional movement continues to evade its responsibilities to the many victims of their own violence.

How must it have felt, for example, for families of victims around Northern Ireland to hear recently the PIRA announce, 34 years after her disappearance, brutal torture and death, that Jean McConville was a tout? Not an admittance of guilt and remorse on their part, but a statement 34 years after her disappearance, torture and death that they had been *right* to do what they did?

There are many many other cases of injustice and pain about which too little has been said. Thirty-four years ago, Belfast was convulsed following 20 explosions and nine murders – how many people here can name those victims?

Who, apart from their broken families and friends and neighbours, is thinking of them tonight? It is increasingly hard to argue with those who claim that there has emerged a hierarchy of victims. And that is a terrible thing. It is also the single most insidious and damaging barrier to any real reconciliation. The double vision, double standards, call it what you want, of the paramilitary gangs has long frustrated me.

The provisional movement knows well and exploits the power and emotion of ancient wrongs against the Irish people. I recently received an email from the Sinn Féin bookshop offering me a DVD about the *famine*, but they seem entirely unable to understand the awful effect of their own actions on their neighbours.

What they have done in the name of the green may have sparked *generations* of mistrust about the cause of Irish nationalism, may have delayed the possibility of reunification of our people by more than a generation.

Similarly, I watch Loyalist bands march through Belfast, incensed that anyone would dare question their commemoration of murderers like the UVF's Brian Robinson or the Rathcoole Kill All Irish gang.

"Why can Nationalist residents not realise that these are historical figures and get over it?" they ask, seemingly oblivious to the fact that

**It is increasingly hard to argue with those who claim that there has emerged a hierarchy of victims. And that is a terrible thing. It is also the single most insidious and damaging barrier to any real reconciliation.**

the reason they are marching, the reason why thousands of them congregate around bonfires and burn tricolours and dishonour the memory of innocent victims like Michael McIlveen is to commemorate a battle that took place a short 316 years ago. In their insane efforts to "save Ulster" they have destroyed the very Ulster that they purport to save.

This disconnect – the sense of shared grievance about what was done upon you without any sense of what was done in the name of your community – adds to the dysfunction of Northern society and it needs to be confronted, it needs to be challenged.

In the SDLP we recognise the role we played in supporting prisoner releases in the context of the Good Friday Agreement. But we also recognise that we must play a central role in taking up that challenge. It is a challenge we embrace.

Our successful opposition to the "On the Runs" legislation means that state and paramilitary killers must be held to account.

Our opposition to the multimillion-pound ransom payment to Loyalist paramilitaries will seek to hold those gangs to account.

Our questions about so-called Community Restorative Justice schemes will seek to make sure justice is held to account, and our support for the Office of the Victims Commissioner is to make sure that, finally, the voices of all victims will be heard and will count.

The second of the roadblocks to reconciliation, as I see it, is the lack of shared space in Northern Ireland and the lack of cultural awareness that underpins this.

It shouldn't come as any surprise that there is a gulf of understanding between both sides of our community – in addition to the violence I've already talked about, we have had a generation of segregated education, segregated housing, segregated sport, segregated life. In dark times, we took comfort in the safety of our own traditions and stayed well clear of others.

With communities at each other's throats, there was little point in trying to understand or appreciate what was important to "the other side". But these are brighter days, and for the days to become brighter still, we must all begin to make an effort to understand each other a little better, we must make genuine accommodation for the needs of others, we must try to make the idea of "shared space" more than just a bit of jargon, a handy government-approved soundbyte.

As a Nationalist, I can put my hand on my heart and say that the beliefs of Orangeism have long been alien to me. I can say that for a very long time my gut reaction to what it was, or what I thought it was, was very negative. Of course, that shoe fitted very often when Orangemen blocked roads and encouraged civil disorder rather than talk to residents, or when they offered weasel words rather

> ... we have had a generation of segregated education, segregated housing, segregated sport, segregated life. In dark times, we took comfort in the safety of our own traditions and stayed well clear of others.

than condemnation when people were killed in Orange-related disturbances, for example.

But it can no longer be enough for nationalists to fall back on the old easy stereotypes. To talk about "sectarian coat trailing" or describe the proposed "Orangefest" as a "bigotfest" as a Newry SF councillor has done, might be comfortable and might raise an easy cheer, but does it do anything to reconcile our traditions?

Are there bigots in the Orange Order? Unfortunately, yes. Are there decent men in the Orange Order? Fortunately, yes.

If as Nationalists we believe the unification of the people of Ireland and the island of Ireland is a worthy goal, when are we going to come to grips with the fact that Orangeism is part of this island's life? When are we going to take up the challenge posed by accommodating this minority right?

While there is no parallel with Orangeism in the Nationalist side of cultural life, there is within Unionism and Loyalism a similar ignorance and intolerance about cultural activities important to Nationalist people.

We need only look as far as the long list of murders of GAA people and attacks on GAA premises to see how little militant Loyalism understands the work and life of that Association or the values and attitudes of ordinary Gaels.

Until more is done to build understanding about each other's lives, unless political representatives do more to lead and shape attitudes, rather than always looking for the lowest common denominator, unless, as St Paul wrote to the Ephesians, we learn to "be subject to one another", there will be no shared space. There will only be a growing chasm between orange and green and an endless cycle of resentment, bitterness and recrimination about which side gets what.

In my maiden speech at the House of Commons I said that when the Provisionals and the Paisleyites were in the driving seats, everyone would suffer. That was 14 months ago and I'm sorry to say that, unfortunately, I have been proven right. The real injustice to the people who suffer, the ordinary working families trying to get on with their lives, is that puke politics are being actively encouraged by Peter Hain and the Northern Ireland Office. We've seen it in the side deals with Sinn Féin, we've seen it in the gymnastics performed by Peter Hain every time the DUP demand more "confidence building" measures.

The problem with pandering to puke politics is that it brings out the worst in the people who practise that game and gets us nowhere good, fast. The cynicism, the "strokes", serve only the narrow short-term political interests of the parties who manipulate the process – not the process itself and certainly not the people it was designed to serve.

In the context of this discussion tonight, puke politics setting the agenda means that the balkanisation of Northern Ireland, warned of by my colleague, Seamus Mallon, continues, greater understanding between our traditions is avoided at all costs and the great promise of the Irish flag remains unfulfilled. It's sometimes hard to shake the feeling that that's part of the point.

**The cynicism, the "strokes" serve only the narrow short-term political interests of the parties who manipulate the process – not the process itself and certainly not the people it was designed to serve.**

My former leader, and great friend of this summer school, John Hume, often talked about his experience of standing on that bridge in Strasbourg. He marvelled that the people of Germany and France who had done so much bad to each other could come together again to work for a common good. While John may have moved off the political stage, that message and image are as relevant today as they were when he first challenged the status quo.

While it may be unrealistic to talk about a full reconciliation between orange and green in the short term while only the most ambitious optimists can imagine full partnership between the two any time soon, surely those of us who can see what unites us, despise what divides us and still believe in the promise of the tricolour. Surely we can be subject to one another and reclaim the agenda from those who profit from division and whose narrow agenda ultimately serves no one, not even themselves if they had the wit to recognise it. Surely we can come together again and work for a common good.

# Gregory Campbell MP, MLA

## Democratic Unionist Party Spokesperson on Security

*Born in 1953 and educated at Londonderry Technical College. Left the civil service to start his own business. Elected to Londonderry City Council in 1981 and to the Northern Ireland Assembly in 1982 of which he was a member to 1986. Member of the New Assembly 1998-2003. DUP security spokesperson since 1994. Minister for Regional Development in the power-sharing Executive July 2000-September 2001. Has been a member at Westminster of the Northern Ireland Affairs Select Committee.*

## Eradicating Sectarianism Will Be a Huge Step

The problem we face is not a new one. It is less of a focus of attention in the Republic only because the orange element in the South has largely disappeared. Removal rather than reconciliation has been the outcome here in this state.

In Northern Ireland it is different. The problems in Northern Ireland did not begin with the outbreak of the Troubles in the late 1960s, but undoubtedly the terrorist campaigns have proved to be the single greatest obstacle to better community relations.

Indeed, even after the day comes if and when terrorism has ended and the paramilitary organisations have disappeared from the scene, the bitter legacy of the last 36 years will live on. Community divisions, which are now so firmly entrenched, were not created overnight and will not disappear overnight either. It is a mistake to imagine that they might.

I believe the reasonable height of our ambitions in the next few years is to remove the causes for this division and begin to deal with the symptoms, but it will not be an easy task. It is one which is closely related to the success of the political process.

Those in the Republican movement say they want change to show their people that politics works. I want change, but of a quite different kind. I do not want a society where thousands of young people from my community don't get employment with the police because they are Protestant. My community does not get a fully funded educational system from the State with a particularly Protestant outlook, but Roman Catholics do. My community's Ulster Scots' cultural rights receive scant attention while the Irish language of a small minority of Roman Catholics receives much more. Those who consider themselves Irish in Northern Ireland can easily obtain Irish passports; those who consider themselves British in the

Indeed, even after the day comes if and when terrorism has ended and the paramilitary organisations have disappeared from the scene, the bitter legacy of the last 36 years will live on.

Republic cannot do so as easily. In fact, even those born here and who have lived all their lives in NI have some difficulty in obtaining a British passport. Your Head of State can and does visit my country frequently. My Head of State has not yet been able to do the same in your country. My community wants change – that's why we want devolved government – but not terror at the heart of it.

In some cases, the end of the worst years of violence and the start of the so-called peace process have coincided with even greater divisions within our society. Terrorism in its most overt form has diminished but the mindset which helped create it has not.

Unless this is concluded we may achieve peace but we will not achieve reconciliation. Sectarianism continues to be a serious problem in Northern Ireland, the effects of which are felt every day. Eradicating sectarianism will be a huge step in seeking to bring about reconciliation.

This year has seen a relatively peaceful marching season so far but the last ten years saw tensions surrounding parades grow, with Unionists believing that for the most part these tensions have been whipped up by Republicans for political reasons. This is not a recipe for positive community relations.

> **The notion that crimes should not be reported to the police and that a political principle of not dealing with the police should be put ahead of a victim of rape, for instance, is frankly perverse.**

Equally, Unionists find it very difficult to understand, never mind sympathise with, the approach which is often taken by Republicans in relation to policing. The notion that crimes should not be reported to the police and that a political principle of not dealing with the police should be put ahead of a victim of rape, for instance, is frankly perverse. How can it be right to report a burglary to the police for insurance purposes but not rape? No matter how plausible the Republican movement's public relations efforts are, this will continue to be an Achilles heel for them until it is resolved.

No stable administration in Northern Ireland could be formed while this position continued. Indeed, what confidence could the Unionist community have if Sinn Féin were in Government while dissident Republican activity continued and Sinn Féin was not prepared to say that people should report what they know to the police?

The Jean McConville case has also generated significant publicity recently with the debate over whether or not she was an informer. Once again, the very existence of this debate is not easily understood by Unionists. Whether or not she was an informer is not the issue. There are those in Sinn Féin who say if she was an informer then it wasn't a crime to murder her! This is why we have been so clear in insisting that paramilitary and criminal activity by terrorist groups must be ended once and for all and there must be no ambiguity about support for the lawful agencies of the state.

There are those who would urge us to move ahead before this has been achieved. I believe that they are fundamentally wrong. They are also making the same mistakes that plagued the process from 1998.

Progress has been made on the terrorism front, I accept that and welcome it, but, equally, I expect others to accept that the journey of paramilitary groups is far from complete. The cross-party Northern Ireland Affairs Select Committee Report on organised crime earlier this month made that absolutely clear. The International Monitoring Commission (IMC) has also been clear about the activities which are engaged in by all paramilitary organisations.

Unionists are not surprised when they hear people urge us to move on now, before all acts of completion are finished. We remember the same people were urging us to move even before the acts of completion had begun.

The problem that our Government and yours have in this area is that they have fallen into the opposite problem of the boy who cried wolf. Instead, they were saying that things were OK before problems were even addressed, never mind resolved.

Throughout this process the DUP has been castigated for requiring the complete end of organised paramilitary and criminal activity. It did not suit the agendas or timetables of our Government or the other parties but ultimately I believe that history will show that the process and the peace will be stronger for it.

The unarguable reality is that the DUP strategy has worked and is working and we intend to keep it working. What is needed now is not for us to take our eye off the ball but to keep the focus on it. The pace of delivery on these issues is not in our hands and those who pretend that it is, or that we are the obstacle, are merely delaying the day of paramilitary groups delivering.

Anyone who understands Unionist politics will know that the pressure on us is not to do things quickly, but to do them right. There is an old saying, "Fool me once, shame on you, fool me twice, shame on me". The Ulster Unionist Party learnt the hard way the truth of that remark when dealing with Sinn Féin and the IRA. We do not intend to emulate them.

While progress seems slow in terms of reconciliation within Northern Ireland, I believe that Unionist relationships with the Irish Republic are probably better than they have been at any point in the past.

I have no doubt that the spectre of Sinn Féin in Government in the Republic has played a large part in concentrating minds about the true nature of the republican movement. Bertie Ahern's new objection to a place for Sinn Féin in coalition with his own party will be seen for what it is by all but the most gullible in the Irish Republic. His true objection is not Sinn Féin's aversion to the European Union

**The problem that our Government and yours have in this area is that they have fallen into the opposite problem of the boy who cried wolf. Instead, they were saying that things were OK before problems were even addressed, never mind resolved.**

but the Irish electorate's aversion to having terrorist gangsters in its government.

It is not just Republican paramilitary and criminal activity that must end but similar Loyalist activity as well. In many ways, loyalists have still further to come but, without the leverage of political advantage, this will be a difficult problem to resolve. Some Loyalists have a range of difficult choices to face because, whilst there was never any justification for their activities, it now doesn't even have a hint of political rationale about it either.

**There is a very fine line between encouraging and assisting people away from violence and criminality and being seen to legitimise the behaviour they are trying to stop.**

Governments must be cautious, in seeking to solve this problem, not to elevate those who have terrorised the whole community over the past three decades. There is a very fine line between encouraging and assisting people away from violence and criminality and being seen to legitimise the behaviour they are trying to stop. It is a balance which has not been found by many and it is one we are acutely aware of. Having said what I have, I believe that if we stay the course there is massive potential for all the people of Northern Ireland.

With due respect to both our Government and yours, regardless of the legacies of individuals or elections in the Republic or changes of prime minister in the UK, history would not forgive us if we settled now for an imperfect peace in which we had little better than a mafia-style society.

If setting arbitrary dates was the solution to deep-seated, centuries-old problems on this island I am sure things would have been sorted long ago.

Whatever happens, either before or after the 25th of November, we remain committed to seeing this through. The history of Northern Ireland will neither begin nor end on that date and the concentration on it is really a distraction away from the focus which should be on ensuring that the conditions exist which enhance progress.

If that is done then I believe that, sooner rather than later, the long-term goal of reconciling people in Northern Ireland can become a reality.

# Martin McGuinness MP, MLA

## Chief Negotiator, Sinn Féin

*Born in Derry. Left school at fifteen to work as butcher's assistant. Became involved in the civil rights protests and, following the outbreak of unrest in the North, became involved in Republican politics. Second-in-command of the IRA in Derry at the time of Bloody Sunday. Was a key figure in negotiations with the British Government in the 80s and played a leading role leading up to the declaration of the IRA ceasefire in 1994. A leader of the Sinn Féin team in the talks that led to the Good Friday Agreement in 1998. Elected MP for Mid-Ulster in 1997 and to the Stormont Assembly in 1999. Minister for Education in the power-sharing Executive up to the suspension of the Executive in 2001. Re-elected as MP for Mid-Ulster in the Westminster elections of 2005.*

## Building Trust and Confidence

Only three weeks ago I visited one of the most heavily militarised regions in the world – the border between the government-held and the rebel-held areas of Sri Lanka. That stark and frightening frontier was a very visible expression of the political legacy of colonial occupation in that small island. Ethnic groups, which had co-existed in relative peace for centuries, became sworn enemies as a result of the destructive and divisive effects of imperial domination. In many ways, the divisions in Sri Lanka mirror our own and the method of resolving them is, in my view, the same. A process of national reconciliation and peace-making is essential, and central to that process is dialogue, dialogue and more dialogue.

One big difference between the situation here in Ireland and that in Sri Lanka is the enormous progress we have already made. The absence of a real and credible process of engagement in Sri Lanka threatens all-out civil war. In contrast, the progress we have made over the last 12 years is a direct result of the real and meaningful engagement between Nationalism and the British government, between Unionism and the Irish government and, to a more limited extent, between Unionism and Nationalism on this island. Our peace process is far from perfect but it is an undoubted success. The Ireland we live in now is a very different place from the Ireland of war and conflict that existed 12 years ago. It is a very different place from the totalitarian Orange state that existed in the north 40 years ago. The Irish peace process is in many ways the reworking of the relationships between Unionism and the rest of the people of this island, and between all of us on this island and the British government.

> Our peace process is far from perfect but it is an undoubted success. The Ireland we live in now is a very different place from the Ireland of war and conflict that existed 12 years ago. It is a very different place from the totalitarian Orange state that existed in the north 40 years ago.

British policy in Ireland has historically been the catalyst for conflict and division in our country. That has to end.

A successful peace process is ultimately about ending the divisive influence and effects of the British jurisdiction on this island. That is Sinn Féin's core political objective.

In the interim, the Good Friday Agreement is about removing the most extreme aspects and consequences of partition. It is about delivering acceptable policing arrangements, ending discrimination, protecting cultural and language rights, defending human rights and delivering a demilitarised, politically tolerant and inclusive society.

The current phase of the political talks are not about the future of the Good Friday Agreement. The Good Friday Agreement is non-negotiable. It has the democratic endorsement of referenda both North and South and it is binding on both governments. The Good Friday Agreement must be implemented come what may. So, the current phase of discussion is about whether or not the implementation of the Agreement will include a six-county Assembly – no more and no less.

The only obstacle to the restoration of that Assembly and the power-sharing executive is the refusal of the DUP to be part of these institutions. That is their prerogative but let there be no doubt that the process of change will continue and it is better for all of us in political leadership, and for our constituents, if we are directing and managing that process of change through a functioning power-sharing Executive. That would certainly be preferable to the bad decisions that are being taken every day by British direct rule ministers.

But I also believe that a functioning Assembly, with a power-sharing Executive and cross-community safeguards, is the best and most efficient means of building trust, confidence and mutual understanding between Irish Republicans and Unionists. It is the best way of sustaining and progressing the enormous work already achieved in reconciling Orange and Green.

It is also the best way of tackling the very real issues that affect all of the people of the North – and on the island of Ireland. The reality is that partition has failed. It has failed the people in the South. It has failed Nnationalists in the North. It has failed the very community it was designed to safeguard. It has failed Unionists. Unionist working class communities suffer high unemployment and educational under-achievement.

No one any longer argues that there is any economic merit in the partition of this small island. On the contrary, all economic advantage lies in Ireland as a single island economy.

No Unionist leader can believe that British direct rule is a good thing. It has resulted in job losses, privatisation, increased rates,

**The Good Friday Agreement is non-negotiable. It has the democratic endorsement of referenda both North and South and it is binding on both governments. The Good Friday Agreement must be implemented come what may.**

water charges, education cuts, falling incomes for those working in agriculture, a failure to produce any strategy to deal with suicide prevention, and much more.

The best people to make decisions about the lives of people in the North are the people who live there. That is the case with education, the economy, health, the environment and housing. It is widely recognised that local ministers in the short-lived power-sharing executive, including DUP ministers, did a much better job than part-time British ministers.

So also with policing and justice. Last week, here at the Mac-Gill Summer School, the British Secretary of State addressed this issue and criticised Sinn Féin for demanding that the Good Friday Agreement commitments on policing and justice be implemented and delivered in full. So I want to address this issue directly. Sinn Féin wants to see a community police service, representative of and democratically accountable to the people they serve through a locally elected minister.

People have a basic right to feel safe in their homes and communities. They have a right to a police service which will act impartially and which will behave in a responsible and accountable way. They have a right to a police service which does not engage in political policing. They have a right to a police service which is not run by MI5 or any other British security agency.

Sinn Féin is not holding back on policing, as Peter Hain tried to suggest. Indeed, many Nationalists are puzzled by the foot dragging of the British government and ask why, seven years on from the Patten Commission's report, we are still awaiting further policing legislation. Has it anything to do with Britain's efforts to cover up decades of state collusion with Loyalist death squads?

Republicans have a vested interest in the creation and delivery of proper policing. It is our communities which have suffered most as a result of decades of a Unionist militia posing as a police service. We are determined that an effective police service, which is democratic and accountable, becomes part of the fabric of life in the Six Counties and the entire island. Substantial progress has been made in relation to policing because of the work of Republicans. We have made sure that the British can't walk away from this issue. Policing has been, and continues to be, a central part of ongoing political negotiations.

I am absolutely convinced that the final pieces can be put in place if the two governments live up to their commitments on transfer of powers and if the political will exists amongst all the political parties.

I have no doubt that we can achieve with others a transformation on policing which will make it democratic, accountable and which enjoys community support.

> Republicans have a vested interest in the creation and delivery of proper policing. It is our communities which have suffered most as a result of decades of a unionist militia posing as a police service.

Republicans and Nationalists who have suffered from partisan policing want, more than anyone else, a new beginning based on impartiality and accountability.

I have no doubt that some day a Republican could hold ministerial responsibility for policing North and South. The need for accountable policing is nowhere more obvious than in the activities of some members of the Gárda Siochána in County Donegal over many, many years. The focus of Sinn Féin is on transforming policing, not accepting a failed status quo.

Sinn Féin wants to work with Unionists to deliver this and to deliver the wider benefits of a stable and effective local administration. I know that many Unionists care deeply about their community. They want to see stability, peace and prosperity and they have worked with Sinn Féin in committees and in local council chambers. Yet the DUP remains implacably opposed to the restoration of a locally elected and accountable Assembly.

Unionism, and the DUP in particular, needs to come to terms with the new political world in which we are living. There is no excuse any longer for non-engagement.

Last year, the Sinn Féin president appealed to the IRA to take the courageous step of committing themselves to purely political means and resolving the issue of IRA weapons. I endorsed Gerry Adams' appeal in the speech I made here in the Glenties last July. The IRA responded by definitively and comprehensively addressing all of these issues, which had been presented as Unionist concerns about the IRA's future intentions.

Those IRA decisions opened up new and unprecedented opportunities for progress towards national reconciliation and of a historic accommodation between Orange and Green. But Unionism also faces challenges and choices in this project. If they claim to be democrats, then the Democratic Unionist Party has to accept and respect the electoral mandate of Sinn Féin. Sinn Féin is the largest Nationalist party in the North. Sinn Féin is the third largest and the fastest growing party on the island. Republicans and Nationalists have great difficulty in the concept of sharing power with Ian Paisley who, for decades, churned out sectarian and religious extremism. On July 12th this year, we were treated to more of the same. But despite this, Sinn Féin does recognise and accept the DUP's electoral mandate.

These are the current political realities which we all have to come to terms with if we are to put conflict, hatred and division behind us. We can continue to disagree politically but that should not prevent us delivering accountable, democratic government for our shared constituencies. It should certainly not prevent us building a better

**If they claim to be democrats, then the Democratic Unionist Party has to accept and respect the electoral mandate of Sinn Féin. Sinn Féin is the largest nationalist party in the North. Sinn Féin is the third largest and the fastest growing party on the island.**

more peaceful future for all our children. And the only way to do this is through political dialogue.

But whatever the approach of Ian Paisley in the months ahead, the reality is that the process of change will continue. And the best option for Unionists and the rest of us is to collectively manage the changes that are coming.

Regardless of the disposition of the DUP, Republicans will continue to engage with Unionist communities. Republicans and Loyalists are already working together with enormous benefits for their respective communities in interface areas. This summer, these on-the-ground efforts and initiatives delivered the most peaceful marching season in decades. The DUP played no part in any of this. However, the DUP need to acknowledge and learn the positive lessons of these local engagements.

Ten years ago, we would have been talking theoretically about the need to reconcile Orange and Green. In the Ireland of 2006, we are now taking about completing a process that is already well underway and which has already been enormously successful.

The process of reconciling Orange and Green is already happening based on principles of equality, inclusivity and mutual respect.

And, as this process progresses, we have new challenges to deal with. We can no longer talk only about two historic traditions on the island. We now have many new Irish who bring their own traditions, perspectives and cultures to our island. A small minority on this island have responded to these challenges negatively through racist intolerance and violence. We need to confront sectarianism wherever it occurs and we also need to confront, with as much determination and energy, racism wherever it occurs. The New Ireland that we are all part of needs to reconcile Orange and Green but it also needs to embrace new cultures and people. We all need to acknowledge and accept difference – to celebrate the enriching diversity of our modern, multi-cultural Ireland.

**Ten years ago, we would have been talking theoretically about the need to reconcile Orange and Green. In the Ireland of 2006, we are now taking about completing a process that is already well underway and which has already been enormously successful.**

# Joe Mulholland

Director, MacGill Summer School and Arts Week

## The Patrick MacGill Summer School

The Patrick MacGill Summer School has been in existence for 26 years. It was founded in 1981 in Glenties to celebrate the memory of local writer Patrick MacGill, whose work on the plight of emigrant workers in Britain at the beginning of the twentieth century and on the horrors of the Great War in which he fought are still being published and read. The School has, in that time, brought together speakers representing all walks of public life in Ireland – North and South – to analyse and debate topics of major national interest. The School's themes have included "Emigration & Employment" (in 1988), "Education in Ireland" (in 1989), "The Constitution of Ireland 1937-1987", "Northern Ireland – The Future" (1986) and, more recently, "Drugs and Alcohol in Ireland – Use and Abuse" (in 2001). In 2002 the School dealt with the issues surrounding the Nice Referendum, "Nice – The Arguments, The Debate, The Facts" and these proceedings were published. The 2003 proceedings were published under the title: *Why Not? Building a Better Ireland*. In the following year the title of our book was *Political Choice & Democratic Freedom in Ireland* and last year's proceedings were published under the title *Managing Ireland's Future 2005-2030*.

Over the years, speakers at the School have included Taoisigh and Tánaistí and, in 1987, two of the country's most eminent members of the judiciary, now alas no longer with us, Mr. Justice Brian Walsh and Mr. Justice Niall McCarthy of the Supreme Court, contributed to the debate on the Irish Constitution, as did the former President of Ireland, Mrs. Mary Robinson. Ambassadors of the United States and of the United Kingdom have also participated in the School's proceedings. The twenty-fifth aniversary of the School in 2005 was opened by the French Ambassador, H.E. Frédéric Grasset, and provided the occasion, on the twenty-fifth anniversary, not to look back but to look forward to the Ireland of 2030.

In 2001 we inaugurated the Annual John Hume Lecture as a tribute to the work done over the decades by the then leader of the SDLP, John Hume, and particularly his major contribution to the peace process. This has become an important and significant national event.

The MacGill School has honoured two distinguished writers who have been, like Patrick MacGill himself, inspired by their relationship with and love of Donegal: Peadar O'Donnell and Brian Friel. It was in August 1985, when the Donegal writer and political activist was in his nineties, that "The Life and Times of Peadar O'Donnell" was chosen as that year's theme. The author himself was in attendance throughout the week and participated fully in the debate, sometimes having to fend off trenchant criticism of his political legacy. He was to pass away about six months later. Several prominent public figures who contributed to that year's School, among them Sean McBride, Noel Browne and Jim Kemmy, have since departed this life.

In 1995 the School celebrated the outstanding literary achievement of the great contemporary playwright, Brian Friel, some of whose family, on his mother's side, hail from Glenties. The week included appraisals of Friel's work by major figures from the world of theatre and academia including Seamus Heaney, Stephen Rea, Terence Brown and the Donegal playwright, Frank McGuinness, as well as readings and recitals. Few who attended the Abbey Theatre production of Friel's acclaimed play, *Dancing at Lughnasa*, which was based on the lives of the author's aunts in Glenties, will ever forget the extraordinary atmosphere and ambiance in the hall of St. Columba's College in Glenties as Friel introduced from the stage his "opus magnum" to a packed and wildly enthusiastic audience, come to see the play return to the place of its inspiration. The performance led to the premiere of the film by Pat O'Connor and Noel Pearson, adapted from Friel's work, being presented in Glenties with, much to the delight of the local people, Meryl Streep in attendance. Brian Friel himself is a frequent visitor to the MacGill School.

As part of the School's arts programme, which has been a feature almost since the beginning, several artists, whose work has been acclaimed, have been honoured during their lifetimes with exhibitions and lectures including the architect, Liam McCormick, one of whose magnificent churches stands in Glenties, and the painter, Derek Hill, who bequeathed to Donegal and the nation his house and much of his collection. As a tribute to the great Irish dramatist, Samuel Beckett, the Gate Theatre has presented in Glenties *Krapp's Last Tape*, with David Kelly, and *I'll Go On*, with Barry McGovern. Two distinguished Irish artistes, Dr. Bernadette Greevy and and Dr. John O'Conor, have performed at the School.

The MacGill Summer School and Arts Week has grown and developed into a national institution and the quality and range of its deliberations are now widely recognised in Ireland and abroad. Each year it attracts more and more people to its sessions and debates which are completely open to the public.